THE SELF, THE INDIVIDUAL,
AND THE COMMUNITY

The Self, the Individual, and the Community

Liberalism in the Political Thought of
F. A. Hayek and
Sidney and Beatrice Webb

BRIAN LEE CROWLEY

CLARENDON PRESS · OXFORD
1987

Oxford University Press, Walton Street, Oxford OX2 6DP

Oxford New York Toronto
Delhi Bombay Calcutta Madras Karachi
Petaling Jaya Singapore Hong Kong Tokyo
Nairobi Dar es Salaam Cape Town
Melbourne Auckland

and associated companies in
Beirut Berlin Ibadan Nicosia

Oxford is a trade mark of Oxford University Press

Published in the United States
by Oxford University Press, New York

British Library Cataloguing in Publication Data

Crowley, Brian Lee
The self, the individual, and the community:
liberalism in the political thought of F. A.
Hayek and Sidney and Beatrice Webb.
1. Liberalism
1. Title
320.5'1 JC571
ISBN 0-19-827497-1

Library of Congress Cataloging in Publication Data

Crowley, Brian Lee.
The self, the individual, and the community.
Revision of thesis (Ph.D.)—London School of Economics,
1985.
Bibliography: p.
Includes index.
1. Liberalism. 2. Hayek, Friedrich A. von (Friedrich
August), 1899- —Contributions in political science.
3. Webb, Sidney, 1859-1947—Contributions in political
science. 4. Webb, Beatrice Potter, 1858-1943—Contribu-
tions in political science. I. Title.
JC571.C73 1987 320.5'1 87-7642
ISBN 0-19-827497-1

Processed by the Oxford Text System

Printed in Great Britain
at the University Printing House, Oxford
by David Stanford
Printer to the University

PREFACE

There are an hundred faults in this Thing, and an hundred things might be said to prove them beauties. But it is needless. A book may be amusing with numerous errors, or it may be very dull without a single absurdity.
Oliver Goldsmith, *The Vicar of Wakefield*

We can never hope to be right; the most we can hope for is to be wrong in interesting ways.

Anonymous

Liberalism has, for many years, called forth in me a kind of fascination, at once horrified and admiring. The horror finds its origins in the over-intellectualisation of human life on which it seems to be based. Liberalism cannot survive but in an intellectual climate in which men are valued only as anonymous centres of rational calculation. For this reason, and others, many major variants of liberalism are preoccupied with men-as-abstractions, with the social sciences, with 'behaviour' rather than 'actions', with the universal and non-contingent in human life and not with the real problems of concrete men.

The admiration I have felt comes from the same source: the appeal of liberalism lies in its symmetry, its (on one level, at least) explanatory force, its reverence of the tools of critical rational analysis. By these methods, intellectuals learn to enjoy the heady feeling which a modicum of wit whetted on logic makes possible, cutting incisively past the irrelevant, the unconnected, the merely contingent, disdaining both superstition and received wisdom in the single-minded quest for knowledge. Liberalism seems, at first blush, to open up before us the vista of a world of calm rationality, a world quite different from the one we know, beset as it is by the undeniable evil of unbridled passions and uncontrolled desires.

But liberalism can only achieve its goal of creating a rational world by turning men into one-dimensional beings. It is a useful exercise to speculate on what the world would be like if men were purely rational beings; it is a nightmare to force real men to live on this procrustean bed. One of the primary purposes of this book is to try to understand the consequences of the application of liberalism to politics.

In the first part, I have chosen F. A. Hayek and Sidney and Beatrice Webb as models of two particular strains of liberalism in British political thought. It may be of some interest that, at the outset, I was implacably hostile to Hayek and the New Right and temperamentally well disposed towards the intellectual tradition the Webbs represent. The writing of this book however, has resulted in these dispositions being, if not reversed, at least deeply shrouded in doubt. While I still believe Hayek to be fundamentally mistaken in many ways, I have grown to respect and admire him and his work and to see much there to which my own intellectual prejudices had previously blinded me. As for the Webbs, suffice it to say that while they may be good exemplars of a certain kind of utilitarianism, they leave a great deal to be desired as representatives of thoughtful socialism in Britain. To understand the enduring nature and indubitable value of the Webbs' contribution to political life in Britain, one must look elsewhere than their political thought. One must look to their concrete achievements, represented, in varying degrees, by such contemporary institutions as the New Statesman, the Fabian Society, the Labour Party, and the London School of Economics and Political Science, to name but a few.

If it is not paradoxical to say so, then, given the reinforcement of my long-standing disquiet *vis-à-vis* liberalism to which allusion has just been made, writing this book has left me deeply changed. I have talked myself out of many of my old certainties without finding anything nearly so reassuring to take their place.

In a (very tentative) attempt to fill this gap, or at least define its limits, the second half of the book concerns itself with the problem of what politics might look like if we were to shake off the intellectual strait-jacket which liberal rationalism imposes on us. Here history, language, and community are seen as useful correctives to the metaphysical conceit of the liberal self as shadowy abstraction. While there is undoubtedly much that is unsatisfactory in my approach, I feel that the answer to the problem of liberal politics (or anti-politics) must lie in realising just how inseparable men are from the purely contingent and non-universalisable aspects of their lives.

Numerous debts of gratitude remain to be paid. This book is a revised version of a doctoral thesis written at the LSE between 1983 and 1985. My work then was generously supported financially by the Social Sciences and Humanities Research Council of Canada, the Imperial Oil Company of Canada, the Committee of Vice-Chancellors and Principals of the Universities of the United Kingdom, the Royal Society of Canada (the Sir Arthur Sims scholarship), the London School of Economics (the Robert McKenzie memorial scholarship), and the Humanitarian Trust. My thanks must also go, first to the Oxford University Press and Henry Hardy, their Senior Editor for Politics, for having agreed to accept this work for publication, and second to my very patient and painstaking editor, Heather Watson.

Academically and intellectually I would be most remiss if I did not acknowledge with very humble thanks the many debts I owe to friends and teachers. I cannot mention them all, but of those whose claims are too great to permit omission I must begin with J. R. Mallory, Professor Emeritus in the Department of Political Science at McGill University, who, by instruction and personal example, first led me to understand that politics might be a civilised and civilising activity. Second, I wish to mention John Charvet of the Government Department at the LSE, who stimulated and challenged me to think about political theory. John Charvet and Rodney Barker both had the patience and the fortitude to read the manuscript and to make many helpful comments, for which I am very grateful. My greatest thanks must go, however, to my supervisor, Alan Beattie, whose insight, patience, knowledge, and unfailing good humour helped to turn what might have been a toilsome burden into an exciting adventure. If I can honestly say that my enthusiasm for my work never flagged during my years at the LSE, it was in large part due to Alan's wise and judicious guidance and encouragement.

There is probably no need to add that no matter how great the contributions of these friends and colleagues have been, the responsibility for what is to follow rests entirely with me.

Finally, I think it sad that so many works of this kind fail to acknowledge adequately emotional and affective debts as well. I have three I wish to recognise explicitly. The first is to Alan Beattie, for reasons already mentioned. The second is to Judy Neiswander, whose sympathy and faith in me often buoyed me up in difficult times. Without her I would never have completed this book. The third is to my grandfather and grandmother, who were always there when I needed them; the satisfaction I feel at the completion of this book is marred only by the fact that they did not live to see it. Unable to arbitrate impartially between the justice of these various claims, I dedicate this work to them jointly.

CONTENTS

I

LIBERALISM'S OPPOSITION
TO POLITICS

Ideally speaking, art shares with politics precisely that
which distinguishes both from the deliberate rationality
of science and the blueprints of ideological programmes:
that it springs from the elemental human need to discipline
into articulate form and communicable convention the
inarticulate and rationally incommunicable forces of life.

Erich Heller, *Thomas Mann, The Ironic German*

The conventional wisdom in modern British political theory
would have us believe that utilitarian socialist planners like
Sidney and Beatrice Webb on the one hand, and individualist
libertarians like Friederich Hayek on the other, are proponents
of views of politics which are diametrically opposed. The
virtually automatic assumption is that their political philosophies are mutually antagonistic and can only be offered in
contrast to one another.

No matter how easily such an assumption is made, however,
it is misleading and superficial in some very important ways.
Their practical prescriptions in the social, political, and
economic fields certainly differ, but the easy belief that this is
wholly the product of substantially, if not radically, different
premises and convictions does not withstand close examination.
On the contrary, one quickly discovers that many of their
disagreements result from contrasting interpretations of certain
basic assumptions on which they share a surprising identity
of views, assumptions dealing primarily with the desirability
and feasibility of politics as an activity.

With respect to their political theories, then (i.e. the nature
of man and the proper relationship of man to society and to
the state), the Webbs and Hayek may be seen as representatives, not of opposing schools of thought, but rather of
subtly different aspects of a single tradition. This tradition can
accommodate writers who appear to us as diverse as this

because it is regally unaware, or perhaps even disdainful of what Letwin has called the 'distinctive political issue since the eighteenth century': the legitimate sphere of activity of the state.[1] As soon as one dispenses with that point of reference, so crucial today for the classification of political argument, our 'taxonomising' instincts become disoriented. In a world of political theory where disputes of this kind are irrelevant, who is the radical and who the conservative? In which directions do 'left' and 'right' lie?

Without wishing to anticipate the arguments to come, the thrust of this tradition can be easily characterised. It is, perhaps paradoxically, *anti-political* because it seeks to deny the legitimacy of politics as an activity and the relevance of politics to questions of desirable social and economic arrangements. It does so firstly by arguing that there is an ultimate and objective social goal to which all rational men would submit if they understood both the true nature of man and society and the imperatives of long-term social survival. It does so secondly by holding that, since all social activities are to be judged against the unquestioned ultimate value, the *way* in which decisions about social and economic arrangements are made is of little importance compared to the content of those decisions.

One can best understand how a tradition of political argument can be 'anti-political' or can find politics 'irrelevant' by examining the meaning of words. The word 'politics' has at least two meanings, one quite broad, the other narrow, which must be carefully distinguished. The first, popular, sense is in fact so broad that it obscures the difference between what is political and what is not. Roughly what is meant by politics here is that any social relationship involving the exercise of 'power' or 'authority' is necessarily political. It is thus not uncommon to hear discussions concerning, for example, the politics of small groups, of the family, of the organisation, of the school, of death, and so on. When one presses for the definition of a more manageable sphere for politics, one which permits an analytical distinction between politics and the rest of human affairs, recourse is often had to the activities of the

---

[1] S. R. Letwin, *The Pursuit of Certainty* (Cambridge, 1965), p. 1.

state. This is in essence a sort of Morrisonian 'politics is what politicians do', where 'politicians' is intended to refer to political leaders, legislators, civil servants, party members, soldiers, policemen, judges, and voters, etc.

The problem with this response is that while it (helpfully) focuses attention on problems related to the exercise of power and authority and the establishment of an order encompassing an entire society, it still misses one crucial point. Politics has always had a much narrower and more precise meaning, a meaning which allows us to make distinctions of vital importance which are blurred by its more capacious and familiar offspring. This earlier sense of the term 'political' can be traced back at least to Aristotle, for whom politics or 'political rule' was but one possible response to the problem of maintaining order in a society in the face of the fact of the diversity of its members, their interests and opinions.[2]

Several important aspects of this definition of politics are contained in the preceding sentence. The first is that a 'political order' is distinguishable from other kinds of order which are possible in a society, even where such a society has all the hallmarks of a popularly understood political order: a state, politicians, a legislature, and so on. Aristotle himself distinguished it, for example, from oligarchy and tyranny, the first being a class or group ruling in its own interest alone, the second being one man ruling solely in his own interest.[3] A regime of political rule, by contrast, sets itself as an avowed goal to endeavour to rule in the interest of all the individuals and groups which constitute it. Not that a political regime always (or ever) succeeds at this task, for the second important aspect of this definition is that it accepts as a fact conflicting notions of what constitutes a just and expedient social order and hence of desirable collective goals.[4] In other words, a recognition of society's irreducible plurality is essential to a political order.

---

[2] On this see e.g. Bernard Crick, *In Defence of Politics*, 2nd edition (Harmondsworth, 1982), p. 17. See also Sir Ernest Barker (ed.), *The Politics of Aristotle* (Oxford, 1948), p. 51; R. Beiner, *Political Judgment* (London, 1983), *passim*; and Hannah Arendt, *The Human Condition* (Chicago, 1958), Chapter 1, esp. p. 13.

[3] B. Crick, op. cit. p. 18.

[4] Ibid., Chapter 2, and Alan Beattie, 'The Character of English Constitutional Theory', unpublished paper (1979), p. 25.

In his interpretative essay on Harold Lasswell's political writings, Alan Gewirth showed a considerable sensitivity to the issue of the relationship which politics presupposes between values and power, a sensitivity which mirrors the central concern of this book:

> The frequently repeated doctrine that politics is simply power tends to obfuscate the integral position which moral values have as goals of that power and hence as basic determinants of its characteristics ... [I]f politics is defined only in terms of power, then it becomes impossible to distinguish within politics itself between a regime which governs only on the basis of power ... and a regime in which the primary basis is the consent of the governed.[5]

Hence this idea of politics assumes both that a reconciliation of conflicting interests, of rival conceptions of the good life is at least possible, and yet that any conclusion reached in this regard is never of the sort which compels the agreement or acquiescence of rational men. A search for what is in the interest of all men, of course, implies a belief that such an interest exists, that there is a discoverable *common good*. A political society seeks to orient itself, its institutions, and its collective efforts to the discovery and implementation of policies which embody the general good, but it does so in a very particular way, and starts from very specific premises.

The first premise, of course, is that of the common good itself. This perspective sees men as intimately bound up with the society which produces them; it permeates them, creating the potential for a living bond of friendship and community between them which, if it is actualised, leads men to take the interests of all other men in that society to be of an equal status to their own. The fundamental elements of this community are the common values and understandings which must exist if there is to be a common language and institutions. Thus, while the basic ingredients of the common good may exist in every society, the common good itself can only be realised through the active will to pursue it by the members of a community.

[5] A. Gewirth, 'Political Power and Democratic Psychiatry', *Ethics*, 59 (pp. 136–42), p. 138.

This concept of a 'communication community' is a crucial one whose development must wait until a later chapter. For the moment, suffice it to say that the very concept of community is intimately bound up with the notion of an ability to communicate between the members of that community, an ability itself premised on a certain minimum of shared meanings and values attached to common objects and experiences. This is embodied in a language which allows members of the community not only to communicate experiences, but also to learn about one's own interpretations of experience, by comparing them with those whose presentation in a common language makes them intelligible.[6] This idea of shared values and at least a minimum sharing of experiences, is crucial to Aristotle's notion of *koinonia*, or what is roughly translated today as 'community', the highest form of *koinonia* being the *polis*.[7]

The second premise of political society, that of rationality, holds that men are rational in the sense that they are capable of engaging in reasoned deliberation about where their common and individual interests lie, of evaluating arguments based on the premise of the common good. Such arguments are designed to persuade them, through an appeal to their rational faculty, to accept a particular conception of those interests. Arendt suggests that this notion was central to the classical Greek understanding of politics:

> To be political, to live in a *polis*, meant that everything was decided through words and persuasion and not through force and violence. In Greek self-understanding, to force people by violence, to command rather than persuade, were prepolitical ways to deal with people characteristic of life outside the *polis*.[8]

The third premise is that of plural epistemology. It holds that knowledge of society, and therefore of the common good, is not wholly reducible to a factual description of society, but must also depend on the meaning which men attach to their particular social experiences. Since each man occupies a

---

[6] See e.g. M. Taylor, *Community, Anarchy and Liberty* (Cambridge, 1982), p. 27.

[7] See M. I. Finley, 'Aristotle and Economic Analysis' (p. 144) in J. Barnes, M. Schofield, and R. Sorabji (eds.), *Articles on Aristotle*, Vol. II: *Ethics and Politics* (London, 1977). .

[8] Arendt, op. cit., pp. 26-7.

unique place in society and in the world, by virtue both of
the overlapping and cross-cutting roles he plays and of his
particular bundle of talents and attributes, his experience of
society and hence his interpretation of the common good must
be accorded an equal hearing to all others in the search for
an agreed definition of that good. Not that it must necessarily
be incorporated in it: such interpretations may not find favour
with his fellow citizens. As was implied in the first two
premises, the common good is arrived at by a process
of *negotiated meaning* between rational individuals against a
background of certain shared values. It is just as possible that
one will be *dissuaded* from one's own view of where the common
good lies as that others will be *persuaded* to accept it. There is
thus a common object of knowledge (society), which can be
observed from many perspectives by unique individuals, and
the knowledge they will have of it will be partly factual and
partly evaluative or interpretative.

The fourth premise, that of mutual restraint, follows from
the tentative nature of knowledge of the common good, a
nature which is explained by the insight that such knowledge
does not depend primarily on immutable and empirically
demonstrable or measurable facts, but on human interpretation
of them or the values men assign to them. Since the search
for the common good aims at finding some basis on which
rational men can be persuaded to respect those rules which
make certain kinds of social behaviour in a sense non-optional
(i.e. law), this premise holds that it is rarely justified to pursue
a particular policy whose status is keenly contested to the
point where the living relationship of mutual trust and
confidence so crucial to the first premise is irretrievably lost.

Certainly this neo-Aristotelian view does not hold that the
pursuit of the common good is the only possible basis for a
social order. It makes the rather different claim that it is the
only order worthy of rational, civilised men. It was this which
led Aristotle to conceive of politics as a civilised and civilising
activity: the pursuit of the common good as a collective social
project requires men to be convinced of the moral worth of
putting chains on their particular appetites, rising above their
individual place in life, and striving to see the larger pattern

of relationships and goods on which their particular goods depend.

It is important to notice here that a political society invites its members to be just and objective in their public relations with each other by asking them not to give any more weight to their particular interest than to any other interest in the search for the common good. By requiring me to convince my fellow citizens, in public and open rational deliberation, of my vision of the public good if that vision is to become public policy, I must convince them that I have tried to take all relevant interests into account, my own no more than any other. For this reason, justice in a political society is primarily a question of desert: claims to just treatment here can only be framed in terms of what the common good requires be given the claimant. No claim can be based on what the particular interest of an individual requires; rather what is sought is a recognition that anyone who occupied a similar position in society would have a well-founded claim to the treatment sought.

One final point: this search for the common good requires a particular institutional framework if it is to function. Specifically, men must have a recognised status as *public beings*, that is to say that there must be what Arendt calls organised public spaces of appearance⁹ in which they can engage in politics, or the active search for the common good and, where necessary, its embodiment in law. Here is where men in their public persona may 'officially' hear argument and debate and translate their conclusions into rules binding on all.

Unless some fairly direct connection of this kind exists between individual opinions on the common good and the determination of the obligatory rules of social behaviour, political society is impossible. This public aspect of men's lives, that aspect which is bound up with the search for the overarching interest of all men in a particular society, can be thought of as citizenship. It is when men act together in their common capacity as citizens in search of the common good that politics in its narrow, neo-Aristotelian sense, is en-

---

⁹ Arendt, op. cit., *passim*. For Arendt, such public spaces of appearance are essential to the articulation and sharing of values on which the *koinonia* of the *polis*, or 'community' in its political manifestation is to be encountered. See pp. 50–8.

countered. And this kind of active citizenship, in which men are both rulers (those who set the obligatory rules of social relations) and ruled (those called upon to respect those rules),[10] makes possible a society in which the autonomy of each as a social being is given its fullest possible scope and expression.

This last point in particular shows that politics is not exclusively concerned with what are vulgarly called 'outputs' of 'political systems', i.e. with law or public policy. While law is undoubtedly the most important product of politics, the latter is at least as much concerned with fostering the kind of exploration of self and values, and therefore the sense of personal responsibility and autonomy, which the activity of politics requires. Politics is as much concerned with the creation of the conditions in which men are led to explore and (more importantly) to evaluate the desires they hold within the framework of a society dedicated to the fullest possible development of all its members. The deliberative and expressive aspects of politics, as well as the moral discipline of rational self-restraint that it implies, are held to be goods in themselves whatever the particular laws that result. Indeed, one of the objectives of the present work is to show that politics is a process by which one both discovers and affirms oneself as a moral and social being.

Clearly politics, in the sense of an ongoing search for the conciliation of conflicting interests and opinions, exists in *all* societies, but that does not make them all political. The difference is that in a political society the search for consensus, for a social order to which the largest possible number of citizens will give their allegiance, is itself the goal, and is pursued for its own sake.[11] In a regime where the gaining and keeping of power is the ultimate goal, or is necessary to that goal, then the conciliation of interests which does take place is regarded, not as a goal in itself, but as a temporary evil, which will be dispensed with at the first opportunity.

A political regime, therefore, is one where power is to some degree diffused throughout society, and where the legitimate exercise of that power is a matter of public debate. The opposite of this, what one might call civil society, à la Hobbes, is one

---

[10] Aristotle's own phrase to describe the *polis* is that community where men rule and are ruled by turns. See, in particular, Book Three of Aristotle's *Politics*, op. cit.

[11] Arendt, op. cit., pp. 26–7.

where power is concentrated, and where decisions about its use are private. In the first, men are citizens with a right to participate in public debate and whose opinions matter. In the second, they are subjects of a power which is independent of them. In a civil society, men have no public personality because there is no public space in which their reasoned judgments shall be the measure of their common good. The citizen is jointly responsible with the other citizens of his society, for the decisions made in and about the public sphere, just as he is solely responsible for his actions in his capacity as a private person (a subject on which more will be said in Chapter VI).

Non-political man, by contrast, has no share of power and is therefore the object of decisions made by others according to rules utterly beyond his influence. He is a purely private individual, accountable for his conduct to the state, but incapable of dissenting publicly from or directly influencing the standards against which his conduct is judged.[12] Dissent, discussion, and change are only possible where the right to hold different opinions is recognised, and this can only lead to peaceful social change where political institutions are prepared to recognise that the opinions of individual men are of public significance.

Some important objections to this argument must be taken up here. It may, for instance, be objected that what precedes implies either that there are no certainties or facts about the human world at all and that therefore the possibility of a social science is being denied, *or* that even if such certainties are admitted, a political society would be quite free to take no notice of them in its collective decision-making.

If the first objection is true, then the argument so far merely amounts to a rather crude form of scepticism. If the second, then those who possess 'expert' knowledge, economists such as F. A. Hayek and sociologists like Sidney and Beatrice Webb, have no special claim to having their professional opinions accorded special weight under any circumstances and this must appear a difficult position to defend.

---

[12] Of course, judged by this standard, it is entirely possible for a political society to encompass a large number of non-political men. The Greek *polis*, for example, contained slaves, women, and outsiders or foreigners, none of whom had any public personality whatsoever: they were purely private persons, as opposed to the citizen, who enjoyed both a private and a public life.

The argument here is neither of these, and it is important to see in what the difference consists. Both these objections depend heavily on a particular concept of objectivity. The Webbs and Hayek, for instance, would certainly want to argue that there are things that we can know about men in the way we know things about the rest of the empirical world and this knowledge must be taken into account in the fields of politics, economics, and sociology. The 'objective' nature of this knowledge is far from unproblematical, however, and, as we shall see later, man presents certain unique features which make it inappropriate to classify him as a subject of science in quite the same way that the physical world can be. Indeed, much recent writing in the philosophy of science has been devoted to showing that even in the physical sciences certainty and objectivity are myths which cannot withstand examination.[13] A recurring theme of this book will be that a 'science of man' cannot be built of facts which compel agreement as do the facts of nature, but can only be based on extremely tentative interpretations of the nature of man as it manifests itself in the myriad particular circumstances of the world.

Furthermore, this preoccupation with 'factual' knowledge only serves to obscure what Hume so clearly demonstrated: that facts and values are logically distinct. If values cannot be wholly reduced to facts, then disagreements about values cannot, in most instances, be reduced to disagreements about facts. To the extent that this is true, expert opinion will have a very valuable role to play where disputes of a factual nature arise, but will be largely irrelevant where such disputes centre on questions of values. And disputes about values are unavoidable when what is sought is agreement on common ends. Both Hayek and the Webbs believe that such disputes about values can be avoided, but this claim is hard to establish. J. S. Mill struck at the heart of the matter when he observed that all the 'practical arts' such as medicine and architecture, all scientific

[13] Certainty has been most effectively called into question by K. Popper, *The Logic of Scientific Discovery* (London, 1959) and *Conjectures and Refutations* (London, 1963); T. Kuhn, *The Structure of Scientific Revolutions* (Chicago, 1962) and F. A. Hayek, *The Counter-Revolution of Science* (Glencoe, Ill., 1952). On the rather different question of the validity of the concept of scientific *objectivity* see Dr D. Bohm's excellent work *Wholeness and the Implicate Order* (London, 1980). Dr Bohm is Professor of Theoretical Physics at Birkbeck College, London.

enterprises in themselves, have 'one first principle, or major premise, not borrowed from science; that which enunciates the object aimed at, and affirms it to be a desirable object'.[14] So it is with economics and sociology: they may well be able to answer certain kinds of questions, but they cannot answer every kind. They can tell us how to go about achieving those goals we set for ourselves, but they cannot tell us why we *ought* to want those particular goals.

Certainly some goals can be ruled out by the expert on grounds of (say) physical impossibility (e.g. unaided human flight), but the extent to which questions regarding the values we shall have are reducible to this sort of question would appear, prima facie, rather limited.

This should not be taken to suggest that there are no criteria for settling such disputes about values, or the good, but merely that they frequently cannot be settled by appeal to empirical facts and therefore that their resolution requires other, more tentative kinds of knowledge. This should be no disqualification, however, since, as has already been noted, the work of Popper, Kuhn, and others, has served to make us aware that even scientific knowledge is far more provisional and open to question than had hitherto been realised. What is being argued for, then, is not some odd form of scepticism or a doctrinaire egalitarianism which holds all opinions to be equally valid regardless of empirical fact. It is, on the contrary, a more critical stance *vis-à-vis* so-called factual knowledge since 'facts' can often be improperly used to obfuscate debate more properly conducted in other terms.

This must invariably lead us back to the idea of the common good as an integral part of a political order. While a political order *is* about the conditions in which civilised men can pursue their particular goods, that possibility is itself grounded in a prior appreciation of the common good. It is this notion of the necessity of an 'internal point of view'[15] to any plausible conception of the common good which our authors wish to deny. To this end they assert one of two things. Either, as in the case of Hayek, that since the individual desires or wants

---

[14] Quoted in J. Gray, *Mill On Liberty: A Defence* (London, 1983), p. 19.
[15] This term is H. L. A. Hart's. See *The Concept of Law* (Oxford, 1961), particularly Chapter 5. See also Chapter VII below.

that men have are strictly exogenous, and are by their nature incommunicable and inaccessible to reason, concrete 'collective goals' are nothing more than attempts to coerce morally sovereign individuals to contribute to someone else's (arbitrary) chosen goals. In these conditions, the only possible conception of a common good must reduce it to an abstract, end-independent social order to which the assent of hypothetical rational men can be assumed, but to which the assent of real men is unnecessary. Or, as in the case of the Webbs, it can be argued that the common good is not discoverable by the sort of political means adumbrated here, but is scientifically determinable fact, and therefore can be discovered without the political participation of society's members.

To challenge such views requires several things. First, to show why the view of men in a social context on which it is based is false, or at least highly implausible. Second, to show that human affairs are not directly and unproblematically assimilable to ordinary empirical phenomena, and therefore that the scientific analogy, while superficially attractive, becomes inevitably bogged down in contradictions. Third, that there is another view of the nature and status of human knowledge and desires which avoids many of these pitfalls, and which provides a sound foundation for a justification of a pluralistic politics of the common good. Fourth, to show that such a politics of the common good is not based on mere arbitrary subjectivity, for liberal theories such as Hayek's and the Webbs' find their inspiration, as it shall be argued at some length below, in a desire precisely to escape the seeming subjectivity and arbitrariness of such views. No political theory can hope to find acceptance unless it can satisfactorily answer such charges.

This inquiry must therefore proceed in two stages. The first stage is to examine the roots and substance of the views represented by Hayek and the Webbs. I am going to argue not only that these views are *anti-political*, but also that they are *liberal* in an important philosophical sense. Moreover, I will show that such liberal theories are not just *also* anti-political, but necessarily so.

Liberalism is often used as a kind of shorthand term covering a broad range of social and political thought, but that does not imply that it is meaningless. For convenience' sake, I have decided to use the term 'liberal' to describe both Hayek and the Webbs because they hold certain views which clearly place them within different but intimately related streams of liberal thought stretching back to the seventeenth century. Later on in this chapter I will explain why I regard both Hayek and the Webbs as bona fide bearers of the liberal banner and why their respective ethical and utilitarian theories are really mirror images of one another, issuing from certain common preoccupations.

The second half of this book is concerned to show why the theories of the self, knowledge, and social relations on which these liberal views are based cannot be sustained. Particularly crucial will be the argument that these theories cannot accommodate the full depth of the human self and that therefore political arrangements based on either brand of liberalism cannot allow men to display the full measure of moral responsibility for their values which this depth requires.

From this it follows that there are serious flaws in any conception of social and political institutions in which the sole standard of what is to count as 'rational' behaviour is based on a hypothetical and very partial account of what human beings are like. This includes any conceptions which regard the maximisation of market relationships as the sole criterion of policy (Hayek), or those which naïvely attempt to analyse all questions of social relations as if they were reducible entirely to empirical facts (the Webbs). It further follows that both these views fail when they see the justification of society and politics as lying solely in the direction of organising society as an engine of material want satisfaction.

The burden of the argument, then, is that while the liberal self may be 'alive' in and appropriate to *some* social relationships, it cannot live in, nor account for, certain other kinds. This raises two questions to which political theory must find a response. The first, assuming that the liberal self does in fact describe a *part* of the human self, and therefore relationships appropriate to it form a legitimate *part* of the full repertoire of human relationships, is: how to draw the line between the areas where expert advice and/or market relationships should end and alternative social and political relationships begin? The second question is: what role should political institutions have in deciding and enforcing this line of demarcation?

It is important, however, to start at the beginning. Simply put, the debate at the centre of this book has to do with the grounds on which politics may be attacked or defended as a way of maintaining a social order; with both the feasibility and desirability of politics as the kind of civilising activity which Aristotle believed it to be. It is a debate about the nature and extent of citizenship, and the degree to which all members of a polity are held competent to reason with one another about the management of their common affairs and the sphere in which the judgment of individual men *qua* men (and not as e.g. technocrats, experts, etc.) about matters of communal importance shall be decisive.

In this debate Hayek and the Webbs come down on the same, anti-political, side; but they do so for different reasons related to their epistemological assumptions. Thus Hayek's 'value non-cognitivism'[16] leads him to exclude altogether the possibility of rational discussion of and deliberation about the values that ought to guide men in their collective actions. While not denying the existence of values, he denies that their source is knowable or can ever be satisfactorily articulated by anyone. Men hold the values they do, not because these values are intrinsically worth while, but because they have proved their worth in the struggle for social survival; they have proven utility. Since no one can know *why* they have this utility, to deliberate on the values men should have is to be guilty of a particularly dangerous hubris. The Webbs, too, deny the legitimacy and relevance of politics because there is no ground for crediting ordinary men and women with access to the knowledge on which the deliberative process is premised. This, however, is not because this knowledge is inaccessible, but rather because it is accessible only to those professionally trained and intellectually equipped to discover it.

They agree, then, that men and women cannot reach valid conclusions about the management of their collective affairs,

---

[16] This term is Thomas Spragen's and is taken from his own excellent discussion of the historical development of the two liberal views of reason in *The Irony of Liberal Reason* (Chicago, 1981), e.g. p. 15.

although Hayek would extend this incapacity to scientific experts and the Webbs would not. They concur in rejecting the claim that the average person is capable of managing the *res publica* in co-operation and consultation with his peers, but again different epistemological assumptions lead Hayek to conclude that *no one* is capable of 'managing' it, and the Webbs to conclude that only social scientists can. They thus agree on a rejection of the reasoned judgment of the members of a polity taken as a whole as a legitimate basis for collective action. In short, they agree on a rejection of politics as a desirable means of maintaining a social order.[17]

Politics, to them, is disruptive, dangerous, and irrational because both ethical or deontological liberals like Hayek and utilitarians like the Webbs believe that there are objective criteria available to guide men in the formulation of public policy and collective goals, and that to deviate from these criteria merely on the grounds of their incompatibility with the error-prone opinions of ordinary men is to countenance irrationality in human affairs.

Clearly, the Webbs and Hayek are not alone in adhering to this anti-political stance, and it is instructive to consider for a moment their intellectual roots in order to see more clearly the concerns they are addressing. For this one needs to turn back at least to the European Enlightenment.

Alasdair MacIntyre, in the entertaining and somewhat eccentric first part of *After Virtue*, argues that the intellectual project of the Enlightenment was to find a rational warrant for our beliefs, freed from mere contingency and subjectivity, aspiring instead to discover an objective morality which was as demonstrable as were the findings of the natural sciences, newly liberated from their Aristotelian limitations.[18]

---

[17] Just as *all* societies must have *some* politics, Hayek and the Webbs both recognise that politics has a role to play, however limited, in their ideal society. Nevertheless, Crick rightly states that 'there are societies whose systems of government do not merely contain some political activity, but normally depend on political activity to function at all. These are properly classified as "political systems" ' (op. cit., p. 162). The respective balances between political and non-political activity for which Hayek and the Webbs argue is such that any society which conformed to one or the other of them would be far indeed from being political.

[18] Alasdair MacIntyre, *After Virtue: A Study in Moral Theory* (London, 1981), *passim* and esp. Chapter 1.

Tracing the evolution and ramifications of this project through to our century, MacIntyre concludes that the paradoxical result has been a culture in which moral values are thoroughly relativised and subjectivised, in which emotivism and intuitionism reign, and the notion of the good, or the good life, is held to be purely private. Each man is free to judge what the good life is for himself, and is free to pursue that private vision to the extent both that that is compatible with a like freedom for all other men and that it does not bring the individual into conflict with objective morality. This abandonment of any search for a larger 'common good', or for an agreed content to the 'good life' in favour of a preoccupation with the rules governing the way in which men will be permitted to pursue their private good has often been heralded as the start of a new era of human freedom, not to say liberation.[19]

This provides us with a first insight into the influence that the Enlightenment has had on subsequent understandings of politics and the practice of the political arts: if a commonly agreed notion of the good life is not only not available, but is held to be impossible, then some other, non-teleological moral standards must be found to justify and criticise social institutions and practices.

Although men may no longer share a teleology, as they did in Antiquity and the Middle Ages, still at a minimum they share a common world and they share a society in which they co-operate in order to multiply the fruits of their labour. To share a world and a society requires some institutional structure for the accomplishment of common tasks and some way of resolving disputes, for disputes, both about claims to the fruits of social co-operation and about the scope of the right to pursue the privately defined good noticed earlier, seem inevitable. Appeals to the good as a basis for these social institutions and the practices which make them operative are excluded since the good is purely subjective and there is no possibility of reconciling the competing visions of it held by private persons.

This has posed no obstacle to debate about the moral justification of current social and political arrangements, for many modern political philosophers (including Hayek) have held

---

[19] See e.g. ibid., Chapter 2.

that the Kantian-inspired Enlightenment claims to absolute respect for the individual as an autonomous, rational subject, valued by others as an end in himself and choosing freely his own ends, provides us with a more objective and hence more rational and universal ground on which political questions may be debated.

The other, utilitarian, variant of Enlightenment liberalism (which embraces social planners like the Webbs), grounds a like claim on the rather different insight into the nature of man as a utility-maximiser, and argues that debates about public policy can only rationally be conducted as a kind of logical deduction from this first premise.

As noticed earlier, these viewpoints are frequently defended primarily on the basis of their *objectivity*; that is to say that such theories make one of two claims. Either they do not require any choice to be made between competing concepts of the good, but can accommodate virtually any such concept held by an individual (the society envisaged lays claim, in some sense, to being 'value free', mediating between competing notions of the good, privileging none); or they provide an objective criterion or criteria for choosing between competing notions of the good, which criterion does not *itself* appeal to any such notion (here it is the 'standard of choice' which is objective or value free). MacIntyre has gone so far as to argue that the result is a bifurcation of the political world into those who favour the unfettered exercise of man's freedom to engage in quite arbitrary choices of values and those who favour the regulation of those choices in the service of some rationally defensible end.[20] The latter position frequently issues, in the twentieth-century Western world at least, in some variant of utilitarianism such as that attributed here to the Webbs; the former in some version of what I, following Sandel,[21] have termed 'deontological liberalism', of which Hayek is a proponent.

However different these two liberal offspring of the Enlightenment appear to us on the outside, by the very fact of their common genealogy they share three central and perennial concerns. By looking at these more closely, one rapidly reduces

---

[20] Ibid., p. 33.
[21] See M. J. Sandel, *Liberalism and the Limits of Justice*. The definition of 'deontological liberalism' is the subject of his 'Introduction', pp. 1-14.

the gulf which is presumed to separate Hayek's ethical liberalism from the Webbs' utilitarianism to unexpectedly small dimensions.

The first of these concerns is a concept of the right. Having dispensed with any claim to be able to judge the goodness of the ends that men pursue, the moral interest of society in individual or collective action turns from the ends to be achieved to focus exclusively on the means chosen to achieve them. A notion of the right which claims to be an objective measure for determining whether or not any particular means to an end is socially acceptable without judging the end itself is the very stuff of the liberal view.[22] And not just any standard of the right will do; the right, unlike the good, is held to be objectively discoverable and universal, because it must command the assent of all rational men freed of all contingent and therefore morally irrelevant considerations.

The second preoccupation of these theories arises from the practical need to apply the objective standard (the right) to a concrete society. A concept of justice is thus crucial because of the ever present possibility of conflict between competing rights claims or, put another way, between interpretations of what the right enjoins specific people and institutions to do or not to do in specific circumstances. As with the right, the notion of justice depends on the objectivity of rational man, but precisely what this means differs somewhat for each theory.

For deontological liberals it takes the form of rational men, freed from all contingent considerations, reflecting on how the right ought to be applied in particular circumstances, having regard only to what the universal, rational, and nonparticularistic right enjoins. The ideal is to discover the principles of justice to which all rational men would assent if they could rise above their contingent position in the real world.

For utilitarians the principle is the same, but the application rather different. While utilitarianism shares the preoccupation with objectivity and universalisability, its insight into the nature of rational man is the simpler utility-maximising one. If

---

[22] As Sandel puts it in his article 'Morality and the Liberal Ideal', *New Republic* (7 May 1984), pp. 15-17, 'Only a justification neutral about ends could preserve the liberal resolve not to favour particular ends, or to impose on its citizens a preferred way of life' (p. 16).

maximising the aggregate welfare is what the utilitarian right enjoins, then utilitarian justice seeks to apply this in particular circumstances.

Some forms of deontological liberalism, then, hold the right, and therefore justice, to be *discoverable* by all rational men by virtue of their rational faculty alone. Hayek's position differs somewhat from this. Suffice it to say that for him, men do not know enough to be able to discover justice directly, but a spontaneous social order like the market allows them to approach it indirectly. The form of argument is thus the same: the rules of just conduct are discoverable, but only by the superior rationality of certain sociological processes. Human rationality still plays a crucial role, however, in that it is only man's rational faculty which allows him to subordinate his primitive emotions to the dictates of just and rational behaviour.

Utilitarians, by contrast, assume utilitarianism to follow directly from their insight into the universal nature of man. The objective standard which utilitarian justice seeks to apply is thus a human-centred one, and is based on the assumption that that which will result in the greatest aggregate of utility is objectively discoverable because it is measurable.[23]

The third concern of both streams of liberalism, as is by now apparent, is universalisability. Since the standard invoked in both cases is the rational man who rises above contingency, there must be nothing particularistic about these claims, nothing that would make them more appropriate for one kind of society or one kind of man than for another. Liberalism seeks precisely to escape the kind of particularism in which liberals believe political philosophies based on the good were trapped: they could not claim to be valid for all men because they presupposed agreement on ends—a chimerical idea to liberal eyes.

One evident consequence of these three preoccupations has been that this tradition of political philosophy has concerned itself with the discovery and application of *rules* governing social relations of rational individuals, which rules embody the

---

[23] The most obvious example of this is Bentham's famous attempt to devise a 'calculus of felicity', whose whole purpose was to enable men to quantify in a common medium all possible pleasures and provide a method which would allow one, by a mechanistic calculation, to determine in all circumstances which action would produce the greatest aggregate happiness. See Letwin, op. cit., Part II.

value-free objectivity that is sought. Justice and morality are seen to consist in the observance of rules, quite independent of the motivation which may lead individuals to observe them. Put another way, justice and social morality are seen as external rules which one follows in choosing the means to realise one's ends. Private ethics and public morality are not only not co-extensive, they have no necessary connection. The former embodies an internal conception of the good which is subjective and therefore not universalisable; the latter provides rules indicating how one must behave in order to be just in one's social relations.

The significance of this difference lies in the different sort of engagement called for on the part of the person seeking to know how to act at those times when moral choices must be made. Such 'conditions of choice' require the choosing subject to determine which considerations will guide him in his decision. This activity can provisionally be identified, following Kant,[24] as a kind of *judging*. Briefly, Kant held that the activity of judging could be defined as the 'subsuming of particulars under universals'[25] or the assigning of particular facts, ideas, or objects to their appropriate category. Within the activity of judging he further distinguished two types, which he called 'determinant' and 'reflective'.

Determinant judgments are those where the appropriate universal is already given and hence where the judging subject's engagement lies merely in subsuming the particular under its correct universal. Kant argues that logical and moral judgments are examples of determinant judgment because their appropriate universal is objectively discoverable and therefore given to the judging subject as something which compels his assent as a rational man. Reflective judgments, by contrast, are those where the particular is given, but the appropriate universal must be found by some means. Kant cites here aesthetic and teleological judgments as cases where the judging subject is required to 'posit' the universal.[26]

---

[24] I. Kant, *The Critique of Judgment*, trans. J. C. Meredith (Oxford, 1952).

[25] R. Beiner, *Political Judgment* (London, 1983), p. 144. In Kant's own words, 'Judgment in general is the faculty of thinking the particular as contained under the universal', quoted in ibid., p. 34.

[26] I am deeply indebted to here to R. Beiner, op. cit., for the substance of this account of Kant's theory of judgment. See in particular Chapters 1, 3, and 7.

Kant is thus arguing that for rational man there are two types of judgment, one which is problematic in its search to subsume particulars under their appropriate universal (reflective judgment), and one which is not (determinant judgment). These two categories of judgment correspond to the difference noticed above between private ethics and public morality under liberalism. For Kant, judging what morality requires is simply a question of rational man exercising his capacity for autonomy; once he has risen above his contingent place in the world and attained the 'enlarged mentality' of a transcendental subject, questions of what the rules of morality require are as straightforward as those concerning the rules of logic. Kant bases his absolute respect for the dignity of the individual on the fact that all men are bearers of this potential to be autonomous and therefore to act in accordance with the a priori moral law.

It seems clear, though, that moral law of this kind cannot dictate to men *all* their choices; at the most it can delineate a certain finite set of choices precluded on grounds of incompatibility with the law, and leaves open another, potentially vast set of choices compatible with it. It is amongst this second set that the autonomous self must choose in attempting to create for itself a good life. Since choosing amongst these is a question of the good (which, amongst the universe of moral actions, are those that most commend themselves to me on aesthetic or other grounds?), and not of the right (which of these possibilities is just?), the objective certainty of the law is unavailable to guide us. We are unavoidably thrown back on the subjective, non-universalisable, and therefore arbitrary judgments we make about the good.

Ronald Beiner has suggested that it is useful to think of the field of reflective judgment given to us by Kant as encompassing two questions: 'What do I want?' and 'How do I get what I want?' or the fields of ends rationality and means rationality respectively.[27] Within the parameters laid down by the Kantian moral law, such judgment is a faculty which permits us to choose what we will regard as good in the absence of a given universal or universals to which all rational men would be compelled to assent by virtue of their rationality.

[27] Ibid., pp. 144–52.

Beiner also draws our attention, however, to the fact that there is another question underlying the previous two, the answer to which will deeply colour the response one gives to them. Kant treats the answer to this question as non-problematical, and yet it is central to his theory. That question is 'Who am I?' or, more precisely, 'Who or what is the rational judging subject?'

The problem this raises is just how satisfactory Kant's account can be if it ignores, or takes for granted, this fundamental question? By holding that there is a universal self contained in each human being which is not constituted by its ties, attachments, and projects (i.e. by any contingent considerations), but is prior to and independent of them, is there enough substance left to this notion of the self that we can plausibly imagine it 'choosing' the ties and attachments it will have? If this notion of the self, which inspires many modern writers in the deontological liberal tradition (such as Nozick, Rawls, Hayek, and others) is so 'thin',[28] how can it carry the moral responsibility for choice which these liberals need it to carry if they are to justify an absolute respect for the individual? By putting into question the plausibility of the 'thin' self, one necessarily calls into question the notion of an objective right discoverable (in principle) by that self, and opens up the possibility not only that the right cannot be prior to the good, but that both the good *and* the right are properly seen as objects of reflective judgment by a very different kind of self.

Utilitarianism makes an even more ambitious claim than deontological liberalism and perhaps for that reason appears even more implausible. Utilitarians certainly consider that the question 'Who am I?' is unproblematic. They hold that Beiner's second question is equally so, but different schools of utilitarianism interpret the import of the question differently. Want-regarding utilitarians, for instance, in keeping with the general liberal desire to respect the autonomy of the individual, take the question exactly as Beiner states it: 'What do I want?' This kind of Benthamite utilitarian holds it to be improper to inquire behind 'revealed preferences', merely accepting their existence and proceeding directly to a consideration of how

---

[28] The term 'thin' used in this sense is, of course, borrowed from J. Rawls, *op. cit.*

these preferences might be reconciled so that the aggregate of utility can be maximised.

On the other hand, need-regarding utilitarians such as Sidney and Beatrice Webb, and many modern social planners, balk at placing such great confidence in what they see as the pure subjectivity of expressed wants. They opt instead to use as their measure of utility an 'objective' scientific analysis of human *needs* which can be arrived at in isolation from the preferences of those directly concerned. Whichever strain of utilitarianism is chosen, of course, makes little difference here, although want-regarding utilitarians shall be the focus in the present argument because of the greater clarity and simplicity of their position. Either way, the utilitarian cannot ask himself either, 'Why do I want/need what I want/need?' nor 'Who am I that I want/need that?'. At most he can take note of his simply given wants/needs and can therefore only ask 'How do I get what I (unproblematically) want/need?'

Even this, for the utilitarian, is a question of determinant judgment, for there is a rule (universal) which is given for choosing what to do in any particular context: the utilitarian is bound to do that which will produce the greatest aggregate of utility in the long run, whether seen in terms of want or need satisfaction. Now it may be true that in any particular situation the action which will produce the greatest such aggregate is not immediately obvious. This means, as was the case with deontological liberalism, that what is given is a rule or a yardstick which permits the discarding of some possible solutions, but which gives no guidance in choosing amongst solutions which prima facie would result in the same amount of utility.

This is one of the great weaknesses of utilitarianism, even of the indirect variety usually associated with J. S. Mill:[29] it requires us to reduce all possible courses of action to a common 'medium of exchange'. One cannot, as a utilitarian, meaningfully characterise actions as noble or base, courageous or cowardly. The utilitarian must see all actions only in terms of their contribution to the maximisation of utility; no other method of evaluation is open to him.

[29] See e.g. John Gray's extremely stimulating restatement of Mill's doctrines of utility and liberty in his op. cit. On the particular point alluded to here, Chapter 4 on Mill's conception of Happiness and the concluding chapter, esp. pp. 125–9, are of great importance.

The strength of utilitarianism has been seen as its provision of a rule which makes no reference to any particular notion of the good for specific individuals, leaving that choice to them. The rule purports to permit an objective choice between privately defined goods. As noted above, utilitarianism shares with deontological liberalism the conviction that reflective judgment can be limited to choosing amongst the possibilities falling within the parameters laid down by the universal, offering the universal as an objective, unquestioned, and unproblematic standard. The difficulty with this particular rule, in opposition to most ethically based liberal ones, is that the aggregative nature of at least some of the cruder forms of utilitarianism prevent it from forming any plausible notion of the individual: men are simply dissolved into a series of centres of pain and pleasure, the only object of concern being the sum of pain or pleasure across all such centres.

The foregoing discussion of some aspects of the two main varieties of liberalism can now be summarised. Attention has been drawn to the liberal obsession with *method*—the belief that the value of any particular knowledge (including moral knowledge) reposes entirely on the validity of the method used to arrive at it. 'The ideal is a method of approach to a given subject that will be foolproof in the sense that anyone can be taught how to use it and to produce valid knowledge at the end of it.'[30] This relates back to the Kantian concern to provide a moral justification of the fullest possible respect for the individual: Kant wished to demonstrate that each man was the bearer of a faculty which made him the moral equal of all other men, the faculty of autonomous choice. Similarly, utilitarians have argued that man's universal, utility-maximising nature gives the wants or needs of each man morally equal weight, and there is no way to choose between them on grounds of intrinsic moral worth.

By limiting themselves to what is universal and abstract in man, both views intentionally exclude any considerations which would allow us to attach any weight or importance to any particular person's or group's notion of the good. Questions of wisdom, experience, and other unquantifiable contingent

---

[30] M. Canovan, *The Political Thought of Hannah Arendt* (London, 1974), p. 2.

factors are held to be irrelevant to politics because they can have no bearing on the reaching of a determinant judgment, which is what judgments about desirable social and political arrangements are held to be. Where man's involvement in such questions is limited to having the will to apply the given universal in a particular situation, this exclusion is undoubtedly valid. The different defences of this exclusion mounted by both Hayek and the Webbs form the substance of the next few chapters.

Before considering their arguments, however, some words of explanation are necessary about the choice of both the topic and the writers to be examined. I have already said that this book is concerned with a tradition in modern British political argument, and that this argument has to do with the possibility and desirability of politics as an activity. The interest of this lies precisely in the fact that it makes startlingly clear that the present preoccupation with debates about the desirable or appropriate sphere of state activity and involvement in society can serve to mask much deeper and more abiding disagreements about politics itself. One of my purposes is to show clearly not only the unbroken continuity of anti-political thought in mainstream British political theory, but to show, by choosing authors normally regarded as polar opposites to make the point, that this debate can and does transcend many contemporary political preoccupations.

A word about the authors themselves. No justification is needed for including Sidney and Beatrice Webb in the categories of British, or, indeed, mainstream political thinkers. Their lifetime preoccupation with political affairs, their involvement with the old LCC, the Fabian Society, and the Labour Party is indisputable, although the extent of their influence is clearly open to differing interpretations.[31] While they wrote voluminously (singly and in collaboration) on an astonishingly wide range of political topics, there are those who question the appropriateness of elevating them to the

---

[31] See, for instance, R. McKibbin's *The Evolution of the Labour Party, 1910-1924*, and particularly his account of the influence of Sidney Webb on the early constitutional debates within the Labour Party.

august status of political or social theorists,[32] because, it is claimed, they are inconsistent in their thought, and because the Webbs themselves eschewed theoretical discussions. This is a somewhat harsh verdict, and in what follows every attempt has been made to show that, far from being inconsistent, the Webbs pursued a line of political thought (at first in parallel and later in tandem) which is astonishing for its unwavering constancy over a period spanning more than fifty years. To be sure, their thought evolved, but always in the direction of an ever greater fidelity to, and single-mindedness about, what they thought important.

On the other hand, some explanation is needed of my decision to treat the Webbs primarily as *utilitarian liberals* rather than as, say, socialists or collectivists, which they certainly also were. This usage is dictated by my wish to draw attention away from contemporary political preoccupations and categories, the better to focus it on other fruitful areas of inquiry. Now it will readily be admitted, I think, that liberalism is traditionally divided into two main streams, one utilitarian, the other ethical or deontological. Yet in their modern incarnations, these schools of thought do not always have an obvious connection. It is often claimed that liberalism is intimately connected with a commitment to individual liberty, but precisely what this means is unclear. Bentham and J. S. Mill are both widely accepted as utilitarians, and yet many of their writings can be interpreted as strongly collectivist.

As I argued earlier, and will argue more fully in Chapter VI, the liberalisms of Hayek and the Webbs represent different modern stages in the decline of the European Enlightenment's search for a rational warrant for our beliefs—a warrant which could be validated by an objective method, applicable by anyone. Of course this decline has lead each school of liberalism in different directions, but it is here that the common thread linking utilitarianism and ethical liberalism is to be found.[33]

In *The Pursuit of Certainty*, Letwin has convincingly traced one such 'line of descent' of the liberal decline from Hume, through Bentham and J. S. Mill, and ending with Beatrice

---

[32] For an account of one such objection, see Margaret Cole, 'The Webbs and Social Theory', *British Journal of Sociology*, 12:2, p. 93.

[33] See e.g. T. Spragens, op. cit., *passim*.

Webb. Such intellectual forebears ought, in themselves, be enough to establish the Webbs as bona fide twentieth-century utilitarians.

Even if this point is accepted, however, it may still be objected that liberalism is not *solely* about such objective method and the search for universal and non-contingent truth. As I have just mentioned, another element is often seen to be a commitment to a negative liberty or freedom from coercion. But if this is held to exclude paternalistic and authoritarian social planners like the Webbs from the utilitarian school of modern liberalism, it may equally endanger what has hitherto been seen as Hayek's unassailable place in the deontological pantheon. The weakness of his definition of coercion is such that, while excluding the coercion of individuals by the state, it sanctions an oppressive and all-pervasive set of social institutions which force men to be free. *Both* the Webbs and Hayek, by concentrating on 'value-free' *methods* for discovering non-contingent social truth, methods inspired by the liberal Enlightenment, have a tendency to want social institutions to reshape men according to some abstract ideal itself beyond rational criticism.

As a final comment on the Webbs, I must make the now obligatory apology for the fact that throughout this book they shall be referred to almost as if they were a single person.[34] This is quite simply due to the fact that the Webbs were so intellectually compatible that when they collaborated on a work it is difficult to separate the contribution of one from that of the other with any certainty.[35] The Webb 'partnership' was a rare and remarkable intellectual achievement which is best honoured by making no distinction between them except where clarity and accuracy demand it.

The choice of F. A. Hayek as one of the subjects in a discussion of modern British political argument is perhaps somewhat more problematic. While it is true that he was born and raised in Austria and is, according to Roger Scruton, 'an economist of the Austrian school',[36] he is now a British citizen

---

[34] See E. J. T. Brennan (ed.), *Education For National Efficiency: The Contribution of Sidney and Beatrice Webb* (London, 1975), pp. 3-4.

[35] Ibid., p. 4.

[36] R. Scruton, *A Dictionary of Political Thought* (London, 1982) p. 196.

and has lived a great part of his life in this country, which he considers his home.[37] Aside from his fairly lengthy stay in America, most of his work and teaching have taken place here. I regard the important place accorded him, for instance, by Rodney Barker in his *Political Ideas in Modern Britain*[38] to be reasonably conclusive proof of Hayek's bona fide membership in the group of contributors to modern British political theory and argument.

There is, of course another, less superficial, justification for Hayek's inclusion in the pantheon of British political theorists than the simple question of his place of residence. In his works Hayek claims to be a part of, and constantly makes appeal to, a tradition of characteristically British political theory in opposition to other, 'Continental'[39] approaches to politics. In the index of authors cited in *The Constitution of Liberty*,[40] for example, to use only one very crude measure, we see J. S. Mill cited 28 times, Marx only 6. Adam Smith is mentioned 16 times, David Hume and Edmund Burke 21 times each, and A. V. Dicey 14. Rousseau makes an appearance only 6 times, Voltaire and Hegel twice, Machiavelli once, and Comte merits not even one mention in over 500 pages. And, of course, the references to people that Hayek sees as outside what he conceives as the broad British tradition are largely hostile.

This is not to say that he endorses this tradition *because* it is British. The names of several German and French thinkers who appear to Hayek to share the liberal presuppositions of the

---

[37] Thus, on p. viii of his *Constitution of Liberty* (London, 1960), Hayek writes: 'My mind has been shaped by a youth spent in my native Austria and by two decades of middle life in Great Britain, of which country I have become and remain a citizen.'

[38] Rodney Barker, *Political Ideas in Modern Britain* (London, 1978), *passim*.

[39] Perhaps understandably, given its date of publication (1944), *The Road to Serfdom* concerns itself most with the German intellectual heritage which contributes to this Continental, collectivist tradition. See particularly Chapters 1 and 13. By 1960, however, the chief opponent seemed to have become the rationalist and positivist French thinkers whose influence later spread to Germany, destroying the latter's nascent attempts to implement the principles of what Hayek calls the 'rule of law', a concept which will be discussed later. In *The Constitution of Liberty*, pp. 54-5, Hayek explicitly contrasts the 'British' and the 'French' traditions: '... one empirical and unsystematic, the other speculative and rationalistic—the first based on an interpretation of traditions and institutions which had spontaneously grown up and were but imperfectly understood, the second aiming at the construction of a utopia, which has often been tried, but never successfully.'

[40] Ibid., pp. 543-51.

British school to which he adheres are invoked in support of his arguments. Thus Ludwig von Mises and Alexis de Tocqueville merited 20 and 17 citations respectively in the index mentioned above.[41] And this pattern of references is by no means limited to *The Constitution of Liberty*; it is on the whole representative of all his major works dealing with political and social themes.

This argument is not intended to defeat John Gray's thesis, advanced in *Hayek on Liberty*,[42] that Hayek's 'general philosophy' is primarily and essentially a neo-Kantian one, for this is clearly right, despite the fact that Kant himself is rarely mentioned by name in Hayek's political works. The present concern is not with the broad sweep of Hayek's general philosophy nor with his philosophical epistemology, but rather with his more specifically *political* theory. If this distinction can be accepted, there are strong grounds for arguing, his Kantian heritage notwithstanding, that Hayek finds the British writers mentioned here a rich source of inspiration—certainly more so than any comparable group of Continental political theorists. He explicitly draws on them for argument and examples far more than their European colleagues, including Kant himself. It should also be noted that Hayek is far from being a *pure* Kantian: as the preceding discussion on the nature of Kantian judgment should have highlighted, Kant places great stock in the individual's rational faculty and capability for autonomous choice. Hayek, believing that a superior rationality is available to guide men in their choices, is extremely sceptical about this faith. What Hayek does adopt quite unreservedly, though, is Kant's argument concerning the essence of justice lying in universalisable rules, or simply 'universals'.[43]

No justification is probably now necessary of the ascription to Hayek of the status of a *mainstream* political theorist in Britain. Not so many years ago his libertarian free market

---

[41] Thus, Hayek has argued (ibid., pp. 54-9) that the British tradition has indeed had its adherents on the Continent, just as the French rationalist tradition has its among English thinkers. Amongst these 'Anglomaniacs' Hayek counts Montesquieu, Constant, de Tocqueville, the younger Turgot, and de Condillac (p. 56 n.). Hobbes and all the English admirers of the French Revolution are among those English thinkers who belong to a 'rationalist' tradition that Hayek is rejecting; ibid., p. 56.

[42] J. Gray, *Hayek on Liberty* (Oxford, 1984), esp. pp. 4-8. It should be noted that Dr Gray's book is a masterly work of considerable scholarly acumen and scope; it is indispensable to any proper appreciation of Hayek's philosophy.

[43] Ibid., p. 7.

philosophy relegated him very much to the margins of political
debate in this country, but the rise in influence and re-
spectability of 'the New Right' and the monetarist bent of Mrs
Thatcher's government have changed all that. In fact it seems
clear that Hayek's role as intellectual inspiration of this movement in Britain is not unlike that of Milton Friedman in relation
to the analogous movement in America.[44] The fact that his
championing of the free market cause spans over forty years in
this country gives an added attraction to his work: unlike some
more recent entrants in the field, Hayek presents us with a
large corpus of works of impressive intellectual consistency. No
other individual or group represents such a rich and established
vein of written material on which to draw for an understanding
of the theoretical underpinnings of the New Right. Finally, it
is worth noting Hayek's particular interest for *political* theorists.
Unlike Friedman and others whose interests lie primarily in
economics, Hayek has made great efforts to relate his free
market philosophy to politics in a serious and sustained way;
he accords major attention in his works to the role and status
of law, constitutions, and the political process. He has, in other
words, thought about political problems in their own right,
and not treated them merely as ancillary to other concerns.

While it is in no way a central part of this thesis, it is of
interest that Hayek and the Webbs were very conscious of each
other's work and that Hayek's interest in the Webbs persisted
long after the members of the partnership died in the 1940s.
The connection was perhaps primarily, but not exclusively,
through the LSE, where Hayek came to teach in the early
thirties.

Hayek is mentioned several times (although his name is
consistently misspelt as 'Hyack') in Beatrice Webb's *Diaries*,
particularly as an abstract economist who '. . . has always been
our antithesis at the school' (entry for 1 May 1937).

While the Webbs seem not to have been impressed by Hayek,
he was far from reciprocating this feeling. On the contrary, as

---

[44] In 'The Resurgence of Ideology', Raymond Plant argues that Hayek's work 'was
a major influence on the recasting of Conservative policy in the period 1974-9'; H.
Drucker (ed.), *Developments in British Politics* (London, 1983), pp. 9-10. See also P.
Cosgrave, *Margaret Thatcher* (London, 1978) and R. Behrens, *The Conservative Party
From Heath to Thatcher* (London, 1979), both of whom argue that Hayek's influence on
Mrs Thatcher's economic thinking is clear.

a man who believes deeply in the long-term influence of both ideas and the thinkers who propose and popularise them, he was strongly impressed by the Webbs' career. In a review of *Our Partnership* he began with the observation that,

It would be difficult to overstate the importance of *Our Partnership* for the understanding of British history in the twentieth century. Beyond this, the story of the Webbs provides a unique lesson of what unselfish and single-minded devotion and the methodical hard work of two people can achieve.[45]

While this may overstate somewhat the influence that the Webbs in fact had, the point is clear: in them Hayek finds confirmed his own belief in the power of ideas and the necessity to work hard at spreading political ideas in which one believes for their own sake, regardless of partisan divisions. Bosanquet plausibly suggests that Hayek's active participation in the founding and perpetuation of the Mount Pelerin society was 'perhaps influenced by the example of Beatrice Webb whose ability to influence opinion he held in great esteem'.[46]

Now while it is easy to establish that there is broad agreement between the Webbs and Hayek on an anti-political approach to politics, it is important not to overstate the case. There are real and serious disagreements between them, especially regarding the conclusions that each of them draws from their (largely agreed) premises. More will be said later about their disagreements, but our first concern must be with their common ground. The place to begin is with an analysis of the main elements of Hayek's political philosophy.

[45] Originally published in *Economica* and reprinted in his *Studies in Philosophy, Politics and Economics* (London, 1967), pp. 341-4.
[46] N. Bosanquet, *After the New Right* (London, 1983), p. 26.

II

THE MARKET, THE INDIVIDUAL,
AND EVOLUTION:
HAYEK'S ETHICAL LIBERALISM

> The paradigm of commerce presented the movement of
> history as being toward the indefinite multi-
> plication of goods and brought the whole progress of
> material, cultural and moral civilisation under this head.
> But so long as it did not contain any equivalent to the
> concept of the *zoon politikon*, of the individual as an
> autonomous, morally and politically choosing being,
> progress must appear to move away from something
> essential to human personality. And this corruption was
> self-generating; society as an engine for the production
> and multiplication of goods was inherently hostile to
> society as the moral foundation of the personality.
>
> J. G. A. Pocock, *The Machiavellian Moment*

Hayekian man is a hedonist, but he has the potential to be a
free and responsible hedonist. Man is a bundle of private
desires, of wants and of goals, all of which he seeks to satisfy
to the greatest degree possible. Man's central problem is that
he is incapable of fully understanding his world or himself,
and is therefore liable to make mistakes in choosing the
appropriate means for effectively pursuing his simply given
goals.[1]

Pre-social man is in a difficult situation: he is free to pursue
his own self-development and fulfilment through the pursuit
of any goal he cares to choose; his liberty to try to be whomever
he wishes is completely unfettered. He often finds, however,
that he is ineffectual in the pursuit of his goals. The first

---

[1] F. A. Hayek, 'The Pretence of Knowledge' (hereinafter cited as 'Pretence', p. 33;
'The Atavism of Social Justice' (hereinafter cited as 'Atavism'), p. 68; and 'The Confusion of Language in Political Thought' (hereinafter cited as 'Confusion'), p. 71. All
these articles may be consulted in F. A. Hayek, *New Studies in Philosophy, Politics,
Economics and the History of Ideas* (London, 1978), hereinafter cited as *New Studies*. See
also F. A. Hayek, *The Sensory Order* (Chicago, 1952), *passim*.

reason for this is that the number of goals he can pursue, within a potentially infinite universe of desires, is limited by the means at his disposal. Where all resources are simply what Nature provides, transformed by his own labour, virtually all man's time is spent in mere survival.

Second, man is ineffectual in satisfying his desires because his knowledge of the world is limited to his own experience of it. Much time and effort is wasted in trying to satisfy his wants in ways which do not prove effective because they generate unintended and undesirable consequences.[2] Hayekian man in the state of nature (although Hayek would not use that term) is free to become whom he will, but is hopelessly ineffective in pursuing his own development or in acting with any degree of certainty in the world. By himself not only can he not accumulate a sufficient understanding of the regularities of the physical universe, but he cannot be aware of more than a fraction of the changes and developments occurring constantly around him.

Third, man lives amongst other men, all of whom are equally seeking to satisfy their wants; but, lacking common rules of behaviour, the actions of pre-social man are unintelligible and unpredictable to his fellows. Men appear to each other as arbitrary and inscrutable. Consequently, even where a man achieves a certain degree of control over the predictable features of his physical environment, his plans may at any moment be upset and destroyed by the capricious acts of other men, mindful not of others' wants and needs, but only of their own. Men are thus a special case of the general problem of unpredictable elements in the human environment.

One possible response to these problems is for man to pool his efforts with others, so that labour is shared, production enhanced, and knowledge of the world more efficiently acquired, accumulated, and passed on. The attraction of this course of action is obvious: by increasing the production of wealth for a comparable outlay of labour, man increases his

² See F. A. Hayek, *Law, Legislation and Liberty*, Vol. I: *Rules and Order* (London, 1982) pp. 35–52; *The Counter-Revolution of Science* (Glencoe, Ill. 1952) p. 100; M. W. Wilhelm, 'The Political Thought of Friederich A. Hayek' in *Political Studies*, 20: 2, p. 171; and S. R. Letwin, 'The Achievement of F. A. Hayek' (hereinafter cited as 'Achievement') in F. Machlup (ed.), *Essays on Hayek* (New York, 1976), pp. 152–3.

aggregate consumption at little or no cost to himself. Similarly, the aggregate of knowledge of what have proved to be effective means of pursuing given goals is greatly multiplied, not only for each member of a single generation, but cumulatively, over many generations. Each man's power to wrest from Nature the means to satisfy his private desires is greatly enhanced over what it would have been in a state of nature. Finally, a social order creates predictability in relations between members of that order because it requires them to act in accordance with certain mutually observed and enforced rules, thereby easing the element of uncertainty attaching to the unpredictable behaviour of others. Social man for Hayek is, above all, a rule-following animal.

While the existence of society makes easier the satisfaction of a certain range of desires, however, it also precludes certain others because society is a co-operative venture depending on relations of interdependence between its members. The fact of this interdependence opens up two possible principles on which social co-operation may be based.

Men may thus, as a first possibility, be coerced to act in accordance with goals they have not themselves chosen, in which case the resulting order is exogenously imposed. Or the social order can avail itself of the potential inherent in man to learn to adjust the pursuit of his particular private ends to those of others. This is done via rules which restrict the range of actions he may take in pursuit of those goals to those compatible with a like pursuit by his fellows. This second order thus arises from the interaction of, on the one hand, all human wills, and certain kinds of rules on the other.

The first option requires someone or some group to impose its particular will (and therefore ends) on the larger social group, authoritatively prescribing its own goals as those of the whole and, a necessary corollary, assigning to individual men the tasks they must perform as members of that order.

The second option, Hayek argues, makes possible a society in which no such authoritative allocation of tasks or goals is necessary or even desirable. Its great strength, on the contrary, is that it allows individual men to use their own knowledge in pursuit of their private goals while still bringing about an overall order or pattern of relationships in which it is possible for men to live together in peace.

The reason that such 'invisible hand' accounts of the growth of social order seem so hard for modern men to accept as factual, according to Hayek, is that we are intellectually imprisoned by a spurious dichotomy between the *natural* and the *artificial*, inherited from the Greeks.[3] Something which is 'natural', is thought of as end-independent, as existing not as the result of someone's particular will, but as the result of the unconscious and undirected interaction of natural forces which *no one* controls.

The word 'artificial', by contrast, conjures up images of things which are the product of human will, artefacts consciously designed by men to serve particular purposes or ends. Hayek's objection to this simple opposition is that it obscures a vital third possibility: that men may create regularities in their social relations as an unintended (and therefore unwilled and unconscious) by-product of their attempts to pursue their own goals. Such a *spontaneous order* is likened to the order which is immanent in certain aspects of nature and which, when realised, results in certain orderly phenomena such as galaxies, solar systems, organisms, and crystals.[4]

It is one of Hayek's central theses that a social order best reduces the uncertainty of the world, and therefore makes it more likely that men will be successful in fulfilling their desires, when it is of the second, spontaneous, sort. The best social order, then, is one in which 'we can produce the conditions for the formation of an order in society, but we cannot arrange the manner in which its elements will order themselves'.[5] Only by allowing men to use their own particular knowledge for their private purposes within a framework of rules can such a spontaneous, non-patterned order be formed.

For such a social order to function, however, man must be prepared to renounce goals which might be personally satisfying but the pursuit of which would require someone else's

---

[3] *Rules and Order*, pp. 20-1.

[4] F. A. Hayek, *The Constitution of Liberty* (hereinafter cited as *Constitution*) (London, 1960), p. 160. See also 'Notes on the Evolution of Systems of Rules of Conduct', p. 74, in F. A. Hayek, *Studies in Philosophy, Politics and Economics* (London, 1967), hereinafter cited as *Studies*.

[5] *Constitution*, p. 161.

contribution against their will.[6] Liberty is defined by Hayek as the 'state in which a man is not subject to coercion by the arbitrary will of another or others'[7] and is not simply, as has been claimed elsewhere,[8] an end in itself. Although it will come in for some criticism later in this chapter, for the moment I shall accept Hayek's own view that liberty is itself morally justified because an individual's wants are sovereign and that they are sovereign because they are the self-prescribed means to each individual's own realisation.[9] 'The individual deserves respect *qua* man and, as such must be given the right to free development, power over his destiny, choice and responsibility'.[10] More precisely, the individual deserves respect as a choosing agent who is free to decide who he shall be, and whose choices in this regard are to be respected because he must live with their consequences.[11]

Given this sovereignty of wants and the self-chosen path to individual fulfilment, Hayek argues that society is morally justified, or political obligation exists, to the extent that man may pursue the goals he has chosen, free from the arbitrary coercion of others.[12]

One could thus say that man leaves the state of nature when he chooses not to pursue certain desires in order to obtain the rather different freedom that a social order might offer. To say that in a social context one is not free to act however one wishes (e.g. to rob or murder one's neighbour) is not to say that one is coerced. Man sees that the aggregate of wants he will be able to satisfy in a social context is greater than what he could achieve outside and, faced with this choice, he chooses to act other than purely selfishly. This is true even if he would prefer to act selfishly, and acts in a socially acceptable manner purely to obtain the means to private

[6] F. A. Hayek, *Law, Legislation and Liberty*, Vol. II: *The Mirage of Social Justice* (hereinafter cited as *Mirage*) (London, 1982) p. 150.

[7] *Constitution*, p. 11.

[8] M. W. Wilhelm, op. cit., p. 172.

[9] F. A. Hayek, *The Road to Serfdom* (hereinafter cited as *Serfdom*) (London, 1944), pp. 11 and 78; *Constitution*, Chapter 5 'Responsibility and Freedom', pp. 71–84; H. Finer, *The Road to Reaction* (London, 1947) p. 77.

[10] M. W. Wilhelm, op. cit., p. 172.

[11] F. A. Hayek, *Serfdom*, pp. 27, 156; *Constitution*, p. 71.

[12] F. A. Hayek, *Serfdom*, p. 27; *Mirage*, p. 57; *Constitution*, pp. 76–81.

satisfactions.[13] Man, then, is not a naturally social creature, but a private selfish one who realises he can be individually better off overall in a social order.[14]

It is this realisation which makes a spontaneous social order possible. Through experience men come to appreciate that co-operation widens the range of possibilities for them as individuals. The more men co-operate successfully, the better they learn to adjust their activities to one another. Those ways of co-operating which prove most successful are retained, even though no one invented them or willed that men co-operate in this way rather than another. The rules of social co-operation are the unintended but indispensable product of ever more successful experiments in social co-operation.

Selfish human nature, the rational faculty in each man, and social institutions: these are the three elements of Hayek's theory of human progress. On this view, there is a conflict between man's wish to realise any and every desire he has, and his rational insight that he can satisfy a greater number of them in a social context than alone.[15] The conflict arises from the fact that to reach the greatest aggregate of want satisfaction, man must choose not to pursue certain (antisocial) goals. This is a wholly different choice from that which he faced outside society. There the choice was simply between whatever consummations were physically possible and could be imagined. For Hayek, the choice to join a social order and therefore to renounce a whole range of conceivable consummations is the true beginning of rationality, for rationality only develops in a context of moral choice, that is to say in a social order.[16]

In other words, Hayek's selfish utility-maximising man takes the first step towards rational behaviour when he realises that he can satisfy more wants overall by giving up some wants in particular. This starts society on an evolutionary trajectory, driven by the twin motors of man's growing capacity to be rational (to renounce certain desires the better to satisfy a

[13] See M. W. Wilhelm, op. cit., p. 171; *Serfdom*, p. 67, *Law, Legislation and Liberty*, Vol. III: *The Political Order of a Free People* (London, 1979) (hereinafter cited as *Political Order*), p. 146.

[14] *Constitution*, pp. 76, 83.

[15] Ibid., Chapter 5; also Wilhelm, op. cit., p. 171.

[16] *Serfdom*, p. 156.

larger number of others) and of man's insatiable desire to satisfy the largest possible aggregate of desires. The 'trajectory' arises from the union of these two aspects of man: the more antisocial desires man can renounce, the greater will be the aggregate of satisfactions he can achieve. The evolution of civilisation is the story of man's growing realisation that all his desires are commensurables, that nothing is to be desired in itself, but only as a means to greater overall satisfaction. If all desires are in principle interchangeable, and each man measures his own welfare in terms of the aggregate of self-chosen consummations, then evolution, the 'competitive selection of cultural institutions'[17] will favour those societies which maximise the production of what may be called socially compatible utilities.

Hayek's theory of progress does not stop here, though, for the subordination of man's antisocial and irrational side to his growing rational insight is a *condition* of progress, not progress itself: '... progress consists in the discovery of the not yet known. ...'.[18] The more men know, the more they can do. This refers not only, or even primarily, to knowledge of the natural world, although this is clearly important. Hayek's attention here is directed to knowledge of a peculiarly social kind.

One such type of knowledge concerns the particular environment in which a man lives which, combined with his particular knowledge and skills, makes him better suited than anyone else to turn those circumstances into productive resources. A society which allows men, indeed encourages them, to use opportunities known only to them to pursue their particular ends will, overall, result in more facts about the physical and social world being known and acted upon than any other arrangement. People will have an incentive to explore every nook and cranny of their particular circumstances in order to discover whether they are making the most of them that they can. This, in its turn, maximises the knowledge men have of their own world. Hayek holds it as axiomatic that the more men know about their environment,

---

[17] 'Atavism', p. 68.
[18] *Constitution*, p. 41.

the greater their chances of bringing their own freely chosen plans to fruition.

The second type of knowledge has to do with the behaviour of men in a social setting. Men here are subject to *rules*, having left the lawless pre-social state. That being the case, to the extent that they observe the rules, their behaviour ceases to be an arbitrary mystery and assumes a regularity on which other men can depend. The success of men's attempts to plan is enhanced not only because they know more about the regularities of the physical environment on which they can depend, but also because they come to understand that the behaviour of men can now be regarded as a 'datum', at least in those respects to which the rules refer. This is knowledge of what Hayek calls 'man made cause-and-effect relations'.[19] This, plus a knowledge of the laws of nature, are what allow men to plan for the future with a reasonable degree of confidence.

What are to be considered socially compatible utilities, or those desires which men may pursue under the social rules, is a central question for Hayek.[20] The answer he gives is to be found in his understanding of the historical development of human society. For Hayek, such evolution falls into three distinct phases: primitive, tribal, and urban/commercial,[21] and each of these corresponds to a particular development of the pattern of human wants, the satisfaction of which are considered proper social aims.

Primitive society was made up of small hunting groups of fifty or so, whose primary purpose was to pool the members' efforts toward a more effective prosecution of the hunt and

---

[19] Ibid., p. 153. See also pp. 156–9.

[20] This does not imply that the rules prescribe a particular desire to be pursued, but rather that rules restrict the range of possible choices. Such a restriction of choices is not, for Hayek, in any sense coercive since it still leaves the agent free to make his own choice. Even if the agent's choice is so restricted as to leave him only one possible course of action as a result of permissible actions on the part of others, this is not seen as coercion unless the other decisions were taken for the purpose of bending the agent to the will of another, so that he no longer may follow his own will but is subject to that of another. A full description of Hayek's account of coercion may be found in *Constitution*, Chapter 9, but compare L. Robbins, 'Hayek on Liberty', *Economica* (Feb. 1961), pp. 66–81 and R. Hamowy, 'Hayek's Conception of Freedom: A Critique', *New Individualist Review* (Apr. 1961), pp. 28–31.

[21] 'Atavism', pp. 58–62; *Constitution*, p. 40.

other ancillary activities. As a society based on face to face contact and a common, accepted, concrete goal, it was somewhat analogous to the family, and in it strong ties of dependence and obligation developed. It was characterised by 'a unitary purpose or a common hierarchy of ends, and a deliberate sharing of means according to a common view of individual merits'.[22] Consequently, its social order was primarily exogenous.

The appeal that such unity and solidarity, such a sense of shared aims, still inspires in many today is due, Hayek contends, to archaic remnants of instincts which were acquired in this period, instincts well suited to that stage of social evolution, but which are now socially inappropriate. In fact he argues that these 'instincts' are probably not learned, but genetically transmitted, human beings having lived under the empire of these social imperatives many thousands of years longer than any other subsequent social form.[23] Most of modern man's so-called moral senses come down to us as an awkward heritage of this time.

Such values were appropriate then because of the unanimous agreement on concrete social aims which small social scale and circumstances made possible; but the unitary, concrete aims of such a society, as well as the certainty and security of social status which were concomitants of a social structure evolved to facilitate the hunt, were not its strength, but its weakness.

Primitive society was doomed from the outset by the imperatives of the evolutionary process, driven by individual selfishness, man's status as an infinite consumer of utilities, and a growing stock of knowledge. The primitive social order could not survive because it required all men to pursue a given goal, identifying their personal goals with the overriding social one. By thus preventing individuals from pursuing other opportunities (e.g. technological innovation in agriculture) in favour of doggedly pursuing a fixed objective, such societies made inefficient use of their resources, failed both to pursue possibilities that might have made all their members better

---

[22] 'Atavism', p. 59; see also e.g. *Mirage*, pp. 143-9.
[23] 'Atavism', p. 59.

off and to learn about other features of their circumstances than those directly relevant to the hunt.

Both by restricting the ability of individuals to exploit opportunities known to them, and by misallocating resources (food, clothing, status, etc.) on the basis of need and merit rather than by the economically efficient criterion of the most effective contribution to overall production, primitive society stifled initiative.[24] In so doing, it obstructed the drive of selfish men to seek the greatest satisfaction for the least effort. Efficiency, seen as the production of the most utilities for the least outlay of resources,[25] was subordinated to a concrete social goal, and this meant the aggregate of consummations available was less than it would have been under an arrangement where '. . . individuals are free in the sense of being allowed to use their own knowledge for their own purposes'.[26]

This notion, which Vernon calls the principle of dispersed knowledge,[27] harks back to Hayek's conviction, expressed at the beginning of this chapter, that man's knowledge of his world, his society, and himself is necessarily partial.[28] There is simply an insuperable epistemological barrier which prevents men from knowing everything about their situation. On the other hand, it does ensure, Hayek maintains, that the man in the concrete situation knows more about it than someone who knows about it only in the abstract or whose knowledge of it is indirect.[29] We have already seen, though, that individuals are often mistaken (e.g. man in the state of nature) about how to exploit most efficiently the opportunities available to them and perhaps known only to them as individuals. One of society's great benefits is the capacity it affords to individuals to accumulate and transmit knowledge, thereby making each man more effective in the pursuit of his private goals.

Primitive society lost out in the evolutionary process of competitive cultural selection, then, because its unitary pursuit

[24] Ibid., p. 60.
[25] Ibid., p. 66.
[26] Ibid., p. 58; see also *Rules and Order*, pp. 48–50 and *Serfdom*, pp. 122–3.
[27] R. Vernon, 'The "Great Society" and the "Open Society": Liberalism in Hayek and Popper', *Canadian Journal of Political Science*, 9: 2, p. 264. On this see also *Constitution, passim*, and esp. Chapter 2; and *Rules and Order, passim*, and esp. Chapter 1.
[28] 'Pretence', pp. 33–4; 'Atavism', p. 68; 'Confusion', p. 71; *Serfdom, passim*; R. Vernon, op. cit., p. 264; Letwin, 'Achievement', op. cit., p. 151.
[29] 'Confusion', p. 71; *Rules and Order*, pp. 11–15.

of a given concrete goal was in conflict with the two basic human urges Hayek has identified. The attempt to prescribe concrete social goals and obligations authoritatively had two effects. First, it actively prevented members of the society from discovering ways of exploiting new opportunities for wealth production known only to themselves as individuals. Since primitive society believed its survival to depend on the unitary pursuit of its own goals, and imposed a patterned distribution of its resources in accordance with them, innovation and learning outside these limits were actively discouraged. This inefficient use of the knowledge available to all members of society was the root cause of the static social order and its material poverty.

The second, passive, effect of the pursuit of socially prescribed and enforced goals was to impoverish and narrow the range of the 'learning programme' that socio-cultural institutions provide.[30] By restricting the field in which information was collected and transmitted to that primarily associated with the hunt and the maintenance of a static social structure, each individual's power to exploit opportunities known to him was largely restricted to his own personal knowledge and ingenuity. And since social contact and exchange were largely intra-band, new ideas and innovations were difficult to import from the outside. Face to face society was and is, for Hayek, a closed society.[31]

Understanding the nature of this dilemma, and the way rational man unwittingly discovered to overcome it, is Hayek's story of the evolution of society. Its solution is the unconscious product of man's growing rationality and accumulated knowledge of the world, and is the criterion by which one distinguishes socially compatible utilities.

The obstacle to human fulfilment in primitive society, on the Hayekian view, was the lack of freedom of its members to pursue self-prescribed goals in preference to the overriding social ones. The resulting system of distribution of resources meant that the band as a whole was worse off than it might have been, because the ability of each man to choose other satisfactions than the socially stipulated ones was restricted.

[30] *Mirage*, p. 111.
[31] 'Atavism', *passim*; *Political Order*, p. 90.

While the rational response was simple, its implementation is still only tenuous and partial after several thousand years of human striving.

That response has been to substitute ever more abstract social aims for concrete ones, and abstract human relations for personal ones. This has been in part the cause, and in part the effect, of the growing scale of human societies.[32]

One of the reasons that man joined society originally was that its division and specialisation of labour greatly broadened the range of his potential consumption of utilities. As long as the band was limited in size by its food gathering techniques, and the division of labour was governed exclusively by the social goal of the hunt rather than by individual desires for private consummations, both the scale of society and its ability to satisfy its members was greatly restricted. Those societies which were able to loosen these restrictions, however, were the ones favoured by evolution. What they did was simply to reduce the range of social obligations gradually from the pursuit of concrete social goals to the observance of abstract rules about what was to be considered socially acceptable behaviour.[33] By leaving men ever freer to choose their own goals (subject to a compatible freedom for all others) and by allowing them to keep an ever larger share of the material reward accruing from their ever more specialised labour, such societies increased their wealth by increasing the freedom of their members and vice versa. We shall see shortly the significance of this interdependence.

Progress along the evolutionary path has been slow, however, because of the reluctance of a part of man to submit to the discipline of rationality. This part yearns for the face-to-face contact and concrete obligations and duties to known people which primitive society afforded. Hayek has relatively little to say about the 'tribal', intermediate phase of social evolution. He does, however, suggest that it was a period of transition during which men's irrational desires struggled with the logic of the coming abstract order for the upper hand.[34] While recognising that such desires may in fact be held by individuals,

[32] *Rules and Order*, pp. 17–19.
[33] *Mirage*, Chapter 11.
[34] Ibid., pp. 88–91; 'Atavism', p. 61.

the necessary incompatibility of those desires with the direction of evolution makes them disruptive of the greatest fulfilment of all members of society, including those who hold them. The moral imperative of evolved society requires every man to see all other members of his society, and of the human race in general, as impersonal and abstract beings with whom he shares only impersonal and abstract ties.[35]

The good of individuals, which is most effectively pursued in a social context, is thus dependent on a rational choice to eschew personal ties and commitments, and so Hayek emphasises, 'the increase in personal freedom which results from the destruction of "organic" or familial ties among men who, as legally secured atoms, can choose their own paths and attachments'.[36]

Rationality and selfishness work in tandem to reduce the range of moral obligations men owe to other, known men and extend the moral obligations one owes to all human beings by virtue of their abstract status as equal but anonymous contributors to everyone's development. The transition from primitive to more evolved and, finally, the Great or Open Society,[37] the transition from pre-rational to rational man, is thus the transition to a society in which men have learned to co-ordinate the pursuit of their private goals within a context of universal abstract rules. A society free from tribal and primitive morals, in which rationality was always gaining the upper hand over irrationality, would be one where each man's private goals were subordinated to abstract, never concrete, social goals. This must mean that the only possible and rational social goal would be the gradual improvement of the framework of abstract rules which co-ordinates human effort by allowing each individual to distinguish socially compatible utilities.

In short, *any* goal that can be pursued without violating a rule of the game of social co-operation is a private satisfaction compatible with the social order. Such goals may be pursued

---

[35] *Mirage*, p. 91; see also 'Atavism', p. 60.

[36] R. Vernon, op. cit., p. 267.

[37] Although Hayek explicitly treats the terms 'Open Society' (in the sense in which Sir Karl Popper uses it) and 'Great Society' (in the sense Hayek intends it to be employed) as synonymous, this is by no means self-evident, and potentially the two terms are even mutually exclusive. On this see R. Vernon, op. cit., pp. 269 ff.

by an individual to the utmost limits of his ability and resources. In so doing the individual realises his true self, because all his goals are self-chosen: none of them result from externally imposed and enforceable obligations and none of them are coercively chosen for him by others. True, the·rules prevent him from pursuing certain goals he might otherwise wish to pursue, but since rational insight assures him of the utter commensurability of different consummations this is not coercion, but merely the supplying of information which makes rational (i.e. socially compatible) choice possible. He is not told what he must choose, but merely what he may not choose. Liberty is thus an essentially negative concept.

Rules are therefore central not only to Hayek's social order, but to his moral philosophy as well. The Great Society, a rule-bound society without concrete collective goals, is the only one in which man's selfish utility-maximising nature can become rational, responsible, and morally fulfilled.

The question arises of how the rules themselves are to be arrived at. Since they are the framework within which all social activity takes place, and since, as we have seen, no man or group of men is capable of the necessary omniscience, such rules cannot be simply the product of conscious thought. The development of rules follows a course parallel to that of the growth of human rationality: they are the accretion of countless generations' attempts to adjust human efforts to one another. Rules are the rational man's way of coping with his irremediable ignorance of the world.[38]

So socio-cultural institutions are programmes providing a way of accumulating and passing on successive generations' experience of the ways of acting which have proved successful. The proper function of rules is to provide rational man with information about how his predecessors solved their problems. Rules, for instance, about how to act socially, how to repair an automobile, and how to write a book represent the experience of the past, handed down to the present. But in order for such rules to be effective, they must genuinely reflect actual accumulated experience far greater than any man or group of men could encompass. Not only that, but they must

---

[38] *Rules and Order*, pp. 17–31; *Political Order*, pp. 155–9.

reflect the experience of free men struggling to realise their
own goals, because then their status as a dependable guide to
the rational and efficient development of resources will be
assured. The 'value of freedom consists mainly in the opportunity it provides for the growth of the undesigned, and
the beneficial functioning of a free society rests largely on the
existence of such freely grown institutions'.[39] By allowing free
men the scope to turn their limited resources into the greatest
possible aggregate of socially compatible utilities, and then
leaving behind the fruit of their experience in the form of
rules, the Great Society offers men a far more comprehensive
and accurate guide to efficacious action in an uncertain world
than any conceivable alternative. And by establishing rules
by which it is normally[40] rational to abide, a further degree
of predictability is introduced into man's life.

While freely grown, undesigned social institutions such as
language, law, custom, and conventional wisdom thus offer
to rational man a good guide to the effective pursuit of his
goals, it is still but a negative one. How does the rational man
decide which opportunities afforded him by his various
resources and his peculiar circumstances will bring him the
greatest aggregate of utilities and therefore the greatest
personal fulfilment? No better answer can be found, claims
Hayek, than the market.

The market's superiority is established here because it
'ensures that all of a society's dispersed knowledge will be
taken into account and used'.[41] It is therefore more efficient
than any known alternative. The market allows men to adjust
their activities in response to an objective and impersonal set
of indicators (free market prices), rather than in response to

---

[39] *Constitution*, p. 61; cited in R. Barker, *Political Ideas in Modern Britain* (London,
1978), p. 200.

[40] 'Normally' because Hayek seems to feel that the best sort of rules are those which
leave some discretion to the individual whether to follow them or to deviate because
the benefits he sees flowing from that decision outweigh the obloquy which he will
incur as a result of non-observance. He thus prefers customary rules to statutory ones,
because the penalties attaching to the former are often less onerous and certain. Such
flexibility reinforces the free competition of ideas in the market-place where the most
effective win out through a process of trial and error. See *Political Order*, pp. 161-3; M.
W. Wilhelm, op. cit., p. 173 and R. Barker, op. cit., p. 200.

[41] 'Atavism', p. 62; also R. Barker, op. cit., p. 135.

the merely perceived needs or wants of known individuals[42] or the coercive orders of an administrative authority. It is therefore more moral than any known alternative. The market,

is the only method by which activities can be adjusted to each other without the coercive and arbitrary intervention of authority ... and it gives the individual a chance to decide whether the prospects of a particular occupation are sufficient to compensate for the disadvantages and risks connected with it.[43]

It therefore offers more choice (and consequently more liberty) than any known alternative. Finally, the market acts so as to encourage all selfish individuals to try to increase the material well-being and therefore personal development, of 'any member of his society, taken at random, as much as possible'.[44] It is therefore more just than any known alternative.

Hayek naturally finds the strongest defence of the market order in the comparison with a centrally planned one, and his development of the contrast is helpful in drawing out his premises.

Planning is based, in the first instance, on a spurious and untenable 'pretence of knowledge'[45] on the part of the planners themselves. Given the epistemological barrier noted earlier, any attempt to understand and foresee society's operation from a central point, or even from a series of more or less decentralised ones, is doomed from the start. It is doomed because such a consciously designed construct cannot possibly utilise as much of society's dispersed knowledge as the spontaneous and freely grown order of the market.[46]

In opposition to most modern planners, then, Hayek argues that the increasing complexity of society, resulting from an ever more specialised division of labour, makes planning less rather than more appropriate to the Great Society when compared with primitive or tribal societies. In the latter two it was possible to achieve a 'synoptic view'[47] of society's operation, but this is simply no longer possible. Thus,

[42] 'Atavism', p. 63 and H. Finer, op. cit., Chapter 8.
[43] *Serfdom*, p. 27.
[44] 'Atavism', p. 62; *Mirage*, pp. 126-8.
[45] 'Pretence', *passim*.
[46] *Serfdom*, p. 74; see also e.g. *Mirage*, *passim*.
[47] *Serfdom*, p. 36.

[a]s decentralisation has become necessary because nobody can consciously balance all the considerations bearing on the decisions of so many individuals, the co-ordination can clearly not be effected by 'conscious control', but only by arrangements which convey to each agent the information he must possess in order effectively to adjust his decisions to those of others.[48]

The superior efficiency of the spontaneous order of free competition thus arises from its ability unconsciously to harness 'the multiplicity of particular, concrete facts which enter this order of human activities because they are known to *some* of its members'.[49]

Hayek's claim for the superior morality of a market social order is again rooted in his vision of individuals whose moral nature is realised through their ability to exercise free choice. He denies that a society as such can be moral or act in a moral manner, for society has no moral nature: this is an exclusive attribute of individuals.[50] If, therefore, society arrogates to itself the right, say, to enforce an ideal-regarding pattern of distribution of wealth, and uses the coercive power of the state to enforce it, this will be an immoral act.

It would be immoral because 'individual moral responsibility ... is incompatible with the realisation of any ... desired overall pattern of distribution',[51] for such a coercively enforced action removes from the individual the ability to choose which alone would confer moral status on it. Because not all the individuals who would contribute to such a state-run scheme would have chosen to do so, the act of redistribution would be immoral because it denies the necessary responsibility for one's actions on which a rational social order reposes. For it to be morally defensible such a scheme would require virtually universal agreement on what constitutes a just pattern of distribution, and such an agreement on concrete social ends, Hayek argues, is not only virtually impossible in the Great Society, but undesirable, for reasons we have seen.

The concern with the visible suffering of individuals, usually at the root of such planning schemes, is a moral sentiment

---

[48] Loc. cit.
[49] 'Confusion', p. 71. Emphasis in original.
[50] *Constitution*, p. 83; *Serfdom*, p. 156; 'Atavism', p. 58.
[51] 'Atavism', p. 58.

which comes to us from the past and is inappropriate to the Great Society. The latter's moral foundation lies in the maximisation of the aggregate of socially compatible utilities available for consumption: by increasing the choices for everyone in society in the abstract (i.e. not just for known persons, but for all), society allows its members the greatest scope for the realisation of their moral nature. The market allows individuals to know what consummations anonymous others wish to have, via the price mechanism which reflects supply and demand, and encourages them to produce that which is most desired but in shortest supply. By efficiently supplying what is most desired, each person not only maximises his power to gratify his own desires, but he increases the aggregate of satisfactions or gratifications in society as a whole.

The market's morality lies in the fact that it leaves men free to choose their own aims while simultaneously encouraging them to offer to all men the greatest possible opportunity to gratify their desires. An authoritatively imposed social goal such as redistribution of income would not only leave everyone worse off, because of its inferior efficiency in distributing resources, but it would reduce freedom for some and undermine responsibility through choice for all.

This still leaves the question of the justice of the market's operation. Even accepting that each individual realises himself through taking responsibility for choice in conditions of scarcity, surely (one could argue) a society which capriciously distributes the economic means of choosing (through the market) is committed to the unequal development of morally equal men and is, therefore, unjust.

Hayek's reply is that this is based on a misunderstanding of justice. The market's largely capricious pattern of distribution of wealth (which he recognises) is absolutely essential for the operation of a society which is just for rich and poor alike.[52]

Since only individual actions may properly be described as moral or just, it is not accurate to characterise the distribution of wealth achieved by the market as just or unjust: results are not the product of anyone's choice in a properly functioning

[52] *Mirage*, pp. 70–3 and 126–8.

market. As long as each individual chooses to act in a moral manner (i.e. in accordance with the abstract rules of the game, themselves not chosen but spontaneously evolved), then society as a whole is just. Note that Hayek's theory of justice is thus a *procedural* one: men act justly to the extent that they respect the rules of social co-operation which, by definition, delimit the sphere of just action. Put the other way around, the rules are designed to prohibit unjust acts by individuals, but to leave them free to choose amongst the alternatives not so proscribed. Hayek is not concerned with the outcome of such rule-observance in particular cases since, so long as no one acted unjustly (broke the rules), *whatever* the outcome is, it is just.[53]

Furthermore, in a properly functioning market order, no one's share of the wealth is assured since it depends on the unpredictable demand for goods and services by free men. But since no one's share is guaranteed, everyone has an incentive to produce as much as possible in order to increase the overall size of the economic pie of which he will get an unpredictable share; this is known as the maximisation principle. The unpredictable nature of the return for one's labour and investment in the market is its strength: if one's income were divorced from one's contribution to satisfying real demand for utilities as expressed through the price mechanism, the incentive to meet that demand would be decreased. If incomes were wholly divorced from it, one's share of the pie might be guaranteed, but the size of the pie would necessarily be smaller because resources would not be used to the most market efficient level possible. Rational man, according to Hayek, would choose a social order in which he was free to do what he would, guided by the superior rationality of rules and the price mechanism, and in return for which he would get an unpredictable share of a production which would be larger than any imaginable alternative could produce.

Even if a poor man under a market order did not find this conclusive, Hayek queries whether the proposed alternative would be more bearable. Under the market, poverty is merely an impersonal result of the operation of just rules: it has no

---

[53] See *Rules and Order*, p. 141.

bearing on need or merit. If, Hayek notes, some other system of distributing income were to be pursued, it would necessarily depend on someone's morally arbitrary view of what constitutes need, merit, or some other subjective criterion. He approvingly echoes J. S. Mill in this regard, who wrote:

A fixed rule, like that of equality, might be acquiesced in, and so might chance, or an external necessity, but that a handful of human beings should weigh everybody in the balance and give more to one and less to another at their sole pleasure and judgment would not be borne unless from persons believed to be more than men, and backed by supernatural terrors.[54]

Since equality reduces the whole of which everyone receives an unpredictable part, and external necessity merely restricts the range of choice available to free men (and can anyway be taken into account in their calculations), the rational man, to Hayek's mind, must choose chance as the only defensible principle for the distribution of wealth. As he notes, the chances of any individual chosen at random are thereby increased over any alternative social order. The fact that individuals known to us personally happen to suffer from the operation of the rule of chance ought not to blind us to the spontaneous order's superiority, for to allow that is to lapse back into the morality of life in the tribe.

A number of interesting questions are suggested by this *tour d'horizon* of Hayek's account of epistemology, anthropology, and morality. The first concerns the logical coherence of his characterisation of the moral nature of society. His arguments sometimes give the appearance of circularity. Freedom or liberty is 'good' because it increases the aggregate of production of which everyone will get an unpredictable share; but maximum wealth production is itself justified in terms of the choice of potential consummations it offers to free individuals, and because it contributes to survival in the evolutionary struggle between societies. Society's survival, in its turn, is only desirable because its continued survival by definition means, in the long run, that society is more efficient in turning

---

[54] Quoted in *Serfdom*, p. 84.

its resources into consumable utilities when compared with its competitors.

Neither liberty, nor wealth as such, nor the survival of society can thus be used as a justification of the spontaneous order, because none of them is logically independent of the others. Now it is true that Hayek asserts the superiority of liberty as a social value, but that does not necessarily resolve the dilemma. He claims, for instance, that a liberal market order will, in all likelihood, make men materially better off in the long run, even if in the short run it does not. What is more, even if it did not, it would still be preferable because under it men enjoy liberty.

A series of problems arise with this. First, it is clear that Hayek does not question the assumption of the productive superiority of the market, but holds it as an implicit article of faith. Yet it is an empirical assertion, and as such susceptible to refutation in principle. It is not sufficient merely to claim that if left alone to function long enough, it will produce more than any alternative. There must be a point at which one has to admit that it has or has not worked. If it were to transpire that the non-market system were the more productive one, this would pose a very real problem for Hayek.

Suppose that a system of authoritative allocation of resources were discovered which produced more and more varied goods for consumption than did the market order. Superficially Hayek would reject it on grounds of reduced liberty, but is liberty so unitary a good? It would appear not on Hayek's own showing. We have already seen that rational man accepts a reduction in the range of potential consummations he may choose in order to maximise the aggregate of consummations. We saw that the notion of the commensurability of gratifications was a crucial element in the growth of Hayek's social rationality.

What if the trade-off were between, on the one hand, the liberty to spend all one's income in the market and get a smaller aggregate of desired gratifications or, on the other hand, being free to spend only a smaller part of one's income in a planned society, but receiving a larger aggregate of desired gratifications in return? That Hayek's rational man would choose the former is not at all self-evident. Nor may

Hayek extricate himself by claiming that some satisfactions in liberal society are uniquely connected to liberty as such and not mediated by the market, for he states explicitly that the 'Great Society is an economic order from which the individual profits by obtaining the means for *all* his ends'.[55]

This of course leaves open the question of the pattern of distribution, but we must recall that to meet Hayek's criterion of justice, it has only to be shown that the pattern improves the chances of any individual, chosen at random, to be better off than under any alternative. If a centrally planned economy were proved more productive overall, this should not prove an insuperable obstacle.

One could take this argument a step further: to the extent that Hayek argues from the assumption that man is a utility-maximiser and from an empirical claim regarding the most efficient form of social organisation, his liberal society rests on a moral foundation which is very shaky indeed. It is not wholly implausible that a society based purely on force might achieve a very high level of material want satisfaction. To this extent at least, Hayek's claims in favour of liberty are empirically refutable, and his moral justification of society weakened.[56]

Hayek's strongest defence against this is usually implicit, although reference has frequently been made to it throughout this chapter. Made explicit, it is simply that his is a philosophy of individual human development. The ultimate defence of liberal market society is the liberty it affords each individual to develop himself through his own free choice of values. This freedom for each to create and change his moral personality is made possible because in this society each man is wholly responsible, through choice, for who he is. To restrict the individual's range of choice (either by coercing him, or by reducing the universe of potential consummations) is to restrict his free moral development, whose untrammelled unfolding is the only possible justification of society. Man is not a pure utility-maximiser, but is 'guided' by rational rules to develop in that direction, the better to achieve maximum development

[55] *Political Order*, p. 146. Emphasis added.
[56] R. Vernon, op. cit., p. 269.

for all. The question of how plausible a route this is for human development will be dealt with at some length in Chapter VI.

For the moment, however, if one recalls Hayek's argument regarding the evolution of societies, then it seems clear that all other values—individual development, liberty, and so forth—must give way to the imperatives of social evolution itself. At the very least there is an implied contradiction, then, when he claims that liberty is the ultimate social and individual value and that he would prefer that even if it meant material impoverishment.

The contradiction arises from his claim that all societies are engaged in a 'competitive selection of cultural institutions'.[57] The effect of such competitive selection is to favour those societies whose institutions prove most efficient in providing a high standard of living for their members and to eliminate (by some largely unspecified means) those societies which fail to keep pace in the evolutionary race. On his own argument, to prefer liberty when it entails comparative inferiority in social productivity is to court social destruction. Continued social survival must be the ultimate goal for Hayek, both because each man's fullest development depends on a social context and because such survival must mean that society is faring well in the struggle with its competitors. But surely any particular social order is then susceptible to rejection on the utilitarian ground that whatever its *moral* merits, to persist with it when it proves inferior in the evolutionary struggle is precisely to court destruction. Presumably rational man would not keep his liberty at this price.

Hayek's case has three elements: first, that individual human development is the highest priority of rational man; second, that development reposes on the aggregate of commensurable consummations and on an element of choice between these; and third, that the first two are dependent on man living in *a* social order. The logical conclusion is that the preservation of social order is the very highest priority. Hayek, though, seeks to convince us that it is not merely society's survival which has priority, but the survival of his favoured society. But a non-liberal society which successfully challenged his two

[57] 'Atavism', p. 68.

empirical claims for market society (that it is more productive and it gives a greater choice between consummations) would, on his own showing, have to displace liberal society. The structure of his argument precludes a strong moral defence of the market order, because it is implicitly based on such a utilitarian individualism. It is in any case unclear from Hayek's account why the survival of liberal market society will help develop the *individual*, which must be the primary basis of his account of political obligation.

Hayek seeks to extricate himself from this difficulty in two ways. First, he attempts to show why he should not be considered a utilitarian on definitional grounds and, second, he suggests that individual desires are socially determined. Let us look at these in turn.

In *The Mirage of Social Justice*, Hayek devotes considerable space to a fairly conventional account of utilitarianism. He condemns 'act-utilitarianism' for its failure to account for the complex system of rules observed in our daily lives and, consequently, for 'the phenomena which we normally describe as morals and law'.[58] Additionally, he reiterates that no one knows enough about their present circumstances, let alone future changes in them, to be able to make any plausible rational calculation with respect to the utility of any particular action.

Next, Hayek turns his attention to 'rule-utilitarianism', which he equally condemns because, 'it is bound to assume the existence of rules not accountable for by utilitarian considerations and thus must abandon the claim that the whole system of moral rules can be derived from their known utility'.[59] Hayek's strongest criticism stems from what he claims is the unjustified utilitarian belief in the omniscience of the rational agent. It is precisely our irremediable ignorance of the world, we may recall, which makes *rules* such a crucial feature of the social environment, for they allow us to make use of knowledge of which we do not have to be conscious.

However, to concentrate so exclusively on the rational, calculating aspect of utilitarianism, especially of the indirect or rule variety, seems rather misleading. While there is much

[58] *Mirage*, p. 19.
[59] Loc. cit.

of value in Hayek's criticism of the omniscience assumption, he appears to believe this to be a necessary aspect of any form of utilitarianism, which it is not. The crucial point of this philosophy, after all, is simply that utility must always be measured against an unquestioned end to be maximised: happiness, need satisfaction, wealth, or social survival.

Hayek is himself a species of irrational or anti-rational rule-utilitarian because he argues that the underlying end to which all 'good'[60] social acts are directed is the prosperity and continuation of the evolutionary order and that the rules developed in our struggle to master our environment all tend toward this end. He merely contends that no one rule's utility can be demonstrated on a purely rational basis because the function that any particular rule plays in maintaining the overall order can never be fully known (and therefore articulated). The whole system stands or falls on the basis of experience, not on the basis of rational analysis.

Hayek has, then, a clear maximising claim and a kind of indirect utilitarian calculus. By acting in accordance with a spontaneously evolved set of rules the ability of any individual chosen at random to realise his ends will be maximised, and so thereby will be the survival chances of society as a whole. The consequences of this indirect and irrational utilitarian aspect of Hayek's thought for his methodological individualism will be considered in some detail below.

At present, we must concern ourselves with Hayek's other argument designed to try to rescue his theory of individual development: that individuals, far from being the true agents of their own development, are in fact the product of their very real and concrete society: their desires are not individually arrived at, but socially determined.[61] This is perhaps more plausible than his radical individualism, and gives society a stronger moral claim on the individual because its role in shaping him is now more firmly recognised. Still, on his

---

[60] Nowhere is Hayek's rather instrumental view of the nature of the terms 'good' and 'bad' brought out more clearly than in *Constitution*, p. 36. In the passage concerned Hayek first appears to deny that values are to be implied by the mere fact of social selection, but this hardly seems to fit in with the rest of his argument, the burden of which is that if we do not accept that what works is for all intents and purposes what is right, that we shall perish in the evolutionary struggle.

[61] *Individualism and Economic Order* (London, 1949), p. 6; see also *Constitution*, p. 25.

account of man's moral nature and responsibility, we are bound to respect an individual's choices because they are *his*, and he is therefore morally responsible for them. If, however, his choices are so constrained by social rules, if his whole nature and character are determined by his existence in society, then in what way are his 'choices' morally significant and sovereign? Hayek's rigidly individual conception of choice and responsibility does not sit well with his vision of the overweening significance of society.[62] It is hard to see how he can strengthen market society's moral claims on men (by not implausibly asserting its formative influence on them) and yet retain integrally the individualism for which he wishes to argue.

Indeed, the relation between Hayek's thesis of social evolution (via the beneficial outputs of a spontaneous social order) on the one hand, and his methodological individualism on the other, is a fruitful area for exploration.[63]

One aspect of this problematic relationship is the nature and force of its explanatory value: Hayek locates the motor of social development and change in the actions, purposes, and choices of individuals, who are the basic units of analysis. But evolution is a species (or at the very least, in the Hayekian account, a societal or group) criterion of development and progress. The fatal (for Hayek) objection that this raises is succinctly stated by Gray:

We have here an analogy with utilitarianism, ... which fails to be morally individualist, ... [*primarily*] because it dissolves or disaggregates individuals into collections or series of episodes of pleasures and pains. The natural-selection theory would seem analogously to displace agents' choices from explanatory centrality by making them a dependent variable of survival chances.[64]

It has just been argued that Hayek's ultimate moral justification of liberal market society lies in the contention that the chances for personal development of any individual chosen at random are maximised where he is free to make use of his own knowledge for his own purposes within a framework

---

[62] '[In Hayek] it was society which was to be free of the state, rather than the individuals who were to be free of society.' R. Barker, *Political Ideas*, p. 200.

[63] As J. Gray has shown in *Hayek on Liberty* (Oxford, 1984), esp. Chapters 2 and 6.

[64] Ibid., p. 53.

of laws neutral with respect to all socially compatible ends. Against this Gray seems to be suggesting (rightly, on my view) that Hayek conflates the fulfilment or development of each individual as a distinct and separate entity, with the 'successful' evolution of the group or society of which they are members. The 'benefit' to the group or society as a whole of the natural selection of cultural institutions is achieved at a high price borne entirely by particular individuals: my unsuccessful attempts to achieve particular goals may leave behind a legacy of knowledge incorporated in the spontaneous order. Not only do I not benefit thereby, I purchase this knowledge for unknown others at (potentially, at least) the cost of great misery and suffering to myself and my family.

The distribution of the means to all satisfactions is not only capricious under Hayek's rules of procedural (or 'commutative') justice, but the spontaneous order which guides us in the attempt to acquire and use these means appears to us like the weather: arbitrary, alienating and uncontrollable. In Hayek's own words, 'the only "utility" which can be said to have determined the rules of conduct is thus not a utility known to the acting persons, or to any one person, but only a hypostatised "utility" to society as a whole'.[65]

The difficulty of reconciling all this with a methodological and moral individualism will appear readily enough, but even the group/society survival aspect seems unconvincing unless it can be shown that the operation of a spontaneous order in fact promotes such survival. Hayek sees the operation of the spontaneous order as necessarily entailing the beneficial influence of something like Adam Smith's famous 'invisible hand': the unplanned and spontaneous operation of such an order causes the actions of individuals to be co-ordinated and adapted to one another, producing desirable consequences unintended by those involved, without this necessitating the coercive intervention of human authority. For this to be convincing, Hayek ought to show that the spontaneous order in fact involves the operation of the invisible hand and not what has been termed the 'invisible boot'![66]

[65] *Mirage*, p. 22.
[66] I am indebted to John Gray for this term, which he used in a paper he presented to the LSE Graduate Political Philosophy seminar in 1984.

This somewhat whimsical term is intended to emphasise two logical truths. First, that the operation of a spontaneous order does not necessarily produce only desirable unintended consequences; and second, that there is no obvious reason to suppose that the balance of good and bad consequences produced must be superior to that of *any* other social order.

Hayek's argument seems to entail the proposition that the natural selection of social and cultural institutions will always function better, thus enhancing group survival prospects, when left to operate 'spontaneously', free from government intervention. This is held to follow directly from Hayek's extremely persuasive epistemological argument against the possibility of centralised economic planning. One can find this latter argument convincing, however, without finding it a firm foundation for the much more far-reaching consequences he deduces from it. At least two reasons justify this scepticism.

In the first place, non-interference is held to result in improved evolutionary survival chances because it maximises the *desirable* unintended consequences of human action. What guarantee do we possess that this is in fact the case? Accepting that the *total* subordination of undirected economic activity to central control would primarily result in undesirable unintended consequences still leaves a whole range of intermediate possibilities; it does not commit us to the non-interference thesis. The latter is again an empirical hypothesis which is difficult to prove but which is certainly open to undermining. To take but one example, Keynesianism is based precisely on the notion that one of the unintended consequences of the unregulated market is the undesirable one of unemployment—the invisible boot. Hayek needs to say much more about why he regards the unintended and undesirable consequences of non-intervention as less damaging to evolutionary prospects than any of the range of interventionist possibilities falling short of full central planning.

Granted, he argues that government intervention (or experimentation) is different in kind from individual experimentation because the former is coercive, making those who disagree with it bear a portion of the cost,[67] but this is not

[67] The fullest statement of Hayek's opposition to authoritative state intervention in

compelling. If the government authoritatively intervenes in a few sectors, its new rules may close off certain possibilities, but leave others open, perhaps even more than existed before. This in itself is not coercion on Hayek's definition and there are many ways in which the state can intervene in the economy without requiring particular individuals to act in a particular way (which *would* be Hayekian coercion). Furthermore, it is not inconceivable that some forms of governmental regulation of some aspects of the market may produce a greater degree of stability and therefore offer firmer guides to rational planning by individuals than a wholly unregulated market.

My second reservation is closely related to the first, and questions Hayek's assumption that only the actions of individuals are to be counted helpful in the struggle for socio-cultural survival. A good case can be made that much of the government intervention that Hayek deplores involves an attempt to achieve limited objectives in response to specific problems within a context of imperfect information: precisely the conditions which make individual actions so crucial to Hayek-ian evolution. There seems little justification, for instance, for attributing to most Western governments the kind of synoptic delusion Hayek deplores. Far from believing that they can predict or control all the consequences of their policies, these policies themselves are often strictly *ad hoc* responses to immediate and pressing problems. In fact, government policy itself is often an unintended consequence of actions taken by individuals and of policies enacted by previous governments. On what basis are we to exclude the possibility that such *ad hoc* and unplanned intervention may on balance generate beneficial unintended consequences? Barry suggests that the NHS serves as a good example, arguing that,

Undeniably, this must have had many indirect effects not anticipated by those who introduced it; but the question is whether, given their original principles, they should have had good reason for regretting its introduction when they saw how it had worked out; and I think the answer is 'no'.[68]

the market is to be found in *Mirage*, Chapter 10, 'The Market Order or Catallaxy', pp. 107–32.
    [68] B. Barry, *Political Argument* (London, 1965), p. 57.

Indeed, Macdonagh, in *A Pattern of Government Growth*[69] persuasively puts the case that much British legislation in the nineteenth century was due almost exclusively to such unplanned and reactive intervention, having neither the intention nor the effect of creating a fully centrally planned economy of the type Hayek convincingly argues against. In short, for Hayek to make the evolutionist case work against *any* intervention in the market, he would need to argue that the unintended consequences of such unplanned governmental activities ought to be regarded as different in kind from analogous actions by individuals, and that a plausible case cannot be made that the former can also improve group survival chances.

A different but intimately related question worth looking at here concerns Hayek's contention that a market social order, as opposed to a political one, enjoys a rationality superior to that of men. We now know that to the extent that this is an empirical claim, it is susceptible to refutation and therefore cannot be accepted as an unquestioned assumption. What this leaves unconsidered is the nature of the claims he is making about various kinds of knowledge.

Hayek starts from the position that men who actually engage in an activity always know more about it than those who know of it only theoretically or indirectly. This is one of the keys to his opposition to economic planning: a planner cannot know as much about any market actor's activity as the actor himself, and still less about the activities of *all* the actors. Any attempt to subordinate the decisions of the 'man on the spot' to those of the planner is bound to result in inefficient production and material impoverishment. By being left to operate unhindered, the market not only co-ordinates all human activities without the need of any conscious human control, but does so in the most productive manner possible.

By analogy, Hayek argues, the spontaneously grown sociopolitical institutions which arise in a market order are to be preferred to consciously designed ones because this allows the dispersed knowledge of society to be harnessed without the intervention of the limited rationality of men, and without agreement being necessary on any social ends save the survival

[69] O. Macdonagh, *A Pattern of Government Growth* (London, 1961).

of a liberal social order. Vernon has persuasively argued, in opposition to this, that the analogy is open to question to the extent that it relies on a notion of social knowledge being dispersed, as opposed to being plural.[70]

In other words, in economic activity, central planning or regulation is inefficient because the object of knowledge of an economic actor (his particular circumstances, opportunities, and resources) is not the same as that of a planner (an optimal distribution of resources according to some abstract criterion). On this view, to the extent that any two people engage in different activities (say, opera singing and shoemaking), their knowledge of those activities may be considered 'dispersed', indicating that each may be knowledgeable in his or her field, but ignorant of the other's. The aggregate of knowledge in society covers all fields, but probably no one man knows a great deal about more than a very few.

Knowledge may be considered plural, however, to the extent that many people engage in the same activity and therefore have a common object of knowledge. All opera singers share a common body of knowledge, as do all shoemakers, although none of them may master it in its entirety. In this case, while opinions may differ about how best to engage in the activity, there is in principle the possibility of those engaged in it reaching an agreed perspective on it, through a comparison of techniques and common experimentation.

Hayek seems to assume, by his analogy, that social knowledge is of the same type as economic knowledge and therefore, by extension, that social man is the same as economic man. Social questions are to be settled indirectly and objectively, through the impersonal medium of the market, rather than through a search for agreement between men who are both social and political as well as economic. Each man's social reality is to be seen as just as personal, private, and incommunicable as his economic circumstances.[71] Analogical argument is, however, notorious for its propensity to focus on unimportant similarities to the exclusion of crucial differences. Hayek appears to have fallen into this logical trap, for in the

[70] R. Vernon, op. cit. p. 267.
[71] *Rules and Order*, p. 34.

economic case we have a genuine instance of dispersed knowledge, whereas in the social case we have, on the contrary, a
good example of plural knowledge. Society is a common reality
to all those who live within it. Each person sees it from his
individual standpoint and consequently sees it in a slightly
different way from his fellows, but the central point is that their
differing perspectives focus on a common reality.

It goes without saying that the market itself is a social mechanism for the production and distribution of goods. To the
extent, then, that a society is prepared to accept the outcome
of the operation of a market mechanism and to abide by its
rules, society's members agree to act as economic men, but only
to that extent. There is a clear difference between, on the one
hand, each person knowing how best to make use of the rules
of the market in order to capitalise on opportunities known
only to him or her; and, on the other hand, each person being
able to form an overall evaluation, a judgment of the social
mechanism itself, which he experiences in common with all
other men.

To the extent, then, that social knowledge is different in
kind from economic knowledge, the market may be a wholly
inappropriate device for regulating certain types of social relations. Or, put another way, it may be inappropriate to treat
certain social relations *as if* they could be adequately characterised as purely market relationships.

Let us look again briefly, in this regard, at the operation of
the market.[72] Hayek would have us believe that the strength
of the price mechanism, as a regulator of social and economic
relations, is its objective impersonality: price results from
myriad independent, anonymous transactions conducted between individuals none of whom, under the rules, are permitted
to have 'market power'. A classic principle of economics holds,
however, that the price mechanism can only establish a true
market value where the objects of exchange are not held to be
intrinsically valuable by market actors. The operation of the
market, being based on a common medium of exchange, is
precluded in the case of any object valued in itself. Indeed,
when we value things in and for themselves, we cease to be the

[72] I am deeply indebted to R. Vernon, op. cit., for much of the argument to follow.

independent market actors for whom all consummations are commensurables.

By likening society to the market, Hayek is in effect arguing that opinions about social and political affairs are analogous to opinions about the market worth of commodities, none of which are valued in themselves. It seems clear, however, even by Hayek's own admission, that people do not regard their opinions or feelings in this light, as merely 'objects of exchange' without intrinsic merit.

Speaking of 'opinion' only, however, is to cast the net too widely. Barry uses a helpful distinction between privately oriented wants and publicly oriented ones which will clarify the point.[73] Here the focus is on the differing kinds of justification for political action implied by different kinds of want or preference.

A privately oriented want, according to Barry, is one that directly affects oneself or one's family in the sense of 'having one's life materially impinged upon by some change in opportunities or routine'.[74] Thus I may have a preference, as an individual, for low rents, cheap food, and high wages, not necessarily because I judge these things intrinsically good, but because my life is 'materially impinged upon' by these things. There is no moral or ideal-regarding judgment involved, merely a calculation of what I regard as making my life, or that of my family, materially better.

Barry argues that a claim to the satisfaction of such wants is precisely that: 'a certain claim to satisfaction *qua* wants',[75] one that takes its genesis and justification from the perceived want itself.

By contrast, publicly oriented wants are in effect not *wants* in this sense at all, for these are a species of ideal-regarding judgment whose satisfaction is claimed not by virtue of the fact that someone *desires* it, but because it is held to be *right*. In support of this he offers the following example:

If the Howard League submits a memorandum to the Home Secretary asking for better conditions in prisons, it will no doubt give a

---

[73] B. Barry, op. cit., Chapter 4, and especially Section 6.
[74] Ibid., p. 63.
[75] Ibid., p. 81 n.

number of reasons why this ought to be done; but among them will not be that the members of the Howard League want it done. On the contrary, its members presumably only want it done because it ought to be done.[76]

Publicly oriented wants, then, refer to some potentially universalisable moral principle which one 'desires' be observed because one believes it to be right and not because it will satisfy some non-universalisable private want.

One feature of such privately oriented wants is that they will, within the limits of each individual's relevant indifference curves,[77] be commensurable, or subject to the logic of the rules of market exchange. To expand on Barry's example, one could say that it would be entirely conceivable for the inmates of Dartmoor Prison to band together, form a 'trade union', and agitate for improved conditions. Any negotiations which took place between inmates and the authorities would involve a trade-off in which the inmates would seek to satisfy the largest number of their privately oriented wants as possible. They might even accept certain 'payments' (improvements in conditions) in exchange for giving up others, or for giving up the agitation tactic altogether.

Members of the Howard League, on the other hand, would not be susceptible to this kind of 'bargaining', because their aim is to achieve something they believe to be right in itself. No offer of money or side payments would lead them to change their mind, if these were genuine publicly oriented wants, because a claim to their satisfaction is not a claim for the provision of some privately consumable good.

Presumably such ideal-regarding publicly oriented wants could only be changed through a process of rational discussion in which reasons for and against the principles could be advanced and people persuaded to change their views. This is different in kind from the case of the prisoners' negotiations: at the end of a market transaction both parties may feel that they got an acceptable deal and yet feel that they wish they had done better; presumably there are always some unfulfilled privately

[76] Ibid., pp. 64-5.
[77] On the economic concept of indifference curves and their application to political debate, see ibid., pp. 4-6. and Chapter VI, below.

oriented wants. In the case of someone who is rationally persuaded to change his mind with regard to a publicly oriented
want, however, it makes no sense for him to wish that he had
'got a better deal', for he is now convinced that his new position
is the right one to hold, not that it was the best he could
manage in the circumstances. This is the difference between
'bargaining' and 'discussion about merits'.

Such ideal-regarding publicly oriented wants, then, are valued for themselves, an essential quality if they are to have any
role to play in a public search for agreement about the nature
and meaning of social relationships. In this, such wants are the
opposite of commodities traded on the market, which must not
be valued in themselves, else they falsify the price mechanism.
It would not make sense to offer someone £1,000 to change a
genuine publicly oriented want—although one might in this
way be successful in getting them to act *as if* they had changed
it—because money and moral principles simply are
incommensurables.

Men in Hayek's world have no common reality, no 'public
space', to use Arendt's phrase again, because knowledge is
private and not fully communicable, and because there are no
common objects of knowledge. Judgments on the rightness of
social and political arrangements are, and can only be, a purely
private matter, of relevance only to the individual holding
them. Such opinions become commodities whose worth is assessed objectively by the superior rationality of the impersonal
market. This superior rationality depends crucially, however,
on there being only one kind of knowledge: individually held
and partially incommunicable knowledge of disparate and
purely private activities pursued as ends in themselves, requiring merely some form of co-ordination. If opinions about
social and economic arrangements are based on plural knowledge of a common object this model will be unable to understand or account for the role of the public world. Such a
public space and shared social reality make possible agreement
amongst men on a conception of how they would like their
social world to be ordered—a process itself dependent on a
political order and political debate in which opinions or ideal-
regarding publicly oriented wants, valued in themselves, can

be exchanged and tested against each other. As Vernon puts it,

... in a market economy, price, ideally, is a result of multiple choices, and not a conclusion reached by an individual or group ... But in the political context, a public opinion, ideally, is a conclusion reached after contrasting positions have been presented, and is related internally, not merely causally, to what has gone before. The notion of different perspectives, in short, is qualitatively different from the market principle of dispersed or local action.[78]

This is equivalent to the difference, he goes on to observe, between the market and the *agora*, and this corresponds quite well to the distinction that has been made here between the proper respective spheres of the market and of politics. If they are indeed two quite separate and distinct activities, then Hayek's attempt to subordinate the latter to the former, by proclaiming the primacy of the market, is very much open to question.[79]

This consideration of Hayek's political and social philosophy can be concluded by examining, very briefly, some of the objections he raises to the sort of 'politicisation' of the social order to which my arguments point. Hayek rejects this line of thought because it places too much confidence in the capacity of men to manage their common affairs in a conscious and deliberate manner. Given their limited rationality, and rational man's desire for certainty, no arrangements will in practice be as efficacious as the market.

The market represents superior rationality and certainty because in it methods for resolving social problems are objectively assessed for their truth value. Similarly, it tests institutions for their utility and efficiency in a way that brings into play a much broader range of human knowledge and experience than any man or group of men could ever hope to amass, exchange,

---

[78] R. Vernon, op. cit., p. 268.

[79] In his very interesting treatment of the problems implicit in applying the standard model of economic analysis of behaviour to political behaviour, Margolis makes some apposite observations in this regard, the conclusion to which is the following: '... although one may be able to go far in economics with models that ignore persuasion, it seems implausible that political theory can go far without explicitly incorporating the role of persuasion in the formal structure of the theory.' H. Margolis, *Selfishness, Altruism and Rationality: A Theory of Social Choice* (Cambridge, 1982), p. 13.

or evaluate. Its superiority in providing men with reliable guides to action in an uncertain world makes it preferable to all consciously designed alternatives: since men cannot foresee the effects of their own actions and decisions, the market order's unceasing testing, adjustment, and self-correction cannot be bettered.

Hayek does see a role for politics, of course, and it would be inaccurate to suggest otherwise.[80] However, politics for him is restricted to a power to make very limited adjustments within the framework of rules built up by the market order: neither the order nor the framework as a whole may themselves be called into question.[81] Even this limited power to tinker with individual rules is severely hedged with restrictions on how and by whom it may be done.[82] In this, democracy can be an expedient order, but it has no intrinsic worth. If autocrats are better able to discipline themselves to respect the framework of rules established by the market, then no one can complain that there is no democratic participation in decision-making.[83] The only form of participation that counts, and which must be protected, is participation in the market as a consumer. In other words, the very limited political sphere in the Great Society is justified because it is the only one compatible with the paramount socio-economic one.

This argument will only stand, however, if it can be shown that the socio-economic order of the Great Society, and its political institutions are, to an important degree, analytically distinct and independent. Otherwise it is logically untenable to justify the latter by reference to the former.[84]

It is clear that such an independence is very difficult for Hayek to demonstrate, for he holds that the operation of a market order is itself dependent on the existence of a certain set of political arrangements which provide an authoritatively

---

[80] See, e.g. *Political Order*, pp. 128–52.

[81] *Mirage*, pp. 24–7.

[82] *Political Order, passim.*

[83] 'We must not deceive ourselves', Hayek argues, on p. 100 of *Serfdom*, 'into believing that all good people must be democrats or will necessarily wish to have a share in the government. Many, no doubt, would rather entrust it to somebody whom they think more competent. Although this might be unwise, there is nothing bad or dishonourable in approving a dictatorship of the good.' See also p. 52.

[84] See R. Vernon, op. cit., p. 266.

prescribed framework of rules which make the market work. Courts, contract, police, and surveillance of monopoly formation are but a few examples of political institutions or activities whose existence is obviously required for a properly functioning market to exist. At least some of these, moreover, would not self-evidently be generated by the market itself. In the proportion that a market order's very existence requires political authorities to take certain conscious decisions, such an order depends on political arrangements, on a political will to maintain such an order, and on the political institutions which evolve or are created to facilitate it. The fact that such political institutions may, by chance or design, prove those most compatible with the operation of a market order does not prove that the political arrangements are thereby *justified*, because they are interdependent with the social order they buttress, and that social order rises or falls with the political arrangements.[85] The notion that all ideas on potential political–economic relations are free to compete in the market order and that those which prove themselves most effective will carry the day, is thus false: certain possibilities are excluded at the outset through the decision to limit political arrangements to those most compatible with the market.

One of the political characteristics of Hayek's Great Society, then, is that it restricts the competition of ideas to those which are compatible with it, leaving the essential order unquestioned. It cannot be right, then, for Hayek to suggest that his society merely harnesses the superior rationality of the market in its quest to find the social arrangements best suited to men, since the mechanism itself is based on a prior agreement not to challenge the established order. By institutionally precluding the consideration of certain alternatives on the purely arbitrary basis of their incompatibility with the present order, the field of free exchange of ideas is limited.

The extra certainty that the market order affords to men through the growth of proven rules is thus purchased at a high

---

[85] Brian Barry, (op. cit., pp. 77–8.) argues further that '... just as the type of economic system inevitably helps determine the sorts of things people want, so the type of economic system a country has depends in the end on its laws and the actions (or inactions) of its government ... But because any economic system must rest on a legal foundation the choice of an economic system must be in the end a political one.'

price. That price is the artificial skewing of the rules against certain alternatives because they are presumed to be inferior to a market order. By thus restricting (not spontaneously, but as an act of political self-denial) the sphere of political debate, the only sphere in which *ideas* can really be tested against one another (as opposed to the establishment of the worth of commodities via a common medium of exchange), Hayek endangers two values he must logically wish to promote. The first is the continued survival of society in the evolutionary struggle, which itself depends on all ideas having their fair chance to prove their worth. The second is maximising of the chance to prove their worth. The second is the maximising of the chances for individual development of any members of society chosen at random, which is his moral justification of political obligation.

theoretical justification of a market social order, I want now to make the discussion much more practical by looking at how he proposes to give concrete form to his analysis. In the next chapter, then, I shall concentrate on Hayek's view of ideal political institutions within the Great Society.

III

IGNORANT MEN AND
BENEFICENT MARKETS:
HAYEK'S POLITICAL INSTITUTIONS

> There is a Greek ideal of self-development which the
> Platonic and Christian ideal of self-government blends
> with, but does not supersede. It may be better to be a
> John Knox than an Alcibiades, but it is better to be a
> Pericles than either; nor would a Pericles, if we had one
> in these days, be without anything good which belonged
> to John Knox.
>
> John Stuart Mill, *On Liberty*

Any attempt to write an adequate account of Hayek's political
philosophy, and consequently of his proposals for concrete
political institutions, immediately meets a major stumbling
block. The problem is that Hayek sees himself first and
foremost as a *social* philosopher.[1] His interest lies in the
understanding and explication of social phenomena which are
the unintended product of human actions, and he clearly
wants the products of spontaneous social processes to override
the strongly rationalistic and constructivistic tendencies of the
political sphere.

In this chapter, I shall argue that Hayek's ethical liberalism,
his belief in an inviolable sphere of liberty for each individual
and his belief in the value of each man as an end in himself,
is a political philosophy dictated by his belief in the primacy
of the social. The derivative nature of his political thought
reveals itself in the fact that while, in the political sphere, he
insists that men be treated as if they were ends in themselves,
in the social sphere this is seen as at least as much an

---

[1] See e.g., *Rules and Order*, p. 5, where Hayek discusses the importance and scope
of what he calls 'social philosophy'; and A. de Crespigny, 'F. A. Hayek: Freedom
for Progress', p. 58 in A. de Crespigny and Kenneth Minogue (eds.), *Contemporary
Political Philosophers* (London, 1976), pp. 49–66.

instrumental calculation as an 'ethical presupposition'.[2] Freedom is simply the *sine qua non* of the efficient operation of the greatest mechanism for the discovery and dissemination of knowledge known to man: the market.

As we have seen, the market allows people to satisfy their own desires by acting on knowledge known to them in their unique social position. Thanks to the kind of freedom possible under the market, men unknowingly act on the greatest possible aggregate of knowledge and produce the greatest possible aggregate of socially compatible utilities. This enhances society's survival chances since the freedom to experiment and acquire new knowledge are what distinguish a dynamic and progressing society from those which are falling behind in the evolutionary struggle.

This clearly makes the notion of liberty or freedom the centre-piece of Hayek's political philosophy. This notion, we can recall, is a purely negative one for Hayek in which men are not subject to coercion by the arbitrary will of other men.[3] Experience has led men to achieve this by granting a monopoly of the use of coercive power to the state and subjecting that state to stringent rules governing the exercise of this monopoly.[4] Hayek's political institutions may thus be seen from one direction as an answer to the problem of how to maximise individual liberty by strictly controlling the only social agency authorised to exercise coercion; and from another direction as an answer to the problem of how to discover those practically and morally justified rules which alone can provide a legitimate pretext for the coercion of free men. The problem is that it is impossible to isolate this as a purely political aspect of Hayek's thought: its derivative nature requires us to refer constantly to his social philosophy. While his politics are clearly about the status and force of various kinds of rules, the origins and functions of those rules cannot be understood except by reference to the predominant social world.

---

[2] *Constitution*, p. 6. In this regard, see also Rodney Barker, *Political Ideas*, p. 200, and Scott Gordon's excellent article 'The Political Economy of F. A. Hayek', *Canadian Journal of Economics*, 14 (1981), pp. 470–87, and esp. p. 472.

[3] See e.g. *Constitution*, p. 11 and *Studies*, p. 229.

[4] For a full statement of Hayek's argument regarding the state's role in exercising a controlled monopoly on legitimate coercion in society, refer to *Constitution*, Chapter 9, 'Coercion and the State', pp. 133–47.

A final preliminary comment: even with the general background of Hayek's thought sketched in the preceding chapter, it will be necessary to develop in greater detail some specific aspects of Hayek's epistemology and other theoretical concerns if we are to grasp the full scope and importance of his proposals for ideal social institutions. The principal focus will be the two central statements of Hayek's political thought, *The Constitution of Liberty* and *Law, Legislation and Liberty*, but other of his works will be drawn on where this will serve to illuminate particular points.[5]

We can begin by seeing what the primacy of the social means for Hayek. In the last chapter I argued that, for him, every society is in a struggle for existence which is dictated by a process of natural selection of cultural institutions. We saw equally how spontaneously grown and undesigned social institutions were the front line troops in this struggle. As society grows steadily more complex and its operations depend on an ever more specialised division of knowledge, the part of the totality of knowledge which one person can know is necessarily reduced and his relative ignorance thereby increased. The only way for man to cope with this unavoidable ignorance is to rely on 'tools', 'traditions', and 'institutions'[6] which supplement conscious knowledge by incorporating within themselves knowledge which has proved useful to others in the past.[7]

Central to this theory is a desire to avoid error and to strive for as much certainty as is realistically available, so that free men can have the best chance of pursuing their self-chosen ends successfully. The accent, however, must be on the 'realistically available'. Since men can only reflect on what they consciously know, the product of any rational process must only take into account the facts of which the particular people involved are aware. For this reason, rationalist constructivism, the belief that men must consciously design anew

[5] *Serfdom*, in particular, is not specifically included because of its essentially negative character: it is an argument against planning rather than for any particular organisation or structure of government, although the negative principles outlined in that work all find many echoes in the later ones.

[6] These terms are used throughout Hayek's work more or less interchangeably, but together they cover the whole field of products of the spontaneous order; cf. *Constitution*, p. 27.

[7] Loc. cit.

for themselves tools adapted for each particular purpose they desire to achieve, is the 'fatal conceit'.[8]

If we are not to reduce our capacities and possibilities to what can be imagined in our limited individual minds, we must put our trust in the 'higher superindividual wisdom ... of spontaneous social growth',[9] for we can thus avail ourselves of the 'knowledge how'[10] which men have adopted through centuries of struggling to master their environment. No one need know the genesis of a particular social institution or practice and even less how or why it works or what purpose it serves. Hayek argues that those social institutions which grow and spread do so because those who use them are successful. Men thus learn and flourish by imitating the more successful, who are those who make use of more certain knowledge than they are themselves aware of.[11]

Men follow rules which are the product of human action but not of human design, then, for two closely related reasons. The first is that, by following such rules, men are assured of a higher chance of success in achieving their goals than if they had consciously to discover all the knowledge necessary for the task. The second is that, because such rules do not prescribe the ends which men must pursue, but merely indicate the ways men must behave if they wish to be successful in whatever they do, the rules can constantly adjust themselves to new facts and discoveries and still leave men free to choose whichever socially compatible consummations they wish.

The supremacy of rules thus derives from their status as products of a sociological discovery procedure which assures men that the knowledge they contain is superior to anything

---

[8] *The Fatal Conceit: The Intellectual Error of Socialism* is, according to John Gray (*Hayek on Liberty*, p. 142), the title of a major new work by Hayek which is now in preparation.

[9] *Constitution*, p. 110.

[10] Hayek is thus making use of the famous distinction between 'knowing how' and 'knowing that' which is frequently associated with the names of Gilbert Ryle (*The Concept of Mind* (London, 1949)) and Michael Oakeshott (*Rationalism in Politics* (London, 1962)). Hayek himself uses this distinction explicitly in *Rules and Order*, p. 76, albeit in a slightly narrower sense.

[11] Hayek argues that the progress of civilisation is directly proportionate to the increase in the number of things men can accomplish without having to devote any thought to them. See the epigraph from A. N. Whitehead to Chapter 2 (p. 22) of *Constitution*.

individual men could know. The beauty of this kind of rule of behaviour for Hayek lies in the fact that it not only leaves men free to pursue their own ends, but it actually incites them actively to pursue the discovery of *new* knowledge which will, in its turn, be incorporated in social institutions.

Progress, for Hayek, 'consists in the discovery of the not yet known',[12] because the discovery of new knowledge allows one to be more effective than one's competitors. By emulating the more successful, individuals unconsciously introduce new knowledge into the social order, and progress occurs. This is where Hayek's insight into the motivation of the free man enters. If 'the preservation of the kind of civilisation we know depends on the operation of forces which, under favourable conditions, produce progress',[13] then a society's chances in the evolutionary struggle and the developmental chances of any individual chosen at random are best improved by letting individual men pit their ingenuity against the world, encouraging them to try to accomplish as much as they can with the knowledge and resources they have.

This may sound like an instrumentalist account of the value of individual liberty, and this is a charge to which Hayek is sensitive. In the 'Introduction' to his *Constitution* he states that,

Some readers will perhaps be disturbed by the impression that I do not take the value of individual liberty as an indisputable ethical presupposition and that, in trying to demonstrate its value, I am possibly making the argument in its support a matter of expediency. This would be a misunderstanding.[14]

Misunderstanding or not, a close reading of Hayek's social philosophy leaves the strong impression that liberty is *primarily* a matter of expediency for the survival of the social order and that it is made an 'indisputable ethical presupposition' in the political sphere in order to prevent men from unwittingly arresting the evolutionary development of their society.

There is considerable textual justification for this scepticism regarding Hayek's claim that liberty is the primary value in the social sphere. To choose only three examples from the

---

[12] *Constitution*, p. 40.
[13] Ibid., pp. 39-40.
[14] Ibid., p. 6.

Constitution, we can see that Hayek argues: 1) '... the case for individual freedom rests chiefly on the recognition of the inevitable ignorance of us all concerning a great many of the factors on which the achievement of our ends and welfare depends';[15] 2) '... the value of freedom consists mainly in the opportunity it provides for the growth of the undesigned ...'; [16] and 3) '... the chief aim of freedom is to provide both the opportunity and the inducement to insure [*sic*] the maximum use of the knowledge that one individual can acquire'.[17] Liberty, then, is valued because it is 'essential to the functioning of the [evolutionary] process',[18] a process whose utility is not only not directly demonstrable for particular individuals, but can at best be indirectly inferred for societal survival.[19]

The rationale for individual liberty within a framework of negative rules is thus *not* any assignable benefit to particular individuals but, quite the contrary, a long-term benefit for society as a whole and for hypothetical individuals. Even if an assignable benefit for individuals could be demonstrated, of course, this would remain a strictly instrumental account which leaves no obvious place for a theory of, say, individual rights.

It is true that this system does allow individuals to benefit from successful experimentation in the past and that we are in general therefore more effective in pursuing certain kinds of goals than our predecessors. The world, however, is an unstable, constantly changing place, so that what once was regarded as certain knowledge can rapidly become outmoded. 'The best we can attain in such a situation is not certainty, but the elimination of avoidable uncertainty.'[20]

We thus come to one of the first turning-points in Hayek's transition from the primary social sphere to the subsidiary political one. Since the results of attempts by individuals to use their own knowledge for their own purposes cannot be predicted,[21] the evolutionarily sound social order will not

---

[15] Ibid., p. 29.
[16] Ibid., p. 61.
[17] Ibid., p. 81.
[18] Ibid., p. 29.
[19] See *Rules and Order*, p. 18 and Chapter II, *passim*, above.
[20] *Mirage*, p. 125.
[21] If they could be predicted, of course, they would by definition have no value

attempt to supplement the satisfactions that men can get for themselves individually. If men are permitted to realise their ends without seeing that this depends exclusively on their striving to exploit opportunities known to them, society as a whole will not act on the basis of as much knowledge as it could. The uncertainty as to what particular individuals will receive as a result of their efforts in a spontaneous social order is thus not an avoidable one.

Similarly, since social planners are just as ignorant as the rest of us, converting the spontaneous order into an organisation which collectively shoulders the burden of experimentation and innovation (thus necessarily reducing the overall effort to discover new knowledge) will result in us knowing less rather than more.

The experience of successful spontaneous social orders, according to Hayek, has been that the only practical way to reduce uncertainty is by allowing men to use their own knowledge for their own purposes within a framework of authoritative rules which plays two functions. The first is to allow men to determine which parts of their environment they may use for their own purposes without interference from others, and under what conditions; this corresponds roughly to the institution of private property. The second is to indicate when others can be expected to act in predictable and dependable ways because *their* behaviour is constrained by obligatory rules.[22] More precisely: these rules set out the ways in which men will be prevented from behaving, or the extent to which they will be restrained from acting, in such a way as to upset the legitimate plans of another. This corresponds to what Hayek calls 'private law' or the rules of 'just conduct' in a free society, of which private property is in fact an important subset.[23]

as a discovery procedure. In *Political Order*, pp. 68-9, Hayek goes into some detail about free competition as the equivalent of scientific experimentation.

[22] See *Constitution*, Chapter 9.

[23] Private property being, for Hayek, nothing other than those rights one has to use what one has without interference. This is not an absolute right; he is careful to distinguish e.g. real and movable property, arguing in the former case that the density of population in urban areas makes it imperative that account be taken of the acute nature of certain neighbourhood effects. See *Constitution*, Chapter 22 'Housing and Town Planning'.

In the previous chapter it was noted that all societies have compulsory rules of behaviour, but that the nature of these rules changes as the *scale* of society grows. In small-scale societies men can agree on common ends, and understand the utility of compulsory rules directed towards the successful pursuit of those ends. The scale and concomitant anonymity and complexity of the Great Society rendering such agreement impossible, men gradually learn that they can agree to co-operate only on the basis of abstract principles which permit social exchange between individuals with different ends. But rising above the pursuit of particular social ends does not mean that a spontaneous social order can dispense with compulsory rules, for these preserve a certain regularity in human behaviour which in the past was provided by the common pursuit of agreed goals. Without such regularities men would be unable to make rational plans because the degree of uncertainty in the world would be too great.[24]

It is of some importance to notice several things about this account of liberty constrained by negative rules. The first is the pivotal role that liberty plays as a *discovery procedure*. The second is that this unique discovery procedure extends to every conceivable area of human existence, morals and ethics as well as productive processes, because knowledge is of one kind only: what appears to us to work or to be useful. Giving men liberty is a way of maximising their knowledge of what has utility.

The first point merely recalls what was established earlier regarding the ultimate social justification of liberty: since we can never know in advance whether someone will discover a better way of doing things and since the only test of efficacy is the ability to resist constant efforts to find something better,[25] leaving men free is the best way of maximising our knowledge and therefore of being successful. While almost all experimentation (exercises of liberty) involves testing the adequacy of a particular rule or established way of doing

---

[24] *Constitution*, pp. 156-7.

[25] The close affinities of Hayek's rules (and especially the rules of just conduct and morality) and Popper's arguments concerning the nature of scientific knowledge (found in both his *Logic of Scientific Discovery* (London, 1955) and *Conjectures and Refutations* (London, 1965) are clearly not coincidental. On p. 43 of *Mirage*, Hayek gives his own account of these similarities.

things, one can only do so within the larger framework of rules that the social order provides. One cannot step outside the framework of rules altogether without depriving oneself, for example, of the rules for organising one's thoughts that make critical analysis, reflection, and innovation possible.[26]

Every successful innovation or thought thus depends on pre-existing tools of thought. Successful experimentation causes a small adjustment within the framework of rules as a whole (as people integrate the new knowledge into their actions) and it is therefore vital that men be as free as possible to challenge existing rules or else progress will be restrained.

It is axiomatic for Hayek, then, that only those rules considered absolutely indispensable for the maintenance of the spontaneous order ought to carry the coercive sanction of the state, because he believes this sanction prevents experimentation with these rules. One could easily assume that these compulsory rules of social co-operation must themselves be justified with reference to some moral code which derived its force from considerations other than utility, especially since Hayek identifies them as rules of *just* conduct and justice is normally seen as a moral concept with a content separate from its usefulness. Hayek, however, denies the possibility of moral knowledge which is qualitatively different from our knowledge of what has utility.

In the epilogue to *Law, Legislation and Liberty*, he makes clear his impatience with philosophies which purport to divine an immutable system of morals implanted in the very nature of men which could give some normative content to terms like justice or ethics. The 'older prophets' failed to recognise that,

... though ... society will find it necessary to enforce its rules of conduct in order to protect itself against disruption, it is not society with a given structure that creates the rules appropriate to it, but the rules which have been practised by a few and then imitated by many which created a social order of a particular kind.[27]

---

[26] For a full discussion of Hayek's view of the important role to be played by such 'immanent criticism' of a framework of rules and how criticism of the framework as a whole assumes a level of knowledge which no man can possibly attain, see *Mirage*, pp. 24–7.

[27] *Political Order*, p. 166.

On my view, however, Hayek wants to make the concept of rules of just conduct carry more weight than it can comfortably bear, and this produces a certain lack of clarity or cohesion in his legal thought. For instance, it is unclear in his account precisely what the relation is between the 'rules of just conduct' which he describes, and those rules which are to carry the coercive sanctions of the state (the law), for clearly the two sets are not fully congruent, or rather the latter is a subset of the former. As we shall see, Hayek wants the courts to enforce certain 'rules of just conduct', but not others, on the grounds that only those rules necessary to the maintenance of an overall order of actions ought to carry coercive sanctions. Rules not enforced by the courts may still be rules of just conduct, but are relatively unimportant to the maintenance of the order and so can be left to informal social sanctions which leave greater scope, according to Hayek, for individual experimentation. In other words, the only coercive sanctions which are justified are those which help to create the conditions in which the least possible coercion is necessary. In Chapter VII it will be shown how this notion of the law prevents Hayek from accounting for certain aspects of the law which are commonplace in most societies.

What I want to take up here is how this one-dimensional view of the law makes Hayek confuse two quite separate aspects of legal rules which govern *individual conduct* and which are enforceable by the courts, a distinction which H. L. A. Hart has captured in the concepts of 'primary' and 'secondary' rules.[28] The essence of the distinction is that primary rules are those concerned with the conditions for the maintenance of social order and hence lay down universal coercive prohibitions of the type 'thou shalt not kill, steal,' etc. Secondary rules either 'facilitate' particular actions by specifying what one must do to secure the law's assistance in enforcing rights and duties voluntarily incurred by individuals (via e.g. contract), or 'confer power' on individuals or bodies (defining how parliament must act to make a valid law or how an individual may make a valid will).

Secondary rules may indirectly involve coercive sanctions, but differ from primary rules in that one can escape the

[28] H. L. A. Hart, *The Concept of Law* (Oxford, 1961), Chapter 5.

sanctions by choosing not to engage in the activities in question: factory legislation places obligations on factory owners, but no one is obliged to be a factory owner. It is thus clear what one must do to avoid the law's coercive aspects. There is nothing one can do, by contrast, to escape the implications of primary rules: these are held to be the minimum conditions of social co-operation and are therefore valid for every member of that society.

Hayek implies that laws governing the activities of individuals can or ought to be exclusively of the *primary* type, i.e. introducing dependable regularities of conduct into the social world by means of coercive sanctions, but maximising freedom by reducing such sanctions to the lowest level compatible with the existence of an overall spontaneous order.[29] As Hart rightly points out, however, this leaves out of account secondary rules, or the possibility that individuals may use the law voluntarily to incur rights and duties which the law will then enforce.[30]

In the case of secondary rules, individuals are constrained to obey certain rules, not because these are essential to the overall order, but because the existence of the law makes possible many forms of voluntary relations which individuals may make binding by observing certain legal forms.

Hayek does, of course, distinguish between the obligations arising under the law and those voluntarily incurred which the law will then enforce. Clearly, though, the law of contract, for instance, is seen by him as having evolved *because* of the dependable regularity it makes possible within the overall social order.[31] While this is clearly an important *aspect* of contract, Hart is clearly right to distinguish it from laws of the type 'thou shalt not kill' which are a minimum condition of any kind of order whatsoever. I can avoid the rules of contract by not entering into any contracts, but I cannot, in this sense, avoid the law against murder except by not

---

[29] On this see in particular Hayek's very interesting reply to Ronald Hamowy's review of *The Constitution of Liberty*. The reply is reprinted in *Studies*, pp. 348–50 under the title 'Freedom and Coercion'.

[30] H. L. A. Hart, op. cit., pp. 89–96.

[31] Hayek thus seems unable to offer a full account of what Hart refers to as the 'internal' and 'external' aspects of rules and particularly the rules of law. This is a subject which will receive a much fuller treatment in Chapter VII.

murdering. In the first case I have no obligation, except by choice; in the second *everyone* has an obligation which will be enforced by the courts.

So while Hayek's rules of just conduct are an important aspect of the law, he obscures its full meaning and function by not distinguishing clearly between informally and formally enforced rules (both of which can, on his account, be rules of just conduct) and between primary and secondary rules. His preoccupation with the difference between rules of individual conduct and commands to government (to be discussed below) is reflected in the wealth of examples he gives as to what kind of law falls into which category, but the confusion regarding different kinds of rules of individual conduct is compounded by the virtual absence of examples. Since the purpose of this chapter is primarily descriptive, Hayek's terminology and usage regarding 'rules of just conduct' will be followed, but where this may create confusion reference will be made to the distinctions discussed above.

In his perceptive review of the *Constitution*, Gordon draws our attention to an important aspect of Hayek's account of the evolutionary development of the rules of *just* conduct:

To say that the basic rules of conduct ... develop in this way is a proposition in sociological theory. To say that such rules are *just* is a proposition in ethics, a very different thing. How are these two propositions linked? Hayek advances the view that the rules that develop in this way are morally proper *because* they are the result of undesigned evolutionary processes: their moral merit is certified by the fact that they are the rules of conduct of societies that have passed the test of competition and survived.[32]

While Gordon and Buchanan[33] are right to point out that this justification of the rules of social conduct appears to confuse success and moral worth, they are perhaps more importantly drawing our attention to Hayek's attempt to rule out disputes about the morality of the rules of just conduct by recognising only one moral criterion against which they can be evaluated. This 'moral monism'[34] derives from Hayek's

[32] Gordon, op. cit., p. 479.

[33] J. M. Buchanan, 'Law and the Invisible Hand', *Freedom in Constitutional Contract* (College Station, Texas, 1977).

[34] This term is Gordon's, op. cit., p. 474.

belief that any attempt to base the compulsory rules of just conduct on substantive moral criteria would necessarily involve an agreement on the particular concrete *ends* which the social order ought to be pursuing, something he believes impossible without coercion.

Given what we know about Hayek's epistemology, he clearly cannot found a theory of justice on any kind of rational reflection or direct knowledge of the just. In the absence of such positive measures, he puts his trust in the negative discovery procedure which is liberty.

The importance of this freedom of the individual ... rests mainly on the fact that the development of custom and morals is an experimental process ... in which alternative rules compete and the more effective are selected by the success of the group obeying them, and may ultimately provide the model for appropriate legislation.[35]

The meaning of the term 'moral monism' should now be clear: by reducing justice and morals to mere considerations of what has proved most successful in men's attempts to prosper, Hayek makes them dependent values of liberty, liberty being the essential condition of discovering what has utility. The burden of Hayek's political philosophy, then, is that the only coercive intervention permissible in the lives of free men is the enforcement of those universal rules of just conduct which experience has shown to be necessary to the orderly search for new knowledge. Since liberty and evolutionary competition are the best way of conducting that search, authoritative rules are morally justified to the exact degree that they secure the greatest possible sphere of free action to the individual compatible with the existence of social co-operation. Justice, morality, and duty are simply descriptive terms for those ways of acting that are conducive to the maintenance of such an order of liberty. For this reason Hayek set himself the task in *Constitution* of showing that 'liberty is not merely one particular value but that it is the source and condition of most moral values'.[36]

Liberty's unique status as not merely one value among many, but the value whose observance makes the discovery

[35] *Mirage*, p. 57.
[36] *Constitution*, p. 6.

of most moral values possible, is of prime importance. Since each man discovers the relative utility of competing values as a result of his unique position in the world and his irreproducible combination of dispersed knowledge, the ends men pursue are inaccessible to reason. This makes the very idea of politics as an attempt to reconcile or aggregate the particular ends men pursue and to agree on a common hierarchy of ends an utterly chimerical idea.[37]

This does not, however, do away with the necessity of showing that rules of just conduct in the Great Society are not merely someone's arbitrary dictates, for the authority of the state which enforces such rules 'rests on and derives its support from the expectation that it will enforce the prevailing opinions concerning what is right'.[38] It appears, then, that men can share 'prevailing opinions' and yet not share common ends. What makes this possible is Hayek's interpretation of an essentially Humean distinction between 'will' and 'opinion'.[39]

'Will' for Hayek is the connection between the desires of a particular individual and the object of those desires. In other words, when a man chooses an *end*, he does so as a result of a combination of his unique knowledge and particular contingent desires: he knows what he values in general, he becomes aware of a particular opportunity to realise one or more of these goods in action, so he *wills* the accomplishment of the appropriate action. The will lasts only until the desired end is achieved. 'Opinion', by contrast, is fixed on no particular object, but is a general set of dispositions concerning appropriate rules of conduct *whatever* the object desired. An opinion cannot bring about action of itself, but only opinion allied with concrete ends, which are quite distinct from the opinion itself.

To use a characteristically Hayekian illustration of the significance of the difference, I could perfectly well say that I am of the opinion that no pattern of distribution of wealth should be imposed on society (an abstract moral judgment)

---

[37] *Political Order*, p. 134.

[38] Ibid., p. 123.

[39] The following account of Hayek's distinction between 'will' and 'opinion' is necessarily a highly condensed one which undoubtedly loses much that he would consider important. For the fully developed version, refer to *Mirage*, pp. 12-17.

but that *if* one is to be imposed anyway, I have a clear idea of which one I would choose.[40] In the first case, the judgment is of a potentially universalisable character. The appetitive character of the second makes it strictly particular and transitory.

Hayek's belief in the existence of a widespread opinion on the principles of just conduct, but the impossibility of agreement on the ends at which just conduct should aim, underpins his entire political and legal theory. Free men will disagree about what particular results are desirable from the operation of a social order and this disagreement will become more intractable as the scale of society grows. Only by discovering the principles on which opinion agrees and then applying them without exception in all particular cases, whatever the result, will men be assured that they are not subject to anyone's arbitrary will.

Of particular concern to Hayek, then, is the fact that governments in Western society are intellectually and institutionally ill-equipped to discover the rules of just conduct appropriate to a spontaneous order. Their intellectual inadequacy arises from the twin influences of democracy and legal positivism. The latter has popularised the belief that any legal rule must simply be a statement of the will of the sovereign and therefore the question 'What is law?' is really asking 'Who is the sovereign whose will is obeyed?' Hayek denies the existence of a sovereign,[41] asserting instead that in a spontaneous order, no one's will is obeyed because true law is merely the articulation of the rules that free men observe in practice *before* anyone states them. The legal positivists have been wrong to suggest that anything which the sovereign decrees is law, because true law is only sanctioned by its conformity with the broad opinion on the abstract principles of what is 'right'.

---

[40] In *Political Order* (p. 37), for instance, Hayek argues that only the *opinion* of a majority prepared to bind itself to a general rule applicable to all future instances of a similar kind, can justify coercive action by the state, even where the majority, which *wills* a non-universalisable particular rule, is larger.

[41] A large part of both the *Constitution* and *Law, Legislation and Liberty* is devoted to an attack on the whole concept of sovereignty, which Hayek clearly regards as one of the most pernicious errors of legal positivism. Particularly good discussions are to be found in Chapter 7 and Part II of the *Constitution* and Chapters 4, 8, and 12 of the trilogy.

The modern view of democracy, which attributes the sovereign legislative power to popularly elected assemblies is thus intellectually muddled, because it elevates a perfectly acceptable procedural convention (only what the majority approves shall be law) to a substantive principle (anything which a majority approves is good law). Hayek clearly marks off his liberalism from democracy, because liberalism is a 'meta-legal doctrine'[42] which proposes limits on what any law should contain.[43] From this Hayek derives his concept of the 'rule of law', which is 'not a rule of the law, but a rule concerning what the law ought to be'.[44] The rule of law exists, for Hayek, when everyone, including those who declare and administer the law, is subject to rules of just behaviour which they cannot change in order to accomplish their particular ends.[45]

This distinction between true law as rules of just conduct based on broad social opinion and law in the vulgar sense as the mere product of a legislature (whether democratic or otherwise), is, for the modern layman, obscured by the fact that the state is called upon to perform two quite separate social roles which we fail to distinguish properly.

These two roles are: on the one hand, the discovery of the rules of just conduct; and the provision of government services on the other. Every society, Hayek suggests, needs a provider of certain public goods which, by their nature, cannot be got through the market, but he does not believe that the only role of government is to overcome market failures. He is prepared to accept a potentially very wide range of government

---

[42] *Constitution*, p. 206.

[43] See ibid., p. 103.

[44] Ibid., p. 206.

[45] It seems odd that Hayek considers his rule of law a 'meta-legal' rule (i.e. it is not *part* of the law) even though it must be taken account of (*inter alia*) *by* judges in the determination of the law if it is to embody true rules of just conduct. Why the rule that judges should not take account of their own or anyone else's particular purposes in finding the law should not be counted a rule *of* the law is not clear. Similarly, given the rule's meta-legal status, Hayek could usefully say much more about its enforceability. Granted that *Law, Legislation and Liberty* is about creating a constitution in which the rule of law is institutionally reinforced through separation of powers and judicial revision, he has relatively little to say about how it can be made operative in general if it itself is not a rule *of* the law.

activities,[46] provided that, in offering these services, the government is bound to observe the ordinary rules of just conduct.

This may seem innocuous enough if it means merely that the government must obey the law, but Hayek's complaint is precisely that modern governments make their own laws. The objection that Hayek raises to this harks back to his distinction between opinion and will. It is normal that governments be free to decide how they will employ the resources put at their disposal by the whole community for common purposes, and these purposes are indeed best discovered by a democratic process in which groups with particular interests vie with one another to set policy. So long as law-making is the preserve of this process as well, however, law will merely serve the temporary will of those in office in the pursuit of their particular aims.[47] This precludes the force of opinion playing its crucial role in the formation of law, and government becomes merely a scramble for particular benefits, granted without reference to moral principles but only with regard to the organisational strength of particular groups.[48]

The ability of the government to rule and to tax is premised, on Hayek's view, on the belief that government, like any other group or individual, shall be constrained by the *pre-existing* rules of just conduct. This the procedural device of democracy cannot by itself guarantee, nor can it ever be guaranteed so long as legislating and the provision of government services are not separated.

This presupposes a distinction between two products of modern legislatures which modern man merges under the common rubric of 'law'.[49] These Hayek carefully separates into 'private law' or the rules of just conduct with which we are now familiar, and the 'public law' or the instructions that

---

[46] He still argues, however, that in most cases people would be better served if the market were allowed to produce these services wherever feasible. See e.g. *Political Order*, p. 140.

[47] *Political Order*, pp. 23-5.

[48] Hayek acknowledges his debt to Mancur Olson's analysis of the nature of collective action (*The Logic of Collective Action* (Cambridge, Mass., 1933)), an analysis which obviously inspires this aspect of Hayek's work. For Hayek's own view of the relationship between the logic of collective action and the principle of unlimited sovereignty in a popularly elected legislature, see *Political Order*, pp. 8-17.

[49] Ibid., p. 22.

government gives to its servants to carry out its commands.[50]
By confusing these two, modern governments often fall victim
to the belief that they are entitled to issue commands to
ordinary individuals to do particular things, quite a different
proposition from giving orders to civil servants to carry out
government policy.

In the first case, government arrogates to itself the right to
do that which government was created to prevent: the coercion
of free individuals. This must turn the spontaneous social order
into an organisation for the pursuit of specified goals. In the
second case, government merely makes decisions about what
it shall do with the limited resources entrusted to it to achieve
common goals compatible with the pre-existing social order.
A spontaneous order is compatible with the existence of any
number of groups whose members pursue common aims
subject only to the rules of just conduct, but is incompatible
with the existence of a state which treats people and their
possessions as if they were instruments of public policy.[51] This
destroys liberty, progress, and the limited certainty found
through observing the ordinary rules of just conduct; it subjects
men to the arbitrary and changeable commands of the
representatives of momentary majorities.[52]

The central constitutional questions for Hayek are thus:
first, how is true law, in the sense of the rules of just conduct
approved by the opinion of the majority, to be discovered?
The second is how may the will of the majority, as manifested
in democratically chosen governments, be subjected to the
rule of law in the same way that everyone else is?

The answer to the first question lies in understanding that
true law is to be observed in operation in the regularities of
behaviour of men in the social order which precedes the state.

The basic source of social order ... is not a deliberate decision to
adopt certain common rules, but the existence among the people of
certain opinions of what is right and wrong. What made the Great
Society possible was not a deliberate imposition of rules of conduct,

---

[50] On the distinction used here between private and public law, see A. de
Crespigny, op. cit., pp. 59–60; M. Wilhelm, op. cit., p. 174; and *Rules and Order*, pp.
131–4.
[51] *Political Order*, pp. 139–41.
[52] *Constitution*, pp. 30–2.

but the growth of such rules among men who had little idea of what would be the consequences of their general observance.[53]

True law may thus be said to grow out of the resolution of conflicts which arise between individuals attempting to pursue their particular ends within a framework of social co-operation, what Hayek calls 'disturbances of [the] order'.[54] Such conflicts normally arise between men of good faith at least one of whose expectations have been upset by the actions of the other.[55] Each believes that he acted justly in the sense that he acted in accordance with generally accepted principles, but the interested parties are obviously ill-suited to decide the issue. For this reason, *judges* play a crucial role in the discovery of the law and their legitimacy derives not from their association with a particular governmental regime, but in their intimate relationship with the enduring framework of rules on which social co-operation depends: 'The judge is in this sense an institution of a spontaneous order'.[56]

A better understanding of the judge's role in finding the law helps to elucidate the character of law itself. The judge is an institution of a spontaneous order because the resolution of disputes from which that order grows requires the intervention of an arbiter who discovers the rule which ought to have guided the actions of the litigating parties, the rule that a reasonable man would expect to guide men in like situations and which therefore provides a universalisable rule. To act unjustly is to act unexpectedly in a situation where someone observing the normal rules could legitimately expect predictability. In other words, the judge determines which customs of the people are of such widespread significance that their non-observance would be injurious to a reasonable man's attempts to form and pursue rational plans.

The significance of customs here is that they give rise to expectations that guide people's actions, and what will be regarded as binding will therefore be those practices which everyone counts on being

[53] *Political Order*, p. 33.
[54] *Rules and Order*, p. 94.
[55] Ibid., p. 100.
[56] Ibid., p. 95.

observed and which have thereby become the condition for the success of most activities.[57]

For the judge's decisions to have legitimacy, however, they cannot be the product of his particular will. He must not base them on what he would prefer to be the outcome in a particular instance or indeed on what he conceives a good substantive outcome to be. The judge administers justice, not by seeking to arrange his decisions to reflect his preferences, but by articulating a rule to cover this particular case, a rule consistent with the overall pattern of rules which everyone already observes. Being bound by legal precedents, the judge's will is effectively insulated from the proceedings, for the final test of the rules so laid down is not the particular results they produce,[58] but 'the self-consistency of the actions which these rules allow if applied to the circumstances of the real world'.[59]

From this we can begin to enumerate some of the qualities that true law must possess. The law that judges discover is valid because it refers to principles, not particulars; one judicial function is to focus attention strictly on the problem of discovering the principle which ought to have guided the litigants' actions if they were to be consistent with the overall social order. While in most cases the principle will be obvious to someone whose work is to apply the known and articulated principles, new cases will always raise questions unforeseen by earlier judges.[60] In these cases, while the judge appears to make law '... where there exists a real gap in the recognised law a new rule will be likely to establish itself only if somebody is charged with the task of finding a rule which after being stated is recognised as appropriate'.[61]

The judge, steeped in the spirit of the accepted rules, is better suited to this task than, say, the legislator. The legitimacy

---

[57] Ibid., p. 97.

[58] *Constitution*, p. 159: '... only the rule as a whole must be ... justified, not its every application'.

[59] *Studies*, p. 166.

[60] This explains why judges will always be an indispensable element in any spontaneous order; the unpredictable nature of the interaction between a changing environment and the new knowledge that men are constantly obtaining about it makes it impossible to arrive at a set of rules which will cover all future eventualities. See *Rules and Order*, p. 100.

[61] Loc. cit.

of the rules he propounds derives from their conformity with public opinion as manifested in the regularities of conduct of the bulk of the people. In this, the judge is merely a sort of specially trained interpreter; since the existing framework of rules is sanctioned by long popular usage, the legitimacy of a newly stated judicial rule will be in direct proportion to its compatibility with the overall order.[62] There still remains a role for the legislator, however, which we shall come to presently.

In common with most products of a spontaneous social order, then, the rules of just conduct, largely, but not exclusively, articulated by judges, are not the product of someone's conscious choice or decision. Like all rules, they evolve as experience suggests new ways in which they can smooth the operation of the overall spontaneous order. The point about the rules with which we are concerned here is that the regularities their universal observance introduces into the world makes it expedient that they be compulsory.[63] Hayek's legal ideal is where certain rules of just conduct are made obligatory because the overall regularity they introduce is an integral part of an abstract order: for this to be the case, they must be applicable to everyone, regardless of station or circumstances. An action which does not contravene a compulsory rule of conduct is by definition permissible and (what is the same thing) just. The first attribute of true law then, is that it must take the form of universal and general rules which merely forbid certain types of behaviour. Again, this is a description of Hartian primary rules which seems to leave other, secondary, rules of the law unaccounted for.

In Hayek's ideal legal world, no *commands* are issued to do or accomplish specific things. Instead, general and abstract rules are laid down prescribing the minimum standards of behaviour *whatever* one decides to do. The genius of the spontaneously generated rules of just conduct is that they

---

[62] There is considerable scholarly support for Hayek's argument that new legal rules drive their legitimacy primarily from their conformity to existing 'coherence'. On this see N. McCormick, *Legal Reasoning and Legal Theory* (Oxford, 1978) and M. Oakeshott's account of the granting of female suffrage contained in his *Political Education*, an inaugural lecture delivered at the LSE on 6 Mar. 1951 (Cambridge, 1951).

[63] *Constitution*, p. 142.

merely set the limits within which all private ends may legitimately be pursued and, in so doing, allow men unconsciously to co-ordinate their activities and make them socially beneficial.[64]

So the second quality of true law is its constancy or certainty. We know that the whole function of authoritative rules with coercive sanctions is to create cause and effect relations as predictable as those of the natural world. For this degree of certainty to prevail, it is much more important that men know that whatever the rules are, they will be applied universally, than that judges or administrators be free to bend the rules where their strict application would cause distress or hardship. No account must be taken of the results in particular cases or of the effects on individual people, for while the latter would require some common agreement on merit, the former alone can be based on opinion.[65]

In other words, while the law protects legitimate expectations, sight must not be lost of the *kind* of expectations it can protect. It cannot, for instance, protect expectations regarding the particular results of just actions. Stated differently, the law can ensure that people act justly (i.e. so as not to cause 'disturbances' in the overall order), but cannot command them to act in such a manner that the results of their actions conform to some abstract idea of a just outcome. Such commands, directed to particular ends and therefore determined by the will, cannot be just.[66]

The third main attribute of law for which Hayek wishes to argue is equality, in the sense of the 'rule of law' discussed earlier: by subjecting everyone, rulers and ruled, to the same negative prohibitions of true law, he believes that true liberty is unlikely to be contravened by the law. As long as rulers and judges know that they too will be subject to the restrictions,

---

[64] Ibid., p. 157. Here again, Hayek's failure to distinguish adequately between primary and secondary rules makes his account unclear, for while this is a good description of primary rules it cannot in itself explain the origin and role of secondary rules.

[65] Ibid., pp. 218–19.

[66] For this reason, judges can never be the instruments of government policy, which aims at particular results, but only servants of a spontaneous order: 'The function of the judge is *confined* to a spontaneous order', *Rules and Order*, p. 118, emphasis added. In general see ibid., pp. 118–22.

they will be unlikely to prohibit things most people may want to do.[67]

Hayek neatly summarises for us the intimate relationship which exists between freedom, the rule of law, and the distinction between opinion and will:

> The conception of freedom under the law ... rests on the contention that when we obey laws in the sense of abstract general rules laid down irrespective of their application to us, we are not subject to another man's will and are therefore free. It is because the lawgiver does not know the particular cases to which his rules will apply, and it is because the judge who applies them has no choice in drawing the conclusions that follow from the existing body of rules and the particular facts of the case, that it can be said that laws and not men rule. Because the rule is laid down in ignorance of the particular case and no man's will decided the coercion used to enforce it, the law is not arbitrary.[68]

We must now turn our attention from the role of judges in the spontaneous order to that of the 'lawgiver' or the true legislator. My account to this point has made little room for the legislator, but this is not to suggest that he does not have an important function. What that function is can best be seen through a comparison with that of the judge who, on Hayek's view, ought to exercise many functions we normally associate with legislators.

While the contemporary view of the judge is of someone applying rules laid down by a legislature, this is, according to Hayek, a mistaken view based on an historical confusion. Judges are the natural product of a spontaneous order which generates its own rules of conduct which need to be interpreted. Eventually such an order must also produce an agency whose function is not only to extend a uniform rule of law throughout

---

[67] While the purpose here *is* primarily descriptive, the unsatisfactory nature of the guarantees of the universal application principle are too apparent to let pass without some comment. The most obvious example, which Hayek himself concedes, is that this leaves no defence against the universal imposition of religious observances. See *Constitution*, pp. 154-5. For more critical commentary on this point, see both L. C. Robbins, 'Hayek on Liberty' in *Economica*, 28 (Feb. 1961), pp. 66-81, and S. Gordon, op. cit., pp. 483-5, in which the author writes that Hayek's 'concept of the rule of law [is] powerless to condemn even the most repressive acts of government as long as they oppress indiscriminately'.

[68] *Constitution*, p. 153.

a particular territory but, more importantly, to supplement the law finding role played by judges. Thus, while legislatures came after law and judges, the mature state of development of modern legal systems gives the appearance that law originates with legislatures. This is merely another error of legal positivism.[69]

The lawgiver's role arises primarily from the constraints on the work of judges. The first such constraint is that the judicial system as a whole works very slowly and gradually, sometimes too slowly for the legal system to adapt itself readily to rapidly changing conditions. While he offers no examples of this, it might be reasonable to think that a development like joint stock and limited liability companies in the last century was something that judges could only with difficulty have evolved on their own. The rapid development which only legislation could have allowed here would presumably be retrospectively justified by the way in which it clearly fitted in with and indeed facilitated the orderly development of the overall order.

Much more important, though, is the fact that a judge can only discover law in order to apply it to past events; his task is essentially backward-looking. What litigants wish to know is who acted according to the rule which, at the time, was sanctioned, or at least implied, by general usage. The certainty and regularity which judges preserve would be destroyed if they were free to innovate, especially where this would involve the reversal of previous judicial decisions. 'The judge is not performing his function if he disappoints reasonable expectations created by earlier decisions'[70] and this is true whether or not the expectations so created seem, in retrospect, ill-suited to the maintenance of a stable order.

The primary function of a true legislature, then, is to continue the work already begun by judges, but with a forward-looking orientation. Where new developments arise which previous judicial decisions had not foreseen, or where the precedent-bound procedures of the judiciary prevent it from extracting itself from an impasse of its own making, a legislature will have an important role to play. This role may even extend to the deliberate redesigning of whole sections of

---

[69] See e.g. *Rules and Order*, p. 117.
[70] Ibid., p. 88; but cf. pp. 116 and 118.

the law, although still constrained by the larger principles discoverable within the framework as a whole. Within these limits a legislature *is* free to innovate because it is laying down new rules which will only apply to future cases and individuals can therefore take these new rules into account in planning their actions. But the limits are still quite restrictive: at best, the task of the true legislator is limited to the need to deal with problems 'with which the judiciary cannot deal adequately'.[71]

This does not prevent the legislature from playing the extremely useful function of periodically giving an authoritative statement of the present law on a particular subject which can serve as a useful reference and guide to judges, legal experts, and laymen. Such compilations may themselves increase the degree of certainty and consistency which individuals can expect from the legal system. It was from this sanction which the early legislatures gave to pre-existing rules that the idea arose that the legislature was the *source* of those rules.[72] As we have already noted, the advent of democracy compounded the problem by giving the aura of popular approval to laws adopted by representative legislatures.

As long as these democratic legislatures are concerned both with governing *and* finding the rules of just conduct, however, the will which guides the first will inevitably overwhelm the opinion which ought to guide the second. The problem then becomes how to reconcile the 'desirable'[73] principle that only what the majority approves shall become law, with the fundamental precept that law is to be distinguished by certain properties it must possess and not by the procedure which declares it.

[71] *Political Order*, p. 124.

[72] This causes Hayek to qualify heavily even the extent to which it is appropriate for the legislature to attempt to codify judicially discovered law. He considers this at length on p. 116 of *Rules and Order*.

[73] *Constitution*, p. 103. It is Hayek's mature position that democracy is the method of reaching collective decisions which is most compatible with liberalism and that it is therefore desirable. On this, the reader is referred to *Constitution*, pp. 106–10 and *Political Order*, pp. 5–13. At the same time, however, if democracy is going to lead to the tyranny of a sovereign, popularly elected assembly, it seems clear that he would prefer some other form of rule. See the comments on Hayek's attitude to democracy in Chapter II, above.

Hayek's *Constitution* and the *Law, Legislation and Liberty* trilogy represent his exploration of this key problem over a number of years. The former, however, is essentially a catalogue of more or less successful historical attempts to realise the liberal ideal of government under the law. On the other hand, if a work as diverse in its conception and execution as *Law, Legislation and Liberty* can be said to have a principal theme, it is the rather more constructivistic one of inventing a set of political institutions that would make the realisation of this ideal possible. The full and final statement is contained in the last volume of the trilogy, in which Hayek proposes a new style of constitution for Western democracies. Drawing its inspiration from the model of the separation of powers, Hayek's ideal constitution proposes a three-tiered hierarchical structure in which the momentary will of the majority is subject to the enduring opinion of a much larger majority concerning the rules of just conduct. Ultimately both are constrained by the fundamental principles of liberty which are the essential condition of the existence of any true opinion on the principles of just conduct.

In delving into the provisions of this ideal constitution, one does well to remember Hayek's observation that the 'effective limitation of power is the most important problem of social order'.[74] This reminds us that all governmental institutions in a spontaneous order are justified solely by what they contribute to the maintenance of that order, and that whatever power they possess is a consequence of that contribution. Power is bestowed on institutions to enable them to play their role; the purpose of a constitution is, on Hayek's view, to limit this power precisely to that required for the maintenance of the order.[75]

It seems appropriate to begin by looking at the pinnacle of the constitutional structure: the written constitution and the body charged with its conception and amendment, the Constitutional Convention. It may seem surprising that Hayek devotes relatively little space to justifying his proposed constitution,[76] but then his moral monism in the political sphere

---

[74] *Political Order*, p. 128.
[75] Ibid., p. 6.
[76] Although, as noted above, the *Constitution* is largely concerned with this in a

makes its provisions a simple matter: since liberty is the ground from which most other values grow and is the sole condition of social progress and individual development, there can be no place for disputes about the values which the constitution ought to embody.

This comes through most clearly when one realises that, unlike the provisions governing the choice of persons authorised to fill the other roles created by the constitution, Hayek gives literally no consideration whatsoever to the question of who ought to belong to his semi-permanent Constitutional Convention.[77] One can only conclude that he considers this a minor point, such a constitution-making body having almost no choices to make, the provisions of the constitution being dictated by the primary logic of liberty. The central article of such a constitution would provide that

... in normal times, and apart from certain clearly defined emergency situations, men could be restrained from doing what they wished, or coerced to do particular things, only in accordance with the recognised rules of just conduct designed to define and protect the individual domain of each; and that the accepted set of rules of this kind could be deliberately altered only by what we shall call the Legislative Assembly.[78]

This 'basic clause' of the constitution would list the qualities such rules would have to possess in order to be just, and these are in essence the three qualities already discussed. It would equally make clear that, while the Legislative Assembly would have the sole authority to make 'alterations of the recognised body of existing rules',[79] the body of law on which its decisions would be based would 'include not only the products of past [*true*] legislation but also those ... conceptions implicit in past decisions by which the courts should be bound and which it would be their task to make explicit'.[80]

In Hayek's opinion, such constitutional provisions are superior to any attempt at an exhaustive Bill of Rights, since

negative way, as a consideration of the failure of actual historical attempts to put effective constitutional limits on the power of the state which so preoccupies him.

[77] *Political Order*, p. 123.
[78] Ibid., p. 109.
[79] Loc. cit.
[80] Loc. cit.

'government under the rule of law' such as this basic clause would create would protect everyone more effectively against the arbitrary use of coercion than any attempt to foresee every particular area in which unwarranted coercive power might be exercised.[81]

The primary function of the written constitution, then, is to set limits on the law. Its second function is to create those institutions which give substantive content to the rules, a content which must not violate the constitutional criteria laid down for rules of just conduct.

To this end, Hayek separates the laying down of such rules from the administering of the resources of government in accordance with them. Two assemblies are created: a legislative one, whose task it is to embody the opinion of the majority in true law; and a governmental one, to represent the will of the majority in the allocation of public resources to common tasks.

By far the most interesting aspect of the constitution is how Hayek suits the organisation of each chamber to its particular task. The Legislative Assembly could, he suggests, be a better representative of the true opinion of the people than current democratic legislatures are, if five hundred mature adults were chosen at random and allowed, for a fixed term of twenty years, to 'devote themselves to the task of improving the law, guided only by their conscience and the desire to be respected'.[82]

He recognises, however, that democratic sentiment would be unlikely to endorse such a procedure in which the legislators had no plausible popular mandate. None the less, it is imperative to insulate the Legislative Assembly from the popular pressures of the moment, to leave it free to concentrate its attention strictly on the principles of just conduct sanctioned by majority opinion and compatible with the formal criteria laid down in the constitution. A fascinating series of artifices work together to achieve this result.

Membership in the Legislative Assembly is indeed to be elective. In keeping with the relatively enduring nature of the

---

[81] For Hayek's criticism of this error in American constitution-making, see *Constitution*, Chapter 12.

[82] *Political Order*, p. 32.

opinion they are supposed to represent, however, legislators would be elected for a fixed term of fifteen years and would be ineligible for re-election, an honorific post being guaranteed to them by the constitution at the end of their term. There are to be annual elections but, to prevent a momentary humour of the electorate fundamentally changing the composition of the Assembly in order to achieve some particular objective, only one-fifteenth of the Assembly would be elected each year, on an indirect, regional, non-party basis. All of these provisions, of course, guarantee that the only pressures that a member of such an assembly would feel would be those of his own conscience: neither constituents, pressure groups, nor political parties could, in theory, at least, influence him improperly.[83]

Independence is not enough, however, to guarantee that the members of the legislature will have the maturity and judgment necessary for their work. Hayek wants representatives of the considered opinion of those who 'had already gained experience and had had an opportunity to make their reputation, but who would still be in their best years',[84] and so proposes that every person have only one vote in his lifetime for the legislature, which would be exercised at the age of forty-five. One would use this vote to choose amongst one's peers of that age the one-fifteenth of the Assembly to be elected in that year.

However careful the process of selection of these legislators, though, it is possible that they may lose sight of their primary purpose and attempt to pass laws which violate the constitutional criteria, such as rules for the achievement of particular purposes or aiming at particular results. To prevent this, a constitutional court is envisaged, one of whose functions would be to ensure that the legislature's laws were always *intra vires*.

The function of laying down the rules of just conduct being now safely hived off from the activity of governing by the creation of a separate chamber for this purpose, government largely as we know it could continue, albeit with some

[83] The general description of all the provisions relating to the election and powers of the legislators, or '*nomothetae*' is to be found in *Political Order*, pp. 111–18.

[84] Ibid., p. 113.

important limitations not foreseen by current interpretations of democracy.

> The different tasks ... require that ... different assemblies should represent the views of the electors in different respects. For the purpose of government proper it seems desirable that the concrete wishes of the citizens for particular results should find expression, ... for the conduct of government a majority committed to a programme of action and 'capable of governing' is thus clearly needed.[85]

In the Governmental Assembly, popular election by the greater part of the presently constituted electorate would be the rule, as would the existence of political parties dedicated to the achievement of particular ends.[86] The difference would be that under the new arrangements, even such a popularly elected government would be powerless to bend the rules of just conduct to suit its particular purposes. 'This is what "government under the law" means.'[87]

The activities of the Governmental Assembly would naturally be equally subject to review by the constitutional court to ensure that they were entirely consonant with the rules of just conduct. Hayek is careful to point out that the purpose of such a court is not merely a jurisdictional one, in the sense of deciding *which* chamber has a particular power. On the contrary, his system is intended to make it abundantly clear that there are some things which no one, and particularly the state, is empowered to do in a free society.[88] It is no coincidence that this constitution virtually eliminates any degree of discretion in the state's dealings with individuals. This is intended to maximise the chances of correct foresight on the part of individuals in laying their plans because they know as certainly as is humanly possible what the state will do to protect or interfere with those plans.

Some consequences of this constitutional order bear noting. Almost any kind of authoritative state intervention in the

---

[85] Ibid., p. 112.

[86] Hayek considers favourably the idea of forbidding former members of the Governmental Assembly taking up seats in the Legislative Assembly, as this might introduce an inappropriate element of partisan feeling. See ibid., p. 114.

[87] Ibid., p. 123.

[88] Ibid., p. 121.

economy is precluded, whether it be rent controls, most government regulation of environmental use, attempts to regulate or dictate incomes and prices, and even state control of the money supply.[89] On the other hand, once a community is well enough off to be able to afford it, Hayek sees no objection in principle to state provision of a universal minimum income floor. It is clear, however, that this must be a flat rate applicable to all irrespective of previous (market determined) incomes.[90]

Except for the degree of progressivity necessary to compensate for the regressive nature of most indirect taxes, however, government services could not be financed through progressive direct taxation.[91] This would eliminate what Hayek sees as the current 'auction' in which political parties promise their supporters benefits to be paid for by others.[92] Not only is progressivity undesirable, then, but it could not be allowed under the rules of just conduct because it introduces an arbitrary distinction between taxpayers which cannot be justified with respect to any universalisable principle.

This does not mean that *no* legal distinctions will be made between people. Certain distinctions are facts of nature which the law merely recognises: Hayek mentions the fact that only women can be raped or 'got with child'.[93] Other distinctions between minorities and majorities are permissible in principle so long as the majority in *both* groups recognises the distinction as an appropriate one. If the minority objects, the distinction is probably discrimination; if the majority, privilege.[94] However,

---

[89] Part III of the *Constitution* is almost exclusively devoted to a discussion of the economic policies which a 'constitution of liberty' would leave open to government, and the most expedient policies which a wise government in those circumstances would pursue. Most of the policy issues mentioned here, as well as many others, receive a full treatment in this section. Hayek has devoted a separate book to the problem of the money supply: *The Denationalisation of Money* (London, 1976). This work is somewhat technical for the present purpose and so, while wishing to acknowledge the importance that Hayek accords to this aspect of restraining the power of the state, no attempt has been made to give his detailed proposals.

[90] The argument for a uniform national minimum outside the market appears in an undeveloped form in *Constitution*, pp. 100-2 and reaches its full development in *Political Order*, pp. 54-6.

[91] Progressive taxation is clearly one of Hayek's *bêtes noires*. Chapter 20 of the *Constitution* is a vigorous attack on its economic, political, and moral implications.

[92] *Political Order*, pp. 51-4.

[93] *Constitution*, p. 154.

[94] Loc. cit.

while he admits this principle for distinguishing acceptable and unacceptable categories within the law, he suggests no specific machinery for putting it into effect. It would presumably be left to the Legislative Assembly to authorise such distinctions; how they could do so without a specific constitutional authority is unclear.

All this raises an interesting point. Up to now attention has been focused on how the new constitution would limit the powers of government. From Hayek's perspective, however, his constitution gives government a new power they were incapable of exercising before: the power to say 'no'.[95] As long as nothing was specifically forbidden to a sovereign state and the decision about what was permissible was mixed with the decision about what was desired, no government which wished to be re-elected could afford to offend anyone by refusing to meet their specific demands even where these appeared unwise in the long run.

By leaving momentary majorities unrestrained by rules in a sovereign legislature, 'foolish human institutions'[96] have led men to believe that the state can protect expectations regarding the outcome of the operation of the social order because they can coerce men to act in specified ways. This, however, destroys the only certainty possible, since such unprincipled and arbitrary exercises of power are by their nature capricious and changeable. Attempts to ensure a particular level of material welfare for specified groups by governmental action, while perhaps gratifying human emotions, cannot be based on any principle, but only on irrational and antisocial desires.[97]

An examination of Hayek's political institutions is, for this reason, an illuminating excursion into the authoritarian nature

---

[95] *Political Order*, pp. 103 and 149.

[96] *Constitution*, p. 30.

[97] One of the two quotations in the epigraph of Chapter 9 of *Law, Legislation and Liberty* (entitled ' "Social" or Distributive Justice') is from Immanuel Kant and sums up what Hayek sees as the inseparability of will and welfare: 'Welfare, however, has no principle, neither for him who receives it, nor for him who distributes it (one will place it here and another there); because it depends on the material content of the will, which is dependent on particular facts and therefore incapable of a general rule.' Hayek takes this quotation up again in *Political Order* (p. 11) to drive home his point that an omnipotent legislature concerned with the distribution of benefits in the welfare state is bound to act arbitrarily and to destroy the foundations of the spontaneous order.

of his dedication to liberty. A revealing comment from the first pages of the third volume of his trilogy sums up this view of Hayek as essentially a disciplinarian, certain that moral values can be reduced to an undemonstrable and indirect social utility. This justifies a constitution protecting the particular kind of pluralism found in the market, at the price of a rigorous moral monism in politics:

Civilisation largely rests on the fact that the individuals have learned to restrain their desires for particular objects and to submit to generally recognised rules of just conduct. Majorities, however, have not yet been civilised in this manner because they do not have to obey rules.[98]

The point, of course, is not that government should obey no rules, but that for Hayek there is only one possible type of rule, whose form and content are revealed by 'the attribution of transcendent merit to spontaneous processes'.[99] It is undoubtedly wrong to assert that whatever the majority decides as a result of rational discussion is right. This does not entail that Hayek's alternative, that one can infer what the majority believes to be right by studying the regularity of their actions, is any more convincing. As Hayek himself makes clear, his rules do not merely reflect the values that people in a spontaneous order would find appropriate, but the rules themselves introduce a discipline in which men have no choice but to be 'free'.

If ... the necessary condition for a free evolution—the spirit of individual initiative—is lacking, then surely without that spirit no viable civilisation can grow anywhere. So far as it is really lacking, the first task must be to waken it; and this a regime of freedom will do, but a system of regimentation will not.[100]

If evolution is to work, in other words, the first task of the political and social order is to inculcate in men a spirit of initiative through the discipline of freedom. The rules create the values and not the other way around: '... a highly developed commercial spirit is itself as much the product as the condition of effective competition, and ... we know of no

[98] Ibid., p. 7.
[99] S. Gordon, op. cit., p. 476.
[100] *Constitution*, p. 3.

other method of producing it than to throw competition open to all...'.[101]

While Hayek's constitutional structure thus appears to allow politics, in the narrow sense defined in Chapter I, it in fact not simply constrains it, but eviscerates it. The search for common values which it presupposes is impossible, being premised on a kind of knowledge whose existence Hayek denies. Rules become a way for Hayek to make people face up to the impossibility of community because the only real knowledge is dispersed knowledge of what has utility.

The *only* ground on which Hayek believes unlimited government can be opposed is an absolute and unswerving commitment to the economic liberty from which all values grow; but this seems unjustified in terms of his arguments. It can be true that the winner-take-all nature of majority decisions requires us to hedge the majority principle with many restrictions, but it is just as plausible to base these on, say, some substantive notion of justice or a combination of values such as liberty, justice, and equality. To admit this, however, is to relegate liberty to the status of one, possibly predominant, value among several.

The doubtful foundations of the discipline to which Hayek wants us all to be subject, beyond the possibility of conscious choice, is crystallised in the following argument:

However little it may often appear to be true, the social world is governed in the long run by certain moral principles on [*sic*] which the people at large believe. The only moral principle which has ever made the growth of an advanced civilisation possible was the principle of individual freedom, which means that the individual is guided in his decisions by rules of just conduct and not by specific commands.[102]

The first sentence offers us the not unpromising suggestion that government should be dependent on opinion and that opinion embodies the moral beliefs of the people. The next, however, goes on to suggest that the *only* moral principle on which a Great Society can be based is individual freedom, as Hayek understands that term, without any attempt being

101 *Political Order*, p. 75.
102 Ibid., p. 151.

made to show that this moral principle is based on the opinion of the majority. Since *this* principle is necessary to his preferred social order, Hayek proposes political institutions which will inculcate this value in people by entrenching the discipline of the abstract market order.

For his definition of government under the law to be acceptable, Hayek must show that law in fact has the *moral* content with which he wants to invest his rules of just conduct. He thus returns constantly to the opinion/will distinction, identifying the enduring moral sense of the majority with his rules. But in his description of the social origins and growth of the rules, no such moral considerations enter because the morality of the rules arises from their utility; they are not validated because they meet any recognisably ethical criterion.

This brings us back to the commensurability of consummations. A market order ceases to function correctly as soon as its members begin to value some things not for their use or exchange value, but as ends in themselves. To Hayek's mind, only brute desires, of no intrinsic moral worth, are to be found in the breast of man. Since not all of them can be realised in a social context, some must be renounced in order that the aggregate be maximised, the only criterion of choice being what will permit the greatest aggregate of satisfactions to any individual chosen at random. But men are too short-sighted to submit to the harsh discipline that this requires. Freedom is, for Hayek, a hard and difficult mistress, a discipline we long to shuffle off;[103] but we cannot without extinguishing all the 'moral responsibility of the individual'[104] which one exercises by subordinating one's primitive emotional desires to the wisdom of spontaneously grown rules.

Whether this can form any adequate account of the nature of the moral responsibility of individuals, and therefore whether the Hayekian limitations on the sphere of deliberation on values which is politics can be morally justified, is the theme of the second half of this book. For the moment, though, I

---

[103] This is one of Hayek's favourite themes. Some interesting textual references include *Constitution*, p. 18, *Rules and Order*, p. 33, *Political Order*, p. 7, as well as the epilogue, pp. 163–76. The main reference is to Chapter 11 of *Mirage*: 'The Discipline of Abstract Rules and the Emotions of the Tribal Society'.

[104] *Political Order*, p. 129.

want to pursue this theme of hostility to politics, which in Hayek's case may appear at first to be the natural and logical development of his market liberalism, in which the satisfaction of revealed preferences is clearly best achieved through the market. In an attempt to make clear just how much deeper this opposition goes and how widespread are its assumptions, the next chapter will examine how crucial it is to a very different brand of liberal: utilitarian social planners whose intellectual antecedents are unmistakably Benthamite. While the Webbs described themselves as Hayek's 'antithesis' at the LSE, I will show that their one undeniable area of fundamental disagreement with him seems much less imposing when seen against the background of their shared assumptions.

IV

SOCIETY, THE EXPERT, AND EVOLUTION: THE WEBBS' UTILITARIANISM

> It was the belief of the positivists and utilitarians ... that the science of nature which Newton had established was due to be completed by a science of man ... For Comte, Bentham and their followers, no less than for the Marxists, the point of understanding society was to change it; there was a rational way of ordering human affairs, and it only required the application of the scientific method to discover it and put it into operation.
>
> A. J. Ayer in 'Man as a Subject for Science'

The difference in the political philosophies of the Webbs and Hayek cannot be explained by their respective views on human nature, for they agree in seeing men as essentially selfish, rational utility-maximisers. Neither does it flow from a different interpretation of the nature and justification of human society in general, or of the industrial division of labour in particular, for on this they share a common view wherein these are seen as indispensable to the greatest fulfilment of human nature in the individual. They even agree that the particular social order they defend is not only morally and ethically justified, but is the product of an evolutionary process which weeds out societies which fail to make efficient use of their available resources. The fundamental dispute between Hayek and the Webbs focuses on the very simple question: what can man know to be true?[1] Perhaps paradoxically, while the diametrically opposed responses they give to this question account in very large part for our image of them as political opponents, the

---

[1] For a full discussion of the centrality of the nature and possibility of human knowledge to political argument, see e.g. R. M. Unger, *Knowledge and Politics* (New York, 1975), pp. 3–5: 'Until the present time, few ideas were so widely shared among thinkers of the most diverse persuasions as the belief that the decisive question for political thought is, What can we know?...'

attitude to politics[2] which they adopt is fundamentally the same. However different may be the ways in which they justify their opposition to politics, the resulting agreement is unmistakable.

In a curious sense, the Webbian political preoccupation is the same as Hayek's: if social relations are not to repose on the unstable and arbitrary use of force, then they must not depend on irrational human will. Men are prey to delusions, mistakes, and fantasies. The problem then is how to extract human will and desires from social relations and decision-making, how to make each individual feel that in making his contribution to the social order he is not merely being coerced into gratifying the delusions of other men at his own expense.

Hayek's response to this dilemma was to remove the irrationality by 'privatising' it. His idea that no concrete end could compel the assent of all rational men led him to conclude that the only morally defensible social order was one in which particular desires could be pursued by individuals, but these desires could not be coercively enforced on others. A market order thus functioned to provide men with the means to realise any desires they wished, compatible with a like liberty for all men. This left all men free to develop their nature as morally autonomous choosing agents, while non-coercively leading them to act so as to make the greatest contribution to society's moral end and justification: the provision of the greatest possible aggregate of means to self-realisation for all.

This 'privatisation' is the natural and inevitable outcome of a radical epistemological claim: not only do men not know enough about themselves and their world to be able to agree on the goals that it would be rational for all men to pursue, but, even further, they can never hope to possess such knowledge.

As with Hayek, the Webbs' concern is intimately connected with the existence of society. As long as men do not depend on the actions of other men for their well-being, their productivity, and their survival, then what each man creates is unproblematically his; what he makes of himself is of no concern to anyone else and he has no claims on the fruits of the labour of others. Both the Webbs and Hayek must therefore be concerned

---

[2] 'Politics', of course, is used here in the sense outlined in Chapter I.

with the effects of the interdependence created by social co-operation, and particularly the division of labour, for as soon as men co-operate in order to multiply their efficacy through functional specialisation, competing claims arise both over how the product of such co-operation can be maximised and how it ought to be distributed.

The Webbs, of course, reached a number of conclusions on how to deal with the conflict inherent in social co-operation, some of them quite the opposite of Hayek's. The Webbian instinct was, as I've already suggested, a utilitarian one, but this does not advance us very far, 'utilitarianism' coming in many varieties. One can, of course, say that utilitarianism for the Webbs was concerned with the maximisation of the aggregate of utility available to the members of a society, but this too tells us little in itself until we know how they defined utility. Although, as McBriar notes, there is some ambiguity in their writings on this, it seems clear what, in the final analysis, they were *not*: 'hedonistic utilitarians'.[3] As Beatrice wrote, with her usual forthrightness,

... we agree that human action must be judged by its results in bringing about certain defined ends ... We altogether reject the 'happiness of the greatest number' as a definition of our own end ... I reject it, because I have no clear vision of what I mean by happiness, or what other people mean by it.[4]

Note the reason behind the rejection of the happiness of the greatest number as the end to which all actions ought to be directed: the utter subjectivity of the concept, its basis in the desire-ridden and emotion-laden part of the self. Something much more concrete was wanted, something whose value was objective, demonstrable, and measurable, for happiness could not carry the justificatory weight for which the Webbs were searching. We shall have occasion to return to this subject shortly.

Because of the ambiguity mentioned earlier, the nature of utility in the Webbs' work can best be discovered indirectly,

[3] A. M. McBriar, *Fabian Socialism and English Politics: 1884-1918* (Cambridge, 1962), pp. 149-50.
[4] B. Webb, *Our Partnership* (London, 1948), p. 210, also quoted in McBriar, op. cit., p. 150.

through a consideration of two elements: their conception of human nature and the proper path to its development on the one hand, and the nature of the interdependence created by the existence of the Great Society[5] on the other.

The Webbs believed men to have a rational, utility-maximising nature. This shows through clearly, for instance, in one of the criticisms of capitalism which the Webbs clearly considered the most damning, namely that, while in its earlier phases it undeniably *was* the best means of producing the greatest aggregate of wealth (i.e. means to the satisfaction of desires), superior forms of social organisation now existed which could surpass what Sidney termed this 'unscientific Individualism'.[6] Socialism's inherently superior productivity is clearly seen as a sufficient and conclusive argument *in itself* for its supplanting capitalism. Thus, in *The Decay of Capitalist Civilisation* and elsewhere, the argument is made time and time again that,

... with all its drawbacks, the dictatorship of the capitalist scored an initial success. It delivered the goods. It created the highly efficient machinery of ever-increasing production. And ... on balance ... the advantages exceeded the drawbacks.[7]

There follows a discussion of the grounds for the most 'fundamental' disagreement between capitalists and socialists. To the capitalist, it is claimed, 'what seems essential is the organisation of the instruments of production in the manner that is continuously the most efficient in maximising output',[8] and this is seen to depend on a system of incentives which, through the use of fear, intimidation, and coercion, produces the desired result. Whereas one might not unreasonably expect that a socialist critique of this position would focus on 'radical' issues

---

[5] On the use of the term the 'Great Society' with respect to the work of the Webbs, see Samuel Beer's 'Introduction' to *A Constitution for the Socialist Commonwealth of Great Britain* (Cambridge, 1975), pp. ix–xxxiii (hereinafter cited as 'Introduction'), in which he traces its origins from the Webbs back to Emile Durkheim via Graham Wallas (p. xv). This serves to drive home yet again the similarity of the concerns being addressed by Hayek and the Webbs, given Hayek's great interest in the 'Great Society' outlined in Chapter II.

[6] S. Webb, 'Lord Roseberry's Escape From Houndsditch', reprinted in E. J. T. Brennan (ed.), *Education For National Efficiency: The Contribution of Sidney and Beatrice Webb* (London, 1975), p. 83.

[7] S. and B. Webb, *The Decay of Capitalist Civilisation* (London, 1923) (hereinafter cited as *Decay*), p. 62.

[8] Ibid., p. 64.

(like the distortion of human nature caused by the capitalist relations of production, for example), the Webbs held that capitalists and socialists disagree on what they see as nothing less than the 'very core of the case': the efficacy of the profit motive in producing this unending and self-evidently desirable increase in material production. In fact, the Webbs take to task certain (unspecified) socialist critics of capitalism for advancing the notion that human happiness and welfare could be increased without any additional increase in production.[9] Every man's interest is clearly held to lie in an increase in material wealth and no social or institutional reform would be acceptable which did not, at a minimum, increase productivity over that achieved by capitalism.

This wealth is necessary because men develop themselves through the passive consumption of commodities. Every possible increase in production is favoured as procuring 'additional personal freedom for each individual citizen, as well as a progressive improvement of the race', on the proviso that it is 'fairly distributed and efficiently consumed'.[10] Similarly, the distribution of income under capitalism is criticised because of the declining marginal utility of incomes, resulting in millionaires possessing the means to realise themselves far in excess of what they can reasonably consume, while paupers have not the means to create 'effective demand', depriving the market of any plausible claim to satisfy 'social requirements' or even to produce subjective 'individual happiness'.[11] Further, the Webbs defined personal freedom as 'the possession of the opportunity to develop our faculties and satisfy our desires', and it is held to follow directly from this that 'inequality of income [*i.e. the power to consume*] ... entails inequality in personal freedom'.[12]

Perhaps the most powerful argument to show that the Webbs held utility-maximisation to be the key to human development lies in their utter preoccupation with 'social' or 'national' efficiency. The 'ideology' of the National Efficiency movement has been summed up as:

[9] Ibid., p. 69.
[10] Loc. cit.
[11] S. Webb, *The Difficulties of Individualism*, Fabian Tract no. 69, p. 11, hereinafter cited as *Difficulties*.
[12] *Decay*, p. 45.

... an attempt to discredit the habits, beliefs and institutions that put the British at a handicap in their competition with foreigners and to commend instead a social organisation that more closely followed the *German* model.[13]

The interest of the Webbs in National Efficiency was twofold. On the one hand there was the matter of a straightforward belief that if another form of social organisation was more materially productive, then its citizens would have access to a greater aggregate of means to their own realisation. The superior 'efficiency' of the Germans was thus a cause for concern because it not only undermined the 'necessary basis of society'[14] (by exposing Britain's relative inability to provide its citizens with the greatest possible means to their individual development), but also for a much deeper reason.

National Efficiency puts the accent on the interdependence of all the members of the nation, on the fact that each man's development, as well as his productivity (on which everyone's development depends), are increasingly the result of the interplay of complex factors far beyond the comprehension and experience of the average man. Here we return to the interdependence which I suggested earlier was the other element offering some insight into the nature of utility in the Webbs' thought.

The Webbs argued that the arrival of industrial society, with its highly developed degree of specialisation and interdependence, had fundamentally and irrevocably shifted, if not inverted, the traditional reciprocal claims that the individual and society have made upon one another. When no one else's well-being depended directly on one's own decisions of what to produce and what to consume, men were freer, but much less productive, because they worked in isolation.[15] Now, however, things had changed. With every man dependent on every other's contribution, not only for his own personal development, but for social survival in the struggle with competitors

---

[13] G. R. Searle, *The Quest for National Efficiency* (Oxford, 1971), p. 54. Emphasis in original.

[14] S. Webb, 'The Necessary Basis of Society' in *Contemporary Review*, June 1908, pp. 665-7, hereinafter cited as 'Basis'. See also Searle, op. cit., p. 63 n.

[15] See, for instance, *Difficulties*, pp. 12-13, and also S. Webb, 'Historic' in G. B. Shaw (ed.), *Fabian Essays* (London, 1948), p. 53.

like Germany, society came to be seen by the Webbs as an organism whose overall well-being was superior to that of the individuals it comprised. Thus, to pick a very typical example, Sidney favoured '... the formulation and rigid enforcement in all spheres of social activity, of a National Minimum below which the individual, *whether he likes it or not*, cannot, in the interests of the well-being of the whole, ever be allowed to fall'.[16]

Similarly, in opposition to Joseph Chamberlain's populist position that the state ought to give to people what they want, Beatrice 'wondered whether it might not be wrong for the governing class to "gratify the sensations of the great social organism", whether it should not rather impose the right remedies "irrespective of the longings of the patient" '.[17]

Increasing interdependence resulting from industrialisation, then, meant that each man was less free to choose what he would do and when, but this loss could be compensated by his superior productivity, if he got an equitable share. This meant that, if the Great Society was to gain the acquiescence of rational men, they needed to be convinced that the decrease in personal freedom to choose whatever consummations they liked was more than balanced by an increase in the generalised power to consume and therefore realise themselves. In a curious way, the imperatives of individual development thus required, on the Webbs' view, that men renounce the desire to do what they wish with themselves[18] and submit to the demands of 'rational' or 'scientific' social organisation. Since development of the individual was conceived in terms of fitting him to play his social role in the most productive and efficient manner, it was society's needs which determined what individuals could have, and not the desires of individuals which determined the form society would take.

---

[16] 'Basis', p. 665. Emphasis added.

[17] B. Webb, diary entry for 26 Sept. 1883; cited in S. R. Letwin, *The Pursuit of Certainty* (Cambridge, 1965), p. 359.

[18] There is some evidence to suggest that this renunciation was intended to apply only to the realm of *production*, that is to say that men would be expected to acquiesce in being told what to do by experts in the workplace in order to maximise production so that they would be able to make the most of themselves as they liked in the privacy of their free time. See *The Consumers' Co-operative Movement* (London, 1921), p. 481, and also McBriar, op. cit., pp. 161–2.

There is no denying that this represents a central tension, indeed inconsistency, within the Webbs' work: on the one hand they appear to argue for the fullest development of the individual according to his lights, and on the other they seem to subscribe to a view which holds that the proper development of men depends on a renunciation of their subjective desires in favour of the needs of the organic whole. While wishing in no way to play down the crucial problem that this presents for the Webbs, my intention in the first half of this chapter is to present *their* arguments as faithfully as possible, leaving the critical analysis for later. This has the double advantage of allowing the Webbs to 'speak for themselves' and of allowing us to form a critical appreciation of their work as it should be seen: as a whole and not as bits wrenched from their context.

The question now arises as to why rational individuals might acquiesce in this holistic and organic view of society, or, put the other way round, how might such an order, which appears to take no cognisance of individual wants, justify itself morally to the individuals whom it comprises? For the Webbs the justification is simple and straightforward, and rests on two premises. The first is that rational men will concur that action in accordance with objectively ascertainable fact is always preferable to action in accordance with purely subjective opinion or desire. The second is that facts and values are separable in an unproblematic way, such that knowledge of men and society can be reduced to empirically demonstrable statements.

To use again a concrete example which will illustrate how these epistemological premises distinguish the Webbs from Hayek, this has important implications for the distribution of income in the Webbs' ideal society. Since the equality of men rests not, as it does with Hayek, on their nature as autonomous choosers, but on the (in principle) equal worth of the contribution each functionally specialised person makes to the operation of the social organism, then income must be distributed on the basis of those objectively measurable *needs* the individual must satisfy in order to perform his social role most efficiently.

From another angle, one could say that the ability to develop oneself to the maximum is clearly dependent on a social context. Since the moral worth of men lies not in themselves *qua* men, but in their role as contributors to the production of the utilities on which each social partner's development hinges, each individual's development is subordinate to the needs of society. In a representative passage, Sidney writes

... the perfect and fitting development of each individual is not necessarily the utmost and highest cultivation of his own personality, but the filling, in the best possible way, of his humble function in the great social machine.[19]

The Webbs' utilitarianism, then, may be seen to depend on a notion of utility which concentrates on the maximisation of the satisfaction of *needs* ascribed to individuals quite independently of their particular wants, needs whose satisfaction is justified because it enables the individual concerned to fulfil properly his specialised role in efficient production.

This is not to say that the Webbs do not recognise that individuals may feel that their own development lies along another path and that they may be prepared to accept or even positively desire a less 'efficient' distribution of resources in order to gratify these desires. The Webbs reject this as a sound basis for a social order, however, on three grounds.

Pride of place here must go to what the Webbs see as the evolutionary imperative. Any diversion of the fruits of social co-operation to less than optimally efficient uses will, on their view, endanger the continued survival of society, which is locked with its competitors in a struggle for survival.

Their second ground for rejecting a want-regarding basis for the distribution of resources is a moral one. Given that all people who play a role, however humble, in the functioning of the Great Society's intricate network of interdependency are thereby considered morally equal members of that society, it is unjust to distribute the means to everyone's development in a way that takes no practical account of this equal claim. A just system requires that each man see that he is receiving exactly that to which he is entitled, no less and certainly no more. 'Just' here means that every man receives the same proportion of the means to satisfy his objectively determined needs, given that society may not be able to supply 100 per cent of all the needs all the time. This of course relates back to the evolutionary imperative noted above, in the sense that the society that is

---

[19] 'Historic', p. 54.

most efficient (best able to provide the means to meet the highest possible proportion of its citizens' needs) will by definition be the most productive (need being measured in relation to one's ability to fulfil one's productive role).

The final ground for the Webbs' opposition to a wants-based politics is an epistemological one. Wants, when seen in opposition to needs, appear to be purely subjective and error-prone. Rational man, naturally preferring the certainty of demonstrable truth to the possibility of error, would want to act, therefore, in accordance with certain knowledge. Now it is precisely the existence of this type of knowledge, knowledge which could guide men in their social decision-making and about which rational man could have no doubt, that Hayek is concerned to deny. The Webbs assert most emphatically that it exists, but that it is hard to gather and interpret. Their famed 'average sensual man' is neither functionally specialised in its discovery, nor able to distance himself enough from his emotions to be able to see it for itself. It can be done, but only by those people fitted by talent and training to the task.

As social scientists, the Webbs maintained that the great increase in productivity made possible by the Great Society permitted the emergence of a new class. This class devoted itself exclusively to the study and understanding, by means of a strictly disinterested scientific method, of the objective forces which shape human society. As positivists they also believed that there was a structure to all human experience which paralleled the structure of the physical world and was reducible to, and explicable in terms of, the same kind of causal laws. In their own words, they were always concerned to verify that the 'order of thought' conformed to the 'order of things'.

These claims are clearly closely linked and together constitute the core of the Webbs' very particular social vision. Taking each in turn we will explore the unity and substance of this vision, focusing particularly on the assumptions that are made about the nature and character of the men who are expected to live under it.

'Socialists', wrote Sidney Webb, 'have learnt the lesson of evolution better than their opponents...'[20] This statement

---

[20] *Difficulties*, p. 3.

summarises the difference between the Webbs and someone like Hayek on the subject of evolution. Each proceeds from the assumption that there is a structure to human experience which is constant and discoverable, but not obvious, and with which man must wrestle in the effort to wring from the 'niggardliness of nature'[21] ever more means to self-development.

Society is thus again seen as a cumulative learning programme, or at the very least as the receptacle of the accumulated knowledge of past men and women. Society teaches men to act rationally, to make their desire for the maximum consumption of utilities dominate over all others, thereby guaranteeing the greatest aggregate fulfilment of each person. To this end, the slowly emerging and painfully acquired knowledge of the empirical world works progressively to undermine, circumscribe, and destroy those irrational aspects of man, his private desires and whims. Such whims only serve to encourage selfish individuals to divert their energies from the goals of mastering nature and maximising production to mere pleasure-ridden self-regarding ends.

At first, men have no choice but to learn slowly and haphazardly, by trial and error, as a kind of 'unconscious process'.[22] This, however, is merely a function of the small amount of knowledge that early societies have accumulated. This, in its turn, is due to the relatively short duration of their struggle to subordinate Nature and themselves to the overarching imperatives of the natural selection of social units. As individuals learn more about the world, but remain in ignorance of the struggle for survival between societies, they naturally turn their attention to profiting individually from the particular knowledge they possess. Capitalism and individualism are thus a natural stage in the evolutionary process, but one to which the ineluctable march of knowledge cannot be indifferent, for the selfish exploitation of knowledge and

---

[21] 'Historic', p. 53

[22] As gradualists and evolutionists, the Webbs lay great stress on the unplanned and spontaneous nature of most evolutionary change, but they differ from Hayek in believing that the growing sophistication of society's scientific knowledge makes it possible to improve on this haphazard process by conscious planning; see 'Historic', p. 29; see also N. Mackenzie, *Socialism and Society: A New View of the Webb Partnership*, lecture delivered at the London School of Economics in 1978, p. 15.

power inherent in capitalism is, in the long run, incompatible with social survival.

As social organisation and the division of labour become more complex, and as interdependence grows, individual natural selection continues but its importance declines as the crucial ' "selected" attribute' becomes the collective one of 'social organisation'. The fall of 'the cultivated Athenians, Saracens, and Provençals' was due to their excessive attention to individual development, whereas their opponents' superiority lay exclusively in their 'more valuable social organisation'.[23] This cannot but lead to the conclusion that it is not the highest possible cultivation of the individual which the Webbs held to be the *telos* of the evolutionary process, but the perfection of a social organisation which maximises the contribution of its members to production.

Accordingly, conscious 'direct adaptation' steadily supplants the unconscious and wasteful 'indirect adaptation' of the earlier form of the struggle for existence; and with every advance in sociological knowledge. Man is seen to assume more and more, not only the mastery of 'things', but also a conscious control over social destiny itself.[24]

When Sidney quotes Huxley approvingly to the effect that evolution *is* the 'substitution of consciously regulated co-ordination among the units of each organism, for blind anarchic competition'[25], the grand scale of the Webbs' conception comes sharply into focus. Sociology, the precise and painstaking observation and collection of social facts, can reveal to men the principles of social organisation which evolution demands, and which human will is powerless to change.[26]

One cannot insist too strongly on this point: for the Webbs there was always, at any moment, one optimal form of organisation for a given society.[27] This is not a permanent ideal state, but rather reflects the number of immutable 'social facts' which are known by that society's leaders. Change is inevitable because the accumulation of knowledge is ceaseless, with society

23 'Historic', p. 54.
24 Loc. cit.
25 Ibid., p. 56.
26 *Difficulties*, p. 3.
27 'Historic', p. 53; also R. Barker, *Political Ideas in Modern Britain*, p. 31.

constantly adjusting to newly acquired knowledge. The process of adjustment, though, can be either unconscious or conscious, spontaneous or planned, once the accumulated knowledge and the division of labour reach a threshold which the England of the Webbs' day had long passed. For them, leaving it to chance and individual whim how and when knowledge would be put to productive use was leaving to the dependent parts the right to dictate to the whole. In opposition to the Hayekian position seen earlier, then, the Webbs believed that the more complex a society was, the more indispensable its self-conscious direction became to its survival chances.

Seeing society as an 'organism', and hence being able to attribute to it the single overriding aim of survival and 'health' made it easy to see what society's, and therefore the individual's, needs were. A widespread awareness of the organic unity of society was itself an evolutionary step which the Webbs believed themselves to be championing; the product of the new insights gained by the rapidly accelerating collection of social facts.[28]

Evolution, in the all-important sense of social, rather than individual adaptation, was the result of a growing consciousness of the structure of the world and the direction in which this channelled human efforts. The Webbs were impatient of philosophical and theoretical discussions about what society ought to be doing because they believed these to be meaningless. A full and correct knowledge of social facts would reveal that evolutionary forces pointed in one direction which had to be followed regardless of individual desires; the alternative was social suicide. Barker sums up this perspective when he writes of the Webbs' belief that 'Philosophers and politicians might be necessary if broad choices were open, but they were not, and so what were called for were men and women with less lofty but more useful talents'.[29] In short, what was needed was the Webbs, people who were interested only in discovering the facts, without fear or favour, and who were prepared to follow the logic of those facts through to their necessary conclusion for the good of all. Accordingly, the Webbs considered themselves the selfless and disinterested midwives of social change

---

[28] 'Historic', *passim.*
[29] Barker, op. cit., p. 31.

brought about by the growth of knowledge. They saw themselves as neither controlling nor directing change, but as merely organising the inevitable.

The famous Webbian belief in the 'inevitability of gradualness' and 'permeation' as a political strategy is an excellent illustration of this notion of the seamless and all-encompassing web of facts. The world was perfectly internally consistent and behaved predictably in accordance with discoverable laws. This being the case, the correct solution to any problem would be perfectly consistent and compatible with the correct solution to any other problem. The evolution of society was, therefore, nothing more than the slow steady accumulation of such solutions, testing them against what is known of the world and, once they have 'proven out', their inclusion in the great body of social facts which set the limits of rational action.[30] Since the Webbs saw 'facts' as value-free and indisputable, they believed that party politics, which were based on selfish, sectional interests and mere opinions, would eventually become redundant where they were not positively harmful. Beatrice 'preferred that social science, "a comprehensive knowledge of social facts, past and present", should come to rule',[31] and both the Webbs believed that the mere discovery and dissemination of facts would be sufficient to secure that men of good faith in all parties would see that only one policy could possibly follow from them.

Clearly, then, evolution had two political implications of capital importance. One was that political action could not depend for its validity on either the pursuit of ideals or on the attempt to satisfy the subjective preferences of men. The other was that because the direction of evolution was discoverable by the methods of sociology, and sociology, 'like all other sciences, can advance only upon the basis of a precise observation of actual facts',[32] social scientists and other experts were to play a pivotal role in society. With each addition to the body of

---

[30] 'Socialism', then, becomes the growing *consciousness* or *awareness* of the pattern and structure of evolutionary change. This viewpoint, far from being limited to the Webbs, was shared by the Fabians generally according to M. Beer, *A History of British Socialism* (London, 1929), Vol. II, pp. 276-7.

[31] B. Webb, diary entry for 6 Nov. 1884; cited in S. Letwin, op. cit., p. 359. I will have more to say on the Webbs' attitude to political parties in Chapter V.

[32] S. and B. Webb, *Industrial Democracy* (London, 1926), p. xix.

social facts, the path of rational action open to men became ever narrower.

At first the Webbs believed that the mere publicising of the facts that experts had collected would be enough to convince men to renounce all irrational modes of behaviour in favour of the scientifically correct one. 'Measurement and Publicity' were thus the watchwords of the ideal constitution of the Webbs' middle years, *A Constitution for the Socialist Commonwealth of Great Britain.* Since experts merely reported the facts, over which they had no control or influence, the Webbs believed that men would be sufficiently rational to see that they ought[33] to act in accordance with expert recommendations. The case for 'measurement and publicity' was put in these terms:

The importance of complete consciousness of the social tendencies of the age lies in the fact that its existence and comprehensiveness often determine the expediency of our particular action: we move with less resistance with the stream than against it.[34]

In the following sense, then, Hayek and the Webbs seem to be in agreement. Human beings must be led to act in a socially rational manner because they are prey to an irrational lower self above which they cannot be expected to rise on their own. The social order is thus crucial to rationality because it provides a context within which men can see that they have an interest in acting rationally: acting to maximise the welfare of all by making the largest possible contribution to efficient production and hence utility maximisation and, ultimately, social and cultural survival.

This is not to overlook that while Hayek and the Webbs might share a common perspective on the mechanism of evolution, Hayek voices a strong ethical or moral concern that this not result in the arbitrary coercion of some men by others. The

---

[33] 'Ought' is used here in *both* the moral and the prudential senses: not only is it prudent to act in accordance with the facts, but since refusing to act in accordance with them would endanger the survival of society, on whose well-being *everyone* depends, it would be immoral to ignore them. Furthermore, since to defy the facts is to be in error, and to be in error is to reduce efficiency from its theoretical maximum, such selfishness is morally blameworthy because it deprives one's fellows of the maximum aggregate of means to their realisation. See 'Historic', p. 53; and *Soviet Communism: A New Civilisation* (London, 1944) (hereinafter cited as *Civilisation*), *passim*, particularly Part II, Chapter XII, Section 14: 'Ethics Emerging From Life'.

[34] 'Historic', p. 47.

fact is that the Webbs too have a similar moral preoccupation, and it is this preoccupation which leads them to oppose a market-based social order as inimical to a moralised society.

The Webbs' moral critique of a social order based on the mere satisfaction of wants takes two distinct forms. The first concerns the liberties or freedoms which rational man may legitimately claim. In this the Webbs were in complete sympathy with Huxley, who said, 'The only freedom I care about is the freedom to do right; the freedom to do wrong I am ready to part with on the cheapest terms to anyone who will take it off me.'[35]

This has important implications for the relations between owners and workers under capitalism. Capitalism, by placing in the hands of owners the power to make decisions about what shall be produced, where and by whom, arbitrarily subjects men to the decisions of others who are qualified neither by training nor background to know how best to do these things. In other words, by leaving such power uncontrolled in the hands of individuals, who exercise it as a result of luck and ruthlessness, capitalism condones the practice of men being obliged to act against their own objective interest. What interests the 'captains of industry', as with all selfish human beings, the Webbs thought, was to achieve their greatest *individual* development, while passing the cost of this on to others. They therefore naturally sought to direct their workers to produce that which would bring them (the capitalists) the greatest possible means to that realisation.[36]

Not only may such production be itself wrongful, in that it does nothing to promote the health of the social organism, but such relations between owners and workers are morally indefensible because they give to an individual the power to direct the labour of others to goals which cannot be rationally justified.[37] The 'chaos of capitalism' was due to the fact that decisions on production and investment were not taken to promote the health of the social organism (thus having one unarguable and obvious conclusion, for those possessing the

---

[35] T. H. Huxley, *Life and Letters*, Vol. I, p. 328; cited in Letwin, op. cit., p. 323.

[36] S. Webb, *The Place of Co-operation in the State of Tomorrow*, undated pamphlet published by The Co-operative Union Ltd., London, p. 2.

[37] *Decay*, pp. 2 and 144–5.

relevant knowledge). Instead, they were taken in the light of the particular arbitrary, fallible, and literally irresponsible[38] desires of the owners of capital. Since such decisions were not taken on a co-ordinated basis, for the measurable common good, capitalism coerced non-owners, the workers who had to labour in order to obtain the means to their own development, into devoting their time and energies to something which in many cases was demonstrably wrong.[39]

This has led at least one Webb scholar to criticise them for having given to 'leadership and authority ... no role in their theory of politics'.[40] This, however, is a misunderstanding. It is not that there was no role for leadership and authority because the Webbs *overlooked* it, but rather that, until 1920, at least (the date of publication of their *Constitution*), they believed these to be largely *pre-rational forms of social relationship*. When rational men realise that strife and disagreement are due to nothing but a remediable ignorance, one can dispense with authority, power, and leadership because men will want to do what is demonstrably rational.[41] The Webbs' moral critique of capitalism can thus be summed up as the belief that it is coercive and arbitrary to allow one man's 'unscientific' decisions to direct the labours of others who acquiesce merely because they must in order to survive.

What particular individuals, sections or classes usually mean by 'freedom of contract', 'freedom of association' or 'freedom of enterprise' is freedom of opportunity to use the power that they happen to possess ... to compel other less powerful people to accept their terms. This sort of personal freedom in a community composed of unequal units is not distinguishable from compulsion ... We ourselves understand by the words 'Liberty' or 'Freedom', not any quantum of natural or inalienable rights, but such conditions of existence in the community as do, in practice, result in the utmost possible development of faculty in the individual human being.[42]

---

[38] 'Hence it is that *irresponsible personal authority* over the action of others—expelled from the throne, the castle and the altar—still reigns, almost unchecked, in the factory and the mine', *Difficulties*, p. 14 (emphasis added).

[39] See Letwin, op. cit., p. 368.

[40] S. Beer, 'Introduction', p. xxviii.

[41] Leonard Woolf writes perceptively in this regard in 'Political Thought and the Webbs' in M. Cole (ed.), *The Webbs and Their Work* (London, 1949), pp. 256–61.

[42] *Industrial Democracy*, p. 847.

There were two ways in which the Webbs found the moral justification of market society inadequate, and the preceding quotation draws our attention to the second as well as the first. Accepting that the fullest possible development of the individual comes through the consumption of the objectively correct package of utilities, the Webbs justified a centrally planned economy on the ground that it would maximise efficiency in both production and consumption. In this, of course, they faced the same obstacle as Hayek in his similar justification of a market order: this is a purely empirical claim, subject to verification in the long run. It cannot be accepted as an article of faith. There is a largely implicit secondary claim that even if expert planning did not result in greater production (a possibility they would never have countenanced), such a centrally planned economy would still be more ethically or morally defensible than a market order because of the way they conceived individual human development working.

Hayek's view, for instance, is that the ability of a man to realise himself depends wholly on his natural abilities or capacities, '*plus* whatever additional power (means to ensure future gratifications) he has acquired by getting command over the energies and skills of other men, or *minus* whatever part of his energies and skills he has lost to some other men'.[43] In other words, such a system does not *guarantee* to anyone the means necessary to their self-realisation. It further accepts that a man's power to realise himself may be transferred to other individuals in a morally unproblematic way.[44]

It is clear that in order to realise oneself, to become the kind of person one wants to be, one requires not only one's own skills and talents (many of which are unequally and capriciously distributed by nature), one normally also needs access to those external resources necessary to that realisation. In the Webbs' view of capitalism, vast masses of men went unrealised (i.e. were wasted as social resources, since self-realisation for the Webbs meant fulfilling one's functional social role) because

[43] This quotation is taken from C. B. Macpherson's article 'The Maximisation of Democracy' in P. Laslett and W. G. Runciman (eds.), *Philosophy, Politics, and Society* (Oxford, 1967), p. 89. While Macpherson is addressing himself to a different question and context, his argument is quite apposite here, and I am indebted to him for much of the reasoning to follow.

[44] *Decay*, pp. 49 and 58.

they were denied access to the means to that realisation. By allowing individual capitalists the power to decide who would work, for how much, and in what conditions, the market in effect allowed employers to coerce workers to work for less than their functional specialisation warranted and allowed them (the employers) to use the surplus thus created for their own private consumption.

The Webbs condemn market society not only because it does not guarantee a universal minimum of access to the means to self-realisation, but also because it condones the achievement of one man's self-realisation by denying another's without rational warrant. He who owns property (which, as Hayek himself recognises, is capriciously distributed under capitalism) can require those who must have access to it in order to develop themselves, to pay him for that access. This means that they must transfer to him some of their power of self-realisation, either directly, as labour, or indirectly, as cash.

From this insight—that a man's ability to realise himself 'depends not only on his natural capacities, but also on his *ability* to exert them [and] therefore includes *access* to whatever things outside himself are requisite to that exertion'[45]—the Webbs concluded that a more rational system of distribution was possible. Their reasoning was the following: if self-realisation is the filling of one's appropriate social role, and this is achieved by the consumption of a scientifically selected package of utilities, then two things follow. First, since the aggregate of self-realisation possible in a society increases in direct proportion to that society's material productivity, the production of utilities must be maximised. Second, everyone who fills his social role must be guaranteed access to those utilities necessary for him to perform that role adequately. This, the Webbs thought, could clearly best be done in a planned economy, directed by experts with no interest but the efficient direction of society's productive efforts.

In their rush to maximise access, however, the Webbs appear to have dismissed what might be considered one of the market order's strongest moral and psychological insights: that *self*-development cannot be achieved *for* someone—it is something

45 Macpherson, op. cit., p. 89.

in which the individual must participate, for which he must accept a degree of responsibility. The Webbs believed that self-realisation was wholly dependent on the social context: in the well-ordered Webbian society not only would everyone be 'adequately healthy, wealthy and wise',[46] but they would become so independently of, and perhaps even in opposition to, what they conceived their own interests and volition to be. Because the 'average sensual man' could not be expected to recognise his own interest, not being functionally specialised in this highly complex business, people came to be *things* to be manipulated in whatever way was necessary in order to create the scientifically correct social order.[47]

This brings us to the third and final ground for the Webbs' opposition to a wants-based politics: the epistemological one. A great deal has already been said about the Webbs' view of the unity of structure of the world, and hence the unity and internal consistency of knowledge, but this poses a central problem. How and by whom is this knowledge to be discovered, and how is the 'rule by experts' which this implies to be reconciled with the Webbs' fervent and frequent expressions of attachment to democracy?

'... [W]ithout the application of the scientific method to social organisation', the Webbs argued, 'the crucial problem of democracy—how we can obviate the arbitrary exercise of one man's will over another—cannot be solved.'[48] Seen against the background of the Webbs' organic social conception, this expresses the heart of their political preoccupation. Knowledge can set men free from arbitrariness and error, but knowledge itself can only be obtained by the strictest observance of scientific method by disinterested experts. These experts were seen as themselves the product of the march of evolution, in the sense that the inevitable result of the increasing functional specialisation of the Great Society was the growth of an 'intellectual proletariat'.[49]

As social relations became more and more complex and interdependent, men became less and less capable of performing,

[46] Woolf, op. cit., p. 263.
[47] See e.g. *Industrial Democracy*, p. 817.
[48] *Decay*, p. 144.
[49] This term is Mackenzie's, op. cit., p. 19.

in addition to their specialised and necessary function, the task of promoting their interests in other roles than that of producer. Such a task depended on the mastery of a body of facts too vast for someone who could not devote himself to their study full time, and who lacked the training to see their true significance. Furthermore, an organic society, engaged in a life and death evolutionary struggle transcending in time and place the life of each individual, required men to take the 'long view' of their interests, something the average sensual man was loath to do.

In the search for the scientifically correct solution to any problem, then, the Webbs were clear that the only opinions which mattered were the relevant expert ones. Their writings on the role and function of trade unions is a particularly good example of this total faith in and reliance on expert opinion. In *Industrial Democracy* it is clear that, in the 'democratic state of tomorrow', the influence of trade unions would be limited to those fields where they could be held to have 'expert' knowledge, namely in how conditions could be improved in order to make workers more productive.[50]

In the same passage it is made equally clear that such expert knowledge would not extend to areas like economic management or political questions like the continued existence of the House of Lords: these are clearly questions on which the direct knowledge gleaned from improving the efficiency of workers can have no bearing. Even within the trade union movement as such, the specialised division of labour would inevitably result in the growth of an expert class whose function it would be to explain to ordinary trade unionists how they might best go about achieving their common objective: increased production. In spite of the early radical egalitarianism of workers' organisations, in their own day the Webbs believed that trade unionists 'have been forced to devolve more and more of "their own business" on a specially selected and specially trained class of professional experts'.[51]

Where might these experts, the new vanguard of evolutionary progress come from, and what fitted them to this role? Wielding the kind of influence that they clearly would in the Webbs' ideal world would require at least some stringent selec-

---

[50] *Industrial Democracy*, p. 839.
[51] Ibid., p. 843.

tion procedure, especially if any recognisable form of democracy were to be compatible with it.

The Webbs' answer to this is characteristic. Only scientific selection of the 'best' would be acceptable, in order to avoid that mere human opinion or preference play a role. Since what democracy requires is that objective truth and not irrational human will rule, the selection of the intellectual élite who would run the system must not be seen to repose on anything so arbitrary as class or wealth. 'An élite hitherto based upon the accident of birth or wealth was to be replaced ... by ... a meritocracy whose goal would be ... the pursuit of "national" and "imperial efficiency".'[52]

What this meant in practice was a meritocratic national school system which would realise the 'really democratic purpose of public education':[53]

... the training of a political élite who would be capable of running the [social] machine efficiently and intelligently; and the education of the 'ordinary' citizen so that he could be fitted squarely and fairly into an appropriate place in the social, but primarily economic machine.[54]

Unsurprisingly, the two abilities that the Webbs believed most essential to the discharge of the function of 'expert' were that of recognising a fact, separating truth from error, and that of accepting the truth and its implications selflessly and objectively, for the good of the social organism. This required experts who were not only trained in the social and natural sciences, but were also not concerned with 'metaphysics' or 'shoddy history' and who had the sole end of promoting the common good before them.

The story of the foundation of the London School of Economics and Political Science provides a good illustration of how the various elements of the Webbs' larger social conception fit together and how true experts were to be brought into the world. While a degree of meritocracy was needed in the national education system, this was at far too low a level truly to create a class of experts capable of mastering the intricate mass

52 Brennan, op. cit., p. 30.
53 Sidney Webb quoted in Brennan, op. cit., p. 30.
54 Woolf, op. cit., p. 258.

of detail that the scientific study of society was already throwing up. What is more, the traditional universities seemed pre-occupied with the vague and empty metaphysical and speculative studies which the Webbs held so useless. With the model of Paris's École libre des Sciences politiques firmly in the forefront of their minds, the Webbs turned their thinking to the creation of a 'London School of Economics and Political Science'. The project became reality with the bequest of a large sum of money to the Fabian Society to be used for purposes of socialist propaganda. Beatrice was 'jubilant that the training of the expert so badly needed in the pursuit of "national efficiency" could now begin in all seriousness'.[55]

Beatrice's thoughts on what the students of the LSE ought to be studying are full of telling insights into their larger outlook on the social and political world. Her diary records how pleased they both were that Sidney had succeeded in having economics recognised

... as a science and not merely as a subject in the Arts Faculty. The preliminary studies for the economics degree will, therefore, be mathematics and biology. This divorce of economics from metaphysics and shoddy history is a great gain. We have always claimed that the study of the structure and function of society was as much a science as the study of any other form of life, and ought to be pursued by the scientific methods used in other organic sciences.[56]

The Webbs' faith in the ability of a 'fact' to speak for itself, without interpretation, and of a social scientist to be trained to recognise a fact by a kind of mechanistic process[57] was central to the social function that the LSE was to play and of the curriculum that they proposed for it. This can be seen with even greater clarity when one considers their detailed conception of the method of the social sciences. The personality and creativity of the individual expert were simply factors which the Webbs considered utterly extraneous to the discovery and understanding of facts. 'The order of thought', Beatrice argued,

[55] B. Webb, diary entry for 21 Sept. 1894; cited in Brennan, op. cit., p. 35.

[56] *Ibid*, p. 41; diary entry for 28 Feb. 1900.

[57] See T. Simey's very perceptive comments on the Webbs' substitution of methodology for judgment in 'The Contribution of Sidney and Beatrice Webb to Sociology', *British Journal of Sociology* (June 1961), p. 114.

was simply determined by the 'order of things'[58] and so the training did not touch on how the social scientist, *as an individual*, might achieve the emotional distance and objectivity which comprehensive social planning required if human will was to play no part in it.

The rule of experts would be a great moral advance on capitalism precisely because it would remove all such arbitrary abuses of power as the attempt to implement ideas not firmly grounded in the facts. The Webbs were certain that this new prominence for the expert would make social relations more rational.

The stream of decisions or orders by which the wheels of industry are kept going will cease to be the exercise of one man's arbitrary will over other men's actions. The independent professional . . . will report according to his knowledge; but he will give no orders and exercise no authority. His function is exhausted when his report is made. His personality will find expression, and his freedom will be exercised without limitation, in the process of discovery and measurement, and in the fearless representation of whatever he finds . . . [59]

It is important to note that the Webbs propose no training in the principles of morality or ethics for their expert class, even though they clearly conceived them to be the vanguard of a newly moralised society. This seeming inconsistency dissolves when one realises, as the foregoing passage makes abundantly clear, that the morality of an expert's actions comes *from* his objectivity and impersonality; as long as he does his job of measuring the facts conscientiously, he acts morally because non-arbitrarily. Morality was not, for the expert, a question of judgment, will, and experience. By the time the Webbs were writing *Civilisation*, however, they had come to see that their optimism with regard to the independent expert's selfless devotion to the truth had been ill-founded and some control mechanism *was* necessary to keep them on the straight and (objectively) narrow path of truth: a monolithic Party structure supplemented by periodic purges of backsliders.

---

[58] B. Webb, *My Apprenticeship* (London, 1926), p. 133. See also Simey, op. cit., June, 1961, p. 114.

[59] *Decay*, p. 145.

Given what we have already seen of the Webbs' work, it is by now clear that they cannot be 'democrats' in any straight-forward way or, more accurately, that their theory of democracy was a 'rather personal' one.[60] The whole thrust of their economic, moral, and epistemological arguments pushes them in a highly élitest and non-participatory direction. Mackenzie is surely right in seeing in the Webbs a conception of democracy totally at variance, for example, with that espoused by the early Labour Party.[61] And yet democracy was a constant watchword of the Webbs' work and they prided themselves on working hard to help evolution bring democracy to industry, just as it had already been brought to politics.[62]

In a world governed by truth which man cannot hope to change, though, it is obvious that democracy cannot be about letting human will rule in government *or* in industry. Webbian democracy was, and could only be, the relationship which exists between the disease-ridden patient (society) and the doctor who can cure all ailments (the expert). The analogy was one the Webbs used themselves to suggest that what democracy was about was providing a kind of feedback mechanism, a channel through which information about problems en-countered by the 'average sensual man' would be com-municated back to the expert for analysis and appropriate action.[63]

Democracy was a mechanism which would make accessible to the planner certain kinds of dispersed knowledge, and as such promoted efficiency. It was more, however. It was a necessary expedient in obtaining the consent of the governed to the de-cisions of the experts.[64] Time and again they argued that it would belong to the people's elected representatives to dispose of the particular measures which it was the province of experts to propose.[65]

[60] J. A. Hall, 'The Roles and Influence of Political Intellectuals: Tawney vs. Sidney Webb', *British Journal of Sociology* (Sept. 1977), p. 353.

[61] Mackenzie, op. cit., p. 14.

[62] *Difficulties*, p. 15.

[63] See e.g. Hall, op. cit., pp. 353–5.

[64] Sidney confided to Graham Wallas that the only good and sufficient justification of elections was that they were 'necessary (or convenient) to get popular consent, i.e. consciousness that they consent', see P. Clarke, *Liberals and Social Democrats* (Cambridge, 1978), p. 143.

[65] *Industrial Democracy*, pp. 844–5.

This could not be allowed to degenerate into a state where 'democratic' institutions obstructed experts in their effort to bring rationality to human affairs. If government was truly to be 'an outside force, ... directed by the ablest minds',[66] and the ablest minds were to be selected on merit and given a special kind of training to fit them for governing, then democracy could not mean the right of citizens to change their rulers. In any case, the rule of truth, as we have already seen, was not the rule of men. It might be possible to change non-expert representatives, but not their expert advisers, for this would be to substitute irrational desire for the calm voice of truth and reason.

Democracy, then, meant experts seeing that the objective needs of the organic community and the ascribed needs of the individual were correctly catered for. 'In the interests of the community as a whole, no ... decisions can be allowed to run counter to the consensus of expert opinion, representing the consumers, ... producers ... and the nation that is paramount over both.'[67] The functional specialisation of the Great Society spread even, or perhaps especially, to the level of experts who knew what men needed better than they knew themselves, and made it rational for men to assent to the 'subordination ... of the person who cannot to the person who can',[68] that is to say of the average sensual man to the omniscient expert. Beatrice sums it all up when she states that, 'it is only consent that is needed, not understanding or intellectual appreciation, i.e. feeling, not thought'.[69]

The trick of democracy was to secure the acquiescence of the masses in what was good for them, by whatever means were necessary, since the good life for man could only be created by altering his social environment in accordance with scientific knowledge; the transformation and moralisation of men could be accomplished through their manipulation as objects and not by an appeal to their intellect.[70] Beatrice, whose belief in the

---

[66] B. Webb, diary entry for 26 Sept. 1883; cited in Letwin, op. cit., p. 359.

[67] *Industrial Democracy*, p. 823.

[68] S. and B. Webb in the *New Statesman* of 3 May 1913, p. 107; cited in Hall, op. cit., p. 353.

[69] Wallas Papers, Box 1; B. Webb to Graham Wallas, 23 July 1908. Quoted in Searle, op. cit., pp. 94-5.

[70] For further comment on the Webbs' instrumental approach to people and institutions, see Woolf, op. cit., p. 258, and Mackenzie, op. cit., p. 21.

possibility of the transformation of men solely through the manipulation of their social environment appears without reservation, leaves us with no doubt as to the ordinary person's role: 'We do not want to unfetter the individual from the obligation of citizenship, we want ... to stimulate and constrain him, by the unfelt pressure of a better social environment, to become a healthier, nobler and more efficient being'.[71]

Based on what we have seen so far, one can readily understand why two particular criticisms figure in every philosophically competent critical evaluation of the Webbs as political thinkers. The first is that they just assumed that society's ends were simply given and discoverable only by experts; the second that they assumed society could be seen as a purposive entity pursuing its own ends. While finding these points both telling and apposite, no purpose would be served by belabouring them further; others have stated the arguments about as well as they can be stated.[72] On the other hand, few of the Webbs' critics seem to have appreciated fully the broader significance of the view of man that underlies these assumptions and this will be the concern in the balance of this chapter. It is in this view of man that is to be found the inarticulate but subtly appealing rhetorical force on which the Webbs founded their opposition to politics.

The central premise of the Webbs' argument in favour of the scientific management of society was the following: Society is an organic whole which is subject to the forces of natural selection, a concept which implies a particular *telos* or idea of 'progress'. That progress proceeds on two fronts: first, the ever greater self-development of the members of the social organism; and second, a growing self-consciousness of the struggle between social organisms, a more and more conscious pursuit of socio-cultural superiority. Because the social organism is construed to have purposes in this way, and because the development of individuals is linked to their contribution to social survival, the purposes, or even more strongly, the *interests* of men as individuals are held to be congruent and coextensive

---

[71] *Our Partnership*, p. 229.
[72] A good summary of these critiques is to be found in Barker, op. cit., esp. Chapter 1. See also e.g. Woolf, op. cit. and Hall, op. cit., *passim*.

with those of the whole. This means that the Webbs are not ordinary *paternalists*, believing that their superior judgment (or 'expert knowledge') justifies them in ignoring the expressed preferences of particular individuals. For the paternalist opposition to subjective want satisfaction to work, the welfare of a particular *identified* individual must be at stake: a parent may deny his small child the extra sweets he desires because the parent *knows* they will make *that* child sick.

The Webbs deny the propriety of satisfying expressed preferences for quite different reasons; the opposition is one of individualism versus holism. The holist treats the social whole as an entity whose good is both separate from and defined independently of the interests (whether subjectively or paternalistically defined) of *any* identified individual. Popper's 'mystical holism',[73] which obliterates any sense of individual identity when viewing the good of 'society', thus corresponds much more to the Webbs' pronouncements than simple paternalism does.

It follows that the Webbs are making a strong claim about the possibility of *certain knowledge* of the interests of the whole (from the objective study of social facts), and on this basis they argue that the purposes and interests of hypothetically rational men can be deduced directly from such social knowledge and ascribed to subrational but real men. It is very important to notice that this is a twofold claim. On the one hand, it is asserted that the fullest possible development of *each* man is sought; on the other, it is suggested society's continued survival must be the ultimate end. No incompatibility is seen to exist between these two maximising claims.

The Webbs are, nevertheless, fundamentally ambiguous about the true nature of human development and this ambiguity is, in the end, fatal to their attempt to separate the subjective wants and desires of individuals from their ascribed 'true' interests as rational men. The attempt founders on the apparently insoluble problems of a theory of human development which takes no account of what individuals believe to be good for them, or to be in their own interests.

---

[73] On Popper's arguments regarding holism, see A. O'Hear's book, *Karl Popper* (London, 1980), esp. Chapter 8, 'Reason and Society'.

The first such problem concerns the possibility of knowledge and of a social science, for the nature and extent of what can be known about man and society is obviously of prime importance. Since this is a very large topic and one, moreover, which is relevant to both Hayek and the Webbs, a large part of Chapter VIII will be devoted to this. At present, my concern is with the second problem: the central suggestion that what is good for man is something that is discoverable solely by the methods of science. I intend to show that many interests of individuals are essentially indeterminate and hence that it is impossible for all or even most of men's interests to be authoritatively prescribed by experts or the state.

It must be admitted at the outset, of course, that the Webbs do not speak in terms of the interests of individual men, but rather of human needs, and this is a significant difference. A consideration of the different meaning of these two terms will, therefore, be helpful in establishing the framework for what is to follow.

Without wishing to compress too much the conventional description of what it means for a person to have an interest,[74] it would not be taking too many liberties to say that the statement 'x is in A's interest' rests on two distinct but related premises. The first might be termed the subjective premise, or, following Minogue,[75] the 'identity condition'. The second, objective premise, might similarly be called the 'reality condition'.

Taking these in order, it is reasonable to say that an indispensable condition of making the statement 'x is in A's interest' is that we be clear who A is. Thus, if A was a miner and member of the NUM, it might be said that it was 'in his interests' that the 1984-5 pit strike succeed, because this would have secured his long-term employment prospects or enhanced the power of workers' organisations or perhaps even advanced

[74] Barry presents the argument in full detail in his *Political Argument*, op. cit., Chapter 10. See also e.g. C. Swanton, 'The Concept of Interests', *Political Theory*, Feb. 1980; R. Flathman, *The Public Interest* (New York, 1966); and A. Hirschman, *The Passions and the Interests* (Princeton, 1977).

[75] K. Minogue, unpublished paper entitled 'Ideology and the Concept of an Interest' presented at the LSE Graduate Seminar in Political Philosophy, 18 Oct. 1984, pp. 4-7. I am indebted to Professor Minogue for much of the argument to follow regarding the essential indeterminacy of human interests.

the cause of socialism (which itself assumes that 'socialism' is in his interests). However, none of these considerations will weigh heavily with *A* in his calculation of his own interests if he does not consider that his membership of a trade union or his objective class status is the pertinent consideration to him here. If *A* felt that the relevant aspect of his *identity* here was not his NUM card, but rather his Conservative political allegiance or his role as mortgage payer or civil libertarian, then he may well have found the strike not to be in his interests. Like the rest of us, *A* inhabits a web of cross-cutting roles and allegiances which do not all pull in the same direction; we have rights and obligations the implications of which are not always compatible.[76]

To say that *x* is in *A*'s interest, then, is to make a judgment about which *aspect* of *A*'s identity is relevant to the interest calculation. In political arguments, this judgment is normally seen to be a subjective one: while we can argue about what aspect of who we are *ought* to be considered relevant,[77] this is a purely rhetorical exercise designed to persuade others what factors to take into account. It rests with each individual to arrive at his own conclusions concerning who he is;[78] and, of course, people take advantage of the fact that they have differing interests depending on the aspect of their identity they choose to regard as relevant. A trade unionist, when seeking to protect and further his interests in that role, may find in Arthur Scargill an ideal representative, but only because he knows that the interests of other, competing aspects of his identity (e.g. as a taxpayer or a Tory voter) can be protected by other, countervailing, means.

[76] Hayek offers a very good treatment of this theme in *Political Order*, pp. 89-97.

[77] Minogue cites here the example of European parliamentary socialists in the period immediately preceding the First World War, arguing that they had to decide whether their *national* identity or their *political or ideological* commitment was the relevant aspect of their identity to refer to in deciding whether or not to support the war, op. cit., p. 4.

[78] This 'identity condition' has clear affinities with Popper's 'methodological individualism' (see e.g. A. O'Hear, *Karl Popper* (London, 1980), pp. 160-9). As Popperian 'mystical holists', the Webbs cannot admit that the identity of individuals is relevant to the definition of the good of the social whole. On the contrary, as an entity quite separate from the individual identities of its members, the pursuit of its good must prohibit the assignment of any weight whatsoever to individual desires where these conflict with the 'social good'.

Even settling the question of *A*'s identity does not in itself settle whether any *x* is in his interest. This is because any calculation of interests includes certain assumptions about what *A* will find to be a desirable state of affairs in his relevant identity. *A* may well believe it to be in his interest to be wealthy and yet find, like Midas, the actual possession of wealth and its consequences to be undesirable. This is what constitutes the *reality condition* of statements regarding *A*'s interests: the world's inherent complexity makes it difficult to know how best to promote *A*'s interest even after the question of subjective identity is settled. *A*, or anyone else, may be simply mistaken about what will promote his interest.

In an effort to avoid the difficulties caused by the subjectivity of the identity condition, the Webbs do not talk in terms of the *interests* of individual men at all. Instead they are at pains to talk about the *needs* of men in the abstract. This move has, at first sight, certain advantages. It gives the impression that there is some objective or scientific criterion of a bona fide need which can justify its satisfaction. Thus, for instance, theories of the equality of man can, with some plausibility, be erected on the foundation of a shared set of basic human needs.[79] The apparently given nature of these needs may thus be appealed to as a justification of their satisfaction, because they do not refer to debatable human purposes and are not subjective because they are measurable.[80]

But need cannot be an independent justificatory principle guiding human actions and policies because, as Barry puts it so well, 'Whenever someone says "*x* is needed" it always makes sense ... to ask what purpose it is needed for'.[81] When the Webbs defend their planned society on the ethical and moral basis that it is more efficient in satisfying the aggregate of

---

[79] Such theories may be found, for instance, in Part IV of D. Miller's *Social Justice*, pp. 122-50; and A. Gewirth, *Reason and Morality* (London, 1978), Chapter 2, particularly p. 63. This is also, in part at least, surely the foundation of J. Rawls' 'thin theory of the good', which is based on the notion of a certain set of goods which any rational man would hold to be essential conditions of the accomplishment of any purposive action whatsoever. See *A Theory of Justice*, Chapter 7, and esp. Section 60.

[80] That is, unless one is speaking in terms of rather subjective and unquantifiable human needs such as for love, community, and so forth. These constitute a somewhat different case which will receive much more attention in later chapters.

[81] Barry, op. cit., p. 48.

human needs, this throws up a smoke-screen of apparent objectivity to obscure the fundamental question they beg: in relation to what end are these to be seen as needs?

No one would dispute that there are certain needs whose satisfaction is necessary to the achievement of any human end whatsoever, in that they are the necessary basis of life itself.[82] But the strong justificatory force this provides for the satisfaction of these particular needs (say, food, clothing, and shelter) derives precisely from the limited nature of the ends in question. The further removed from the most basic necessities of survival one gets in the list of things *necessary* to men, the more one has to justify them in terms other than pure need. What becomes important is the sort of life that they are necessary to, and why that particular sort of life ought to be regarded as desirable.

So the objectivity and measurability of needs must be understood against their absolute dependence on the ends to which they relate. To put it in more formal terms, to say that the possession of *y* is a necessary condition of the accomplishment of *x* is not in itself an argument for doing *x*.

This formal way of stating the problem also helps us to visualise another of the logical inadequacies of the Webbs' position: their complacent assumption that they can always *correctly identify* what *y*s are in fact necessary conditions of doing *x*. While there is perhaps a greater degree of certainty possible in the selection of means once an end has been established, it remains largely a question of degree. To revert to an earlier example, Midas's end was (one assumes) to achieve happiness and he took it that to achieve this end he needed to be wealthy (i.e. this was seen as a necessary condition of happiness). This, in turn, became a subsidiary or incidental end whose necessary condition was, Midas thought, the golden touch.

In practice, however, we know that Midas had correctly identified the golden touch as a means of achieving wealth, but failed to understand that its use would have unintended and unforeseen undesirable consequences which, in the end, precluded the realisation of his one true end: happiness. So no matter how 'objective' the choice of means necessary to the

---

[82] Gewirth is a particularly good example of this sort of argument, op. cit., *passim*.

achievement of an end, what *is* a necessary condition is not always clear or, when acted upon, proved right.

Consequently, the 'objectivity of needs' cannot, on its own, justify the Webbs' proposed social order. This in itself is not fatal to their argument, but it does mean that the structure will now rise or fall on their account of why men ought to regard Webbian social ends as desirable.

We saw that the Webbs had a twofold argument in this regard: they claimed to maximise both the aggregate of human development (and to distribute this more equitably) and to maximise the survival chances of the social organism in the evolutionary struggle.

But there is an ambiguity here, an ambiguity which the Webbs clearly could not resolve for themselves, about the true nature of the path to individual human development. This ambiguity creates a tension between the two aspects of their justification of a concrete social order. When this tension is made explicit, it becomes apparent that, far from being complementary, the developmental and evolutionary arguments are in conflict and that therefore they cannot ultimately sustain the crucial moral aspect of their case.

I have emphasised the Webbs' argument that human beings make the most of themselves by efficiently filling their role in the social machine, thereby both maximising production and establishing an equal claim to the package of utilities necessary for occupying that role. Every man makes the most of himself, not by realising some essence or set of talents and abilities inhering in him as an individual, but by dutifully playing a role not of his choosing in order to achieve objectives that he may not understand, let alone share.

In order to avoid the very obvious political questions that this raises, the Webbs shifted the discussion from one of whether or not this was in the interests of individual men to one of whether or not it filled their objectively determinable needs as anonymous members of the social organism. Subjective identity thus becomes an irrelevancy, and individual development, à la Webb, requires that men renounce the desire to make what they wish of themselves. Put another way, the Webbs seem to expect rational man to accept that, in social organisation at least, his development shall be held to proceed uniquely from his consumption of commodities not of his own choosing. This conception is crucial to the moral justification of the direction of labour and resources by experts, since this is the achievement for men of a development of which they are incapable on their own.

It is clear, however, that the Webbs also retain a more conventional notion of human development in which men strive to realise an essence or set of powers or potentialities which forms part of their identity, of who they are. This conception, a legacy of the classics handed down via medieval Christian thought[83], sees the good life for man not in the mere consumption of ever larger packages of utilities, but rather in the striving of each person to realise the identity and powers which exist as a potential within him.

The Webbs, whether consciously or unconsciously, play on the difference between these two conceptions. They argue, on the one hand, that their society allows the fullest possible development of 'human personality' and the talents and attributes of each person. On the other hand, they see such development as proceeding via each man's passive acceptance of an assigned social position, of a defined package of consummations and of rule by experts who see individuals not as distinct individuals, but as undifferentiated blanks to which a uniform identity may be ascribed.

This can be seen, for instance, in their attitude towards education. They profess to believe in an educational system in which,

> ... every child ... should receive all the education requisite for the full development of its faculties ... Above and beyond [the national] minimum we must see that ample provision is made for varying faculties and divergent tastes.[84]

It is difficult to see how this can be reconciled with an uncompromising view of the primacy of the needs of the social organism over those of full individual development, or indeed with Sidney's comment to Graham Wallas in 1900 that it was

---

[83] Macpherson, op. cit. p. 89.
[84] S. Webb, 'The Education Muddle and the Way Out' (p. 104), reprinted in Brennan, pp. 85–104.

an 'advantage for the ordinary man not to be educated above his station'.[85]

Similarly, how is one to understand the Webbs' already quoted claim to understand by liberty, 'such conditions of existence in the community as do, in practice, result in the utmost possible development of faculty in the individual human being' or their desire to maximise the 'development of individual personality', when they assert with equal force that 'it is of comparatively little importance in the long run that individuals should develop to the utmost if the life of the community in which they live is not thereby served'?[86]

Examples of this kind of ambiguity can be multiplied endlessly, but the point is clear. The Webbs' ethical justification of comprehensive social planning depends on each man seeing that the development of his innate faculties and talents, of his identity and ability to achieve his purposes will be maximised. But these aspects of the self are quickly vitiated of their subjective identity element. What is in fact offered is a society which maximises the development of those human attributes which it finds most useful to *its* purposes and for the achievement of *its* ends, and calls this the maximisation of human development, the achievement of a 'higher individualism'.[87]

There is a clear tension here between the Webbs' individualistic justification of comprehensive planning and their practical collectivism. They justified socialism on the moral grounds that it would prevent owners of capital from abusing their arbitrary power to maximise their own development by passing the cost on to their hapless employees. Under the Webbs' regime everyone would have an equal claim to the resources necessary to their development, but in return every individual would have to surrender the right to choose which parts of his identity to develop. Since only one aspect of human identity was to *count*, the rest was irrelevant to public policy and decision-making.

[85] Letter from S. Webb to G. Wallas of 6 Sept. 1900, Wallas papers; cited in Hall, op. cit., p. 356.

[86] *Difficulties*, p. 16.

[87] For a particularly good specific example of how institutions which one might suppose are designed at least in part to achieve want satisfaction for individuals (i.e. trade unions) are to be subordinated to the rationality of social facts is to be found in *Industrial Democracy*, pp. 703, 816, and 821–3.

The Webbs criticised capitalism for distributing arbitrarily the means to everyone's development without regard for the morally equal claims of all productive members of society. Surely the Webbs commit an error of equal importance by not taking seriously the boundaries between men. It is the aggregate of development across all men which is to count, and one's subjective opinions about one's own development are invalid. Everyone, therefore, has an equal claim on society's resources, but one is not free to determine the best use of those resources to which one is entitled. Such a determination depends on choices which only experts are competent to make, since only our expert-defined collective identity has any 'objective' reality. Whatever 'development' such an equitable distribution of resources makes possible, however, is quite different from that needed by real people seeking to develop complex and multi-faceted identities. The Webbs could not resolve the contradiction which arose from their embracing two incompatible theories of human development: a pure utility-maximising one, and a human potential one, in which utilities are purely instrumental to the development of each person's unique attributes and potentials.

Even this might not topple the Webbian planned society if they could in fact demonstrate that the pursuit by the individual of the development of certain self-chosen aspects of his nature would endanger the long-term viability of the society which sustains both his material well-being and his social identity. But such a claim depends on at least two conditions.

First, the Webbs must be able to show convincingly that there is a unitary and unalterable direction to evolution which man's non-rational desires can frustrate (at least temporarily). Second, they must be able to demonstrate that self-conscious attempts by experts to anticipate this direction meet with at least as much success as leaving human beings free to experiment and choose.

Taking the evolutionary point first, we know that Popper and others[88] have given us strong arguments for questioning

---

[88] K. Popper, *The Poverty of Historicism* (London, 1957), *passim*. See also e.g. F. A. Hayek, *The Counter-Revolution of Science*, and 'History and Politics' (pp. 3–29) in F. A. Hayek (ed.), *Capitalism and the Historians* (London, 1954); a further discussion on this subject will be found in Chapter VIII of this book.

any view of history which purports to identify purposes or even a necessary direction in the unfolding of history. Even if we do not regard such arguments as conclusive, it seems clear that the simple possession of a collection of facts about the past or the present is insufficient to supply us with certain and unquestionable knowledge of such alleged purposes. Here we return to a matter alluded to earlier in this chapter: the Webbs' belief that facts and values are unproblematically separable.

Barker quotes a very illuminating incident in this regard. At the time when Sidney was working with Haldane on the constitution for the new London University, 'he was asked what was his idea of a university and he replied, "I haven't any idea of a university ... Here are the facts" '.[89] This exemplifies the Webbs' belief that facts and expert opinion could in some unspecified way resolve ethical or normative questions, in short, that one could derive 'ought' from 'is'. It is, for instance, difficult to see how a *factual* statement could have any bearing on a discussion of what a university (or anything else, for that matter) *ought* to be like.

Matters of fact can only become relevant to the propriety or correctness of any particular action or policy once the end aimed at is known, and the choice of ends requires a moral discussion in which facts can play but a minor role. To assert that society has a unitary end which can be identified by knowing the facts about that society is therefore to put an end to all discussion about the desirability of any human ends save those which accord with the overarching social ones. This is why the identity condition mentioned earlier becomes irrelevant to the Webbs' understanding of human interests: who I think I am is irrelevant to what is *in fact* good for me.

Not only does this do away with the identity condition (which I have just argued the Webbs cannot do if they are to justify their society morally), but it requires strong assumptions about the reality condition which there is no *prima-facie* reason to suppose the Webbs can make good.

The reality condition of human interests stipulated that even once the question of identity had been settled, that still left open the question of how the person's interests could be promoted in

---

[89] McBriar, op. cit., p. 73; quoted in Barker, op. cit., p. 30.

an inherently complex world. Social facts, like Platonic forms, seemingly immutable and perfectly compatible, offer to the Webbs a possible come-back to this fact/value criticism. They might say that even if it were true that 'the ends of society' is a contestable concept, not to be derived from the facts as such, this is not in itself an argument against rule by experts. On strictly utilitarian, aggregative grounds the latter might still be preferable to politics, say, because it will *in fact* maximise the production of utilities. This would clearly be a much weaker claim, but would still, on my view, be unsuccessful.

This is due to the fact that the reality condition of human interests points clearly to the difficulty of knowing what facts will be relevant to any particular policy decision, plus the fact that ends men consider desirable in the abstract may not turn out to be so in reality.

Expert opinion becomes valid and valuable when it is directed towards the achievement of pre-specified ends or goals, but not only can we be simply mistaken about what our goals are, these may change over time. When I set out on a particular career I may believe that it will achieve for me things I hold valuable: money, prestige, power, and so forth. Once these goals are achieved, however, like the business executive who abandons the competitive commercial life to open a bookstore, I may realise that my previous objects of aspiration leave me unfulfilled. Given that *I* can be mistaken about where my own interests lie, even though I must live with the consequences of my decisions, is there any reason to suppose that my interests will be better served, or my development as a person enhanced by entrusting such decisions to experts?

On a somewhat grander level, there are the all too familiar cases of governments who have sought economic development through so-called prestige projects which have turned out to be expensive white elephants. In spite of the best possible professional advice on *how* to build such projects, they often turn out to be abortive or palsied for reasons that could not have been foreseen with certainty by anyone.[90]

Even the selection of such projects in the first place owes much to a choice of ends or objectives not themselves derived

[90] See, as an example, the case of the Aruba oil refinery cited in the *Economist* newspaper, 10 Nov. 1984, p. 70.

from expert knowledge. Different 'models' of development, based on differing views of the desirability of certain patterns of industrialisation, the comparative worth of agriculture and manufacturing, and the roles of urban and rural dwellers inform such choices. Even where expert opinion may agree that, given a particular set of development priorities, a certain project is desirable, such a calculation may fail to produce the intended results. Such a failure may be due to the inappropriateness of the objectives sought or to unpredictable changes in objective conditions just as much as they may be due to the human expert's error or incompetence.

Not only, then, is there no reason for us to credit planners' claims to produce *superior* economic results to those of the market, Hayek's argument about the growing complexity of the Great Society making planning progressively *less* possible seems rather more plausible than the Webbs' view. The Webbs' utility maximising claim cannot, therefore, be sustained.

Their attempt to eliminate the subjective element from their 'objective' theory of individual human development does not seem to have been any more successful, moreover, than Hayek's attempt to deny any possibility of agreement on ends between utterly subjective selves. Later I shall argue that both these failures stem from their closely related theories of reason, rationality and responsibility, which repose on untenable notions of how human beings arrive at an understanding of their values, and how those values inform social and political discourse. First, though, I want to look at the Webbs' specific constitutional and institutional proposals to see how they intended to prevent 'non-rational' desires encroaching on the growing rationality of their social order and hence how they proposed to exclude politics from society.

V

THE SOVEREIGNTY OF EXPERTS AND THE UNITY OF FACTS: THE WEBBS' CONSTITUTIONAL THOUGHT

> During the last years I ... have had to observe the decline of freedom in societies where rights are shaped by expertise.
>
> Ivan Illich, *Toward A History of Needs*

In the previous chapter, I offered an account of the theoretical basis of the Webbs' attack on politics, and of their justification of the virtually total exclusion of subjective wants from an all-encompassing sphere of social decision-making. As with Hayek, I want now to look at how they envisaged these ideas working in a detailed and concrete manner. In this chapter the institutional implications of the Webbs' political thought will be examined, especially as it appears in the two works most directly concerned with these questions: *A Constitution for the Socialist Commonwealth of Great Britain* and *Soviet Communism: A New Civilisation?*

The inclusion of the latter work deserves some special explanation, given the disagreements amongst Webb scholars regarding its significance. The proper place to begin, then, is by considering the arguments for and against its being bracketed with their *Constitution* as a work concerning the Webbs' constitutional theories *per se*.

This being done, our attention will shift to the theories themselves. A continuity between the principal ideas first expressed in the earlier *Constitution* and *Civilisation*, the first edition of which appeared some fifteen years later, will be established, but the equally important developments represented by the latter work will come in for some special attention. Most notably, we shall see how *Civilisation* came to be seen by the Webbs as making good the shortcomings which they saw in the earlier work.

Samuel Beer has written that '. . . the mind of the Webbs was also in no small degree the mind (though not the heart) of British socialism'.[1] Whatever the truth of this assertion with respect to British socialism, it accurately points up one of the greatest weaknesses of the Webbs' work in the period leading up to and including the *Constitution*: the lack of a 'human dimension'. Unconcerned with individuals, with their motivations, their strengths, and their weaknesses, the Webbs thought almost exclusively in terms of the administrative arrangements which would best suit the kind of society they felt was inevitable.[2]

While this criticism is fully justified regarding their work up to and including the *Constitution* (1920), however, it cannot be allowed to stand as a judgment of the Webbs' work taken as a whole. This is due, in part at least, to the fact that the appearance of the *Constitution* coincides neatly with the drawing to a close of a particular phase of the Webbs' political and intellectual life, coming at the point when Sidney was abandoning the London County Council (LCC) and preparing to stand as a Labour candidate for parliament.

The change from the cosy and somewhat cloistered world of municipal administration and behind the scenes work for the new Labour Party, to the hurly-burly of active national politics (including, eventually, ministerial office) seems to have powerfully affected the rather naïve optimism evinced in their earlier works about the ease with which the evolutionary process would replace the dictatorship of the capitalist with the rule of expert knowledge.

This change comes through clearly in the Webbs' accounts of the disappointments and frustrations of two minority Labour

[1] S. Beer, 'Introduction' (pp. ix-xxxiii) to the 1975 edition of the Webbs' *Constitution* published by the Cambridge University Press in collaboration with the London School of Economics and Political Science, p. ix. It also appeared as an article entitled 'The Webbs Confront the Twentieth Century', *Politics*, 9: 2, 1974.

[2] Both Leonard Woolf and Margaret Cole have written very perceptively on this aspect of the Webbs' work. See L. Woolf, 'Political Thought and the Webbs' (particularly pp. 258 and 260) in M. Cole (ed.), *The Webbs and Their Work*, (London, 1949); and M. Cole, 'The Webbs and Social Theory', *British Journal of Sociology*, June 1961.

administrations, and Ramsay MacDonald's departure and the formation of the National Government, but it is perhaps most evident in what Sidney and Beatrice both felt were the glaring inadequacies and failures of their colleagues in the Labour Party. Most of these men and women were manifestly not pursuing the common welfare in a disinterested manner, any more than they were motivated by a selfless love of public service.[3]

Even though Beatrice was not as directly involved in active public life as Sidney, she shared in the intellectual change which this period produced in him. With Sidney rather distracted by his political duties, the work of the partnership slowed and Beatrice naturally turned her thoughts to larger social questions.[4] During this period she became disillusioned with gradualism and reformism as the crisis of Western capitalism seemed to deepen around her. 'What I am beginning to doubt', she wrote in her diary on 4 February 1931, 'is the inevitability of gradualness or even the practicability of gradualness in the transition from a capitalist to an equalitarian civilisation.'[5]

Both the Webbs were open, then, to new perspectives on how their cherished ideal of a rational and scientific utilitarian society might be brought about. The depth of the crisis convinced Beatrice that the ways of an earlier and gentler age could no longer serve their purposes, and it was in this frame of mind that she began the reassessment of the Russian Revolution and Soviet society in which Sidney came later to participate. The result was an extensive trip to the Soviet Union in 1932 and the appearance in 1935 of the first edition of *Soviet Communism: A New Civilisation?*[6]

The interest of this, in a chapter on the Webbs' proposals for concrete institutional arrangements, is simple, but needs some explanation. I want to argue that one can only obtain a full and complete appreciation of the mature Webb view

[3] According to S. Beer (op. cit., p. xxx), Beatrice saw, 'the corruption of individuals around her—the sneering Snowden, the vain MacDonald, the ranting Lansbury—among civil servants, professional men and trade union leaders, as well as capitalists and landlords and people "living by owning" '.

[4] L. Radice, *Sidney and Beatrice Webb: Fabian Socialists* (London, 1984), p. 230.

[5] Cited in L. Radice, op. cit., p. 292.

[6] The question mark in the title was removed in the 1937 and subsequent editions.

on the subject by comparing their *Constitution*, a theoretical work summing up and concluding a particular phase in their political and intellectual life, and *Civilisation*, their critical appreciation of a particular concrete social order which they held both to embody and supersede their own earlier proposals.

The undoubtedly controversial nature of this thesis does not arise from disagreements amongst Webb scholars over the accuracy of the characterisation of Soviet Communism contained in *Civilisation*, for on this point there is virtual unanimity: the Webbs were quite simply wrong about what had happened, what was happening and what would happen in Russia following the October Revolution.[7] Far from lessening the interest which this work should have for us, however, its failure to portray the Soviet Union of their day accurately makes it repay study all the more. This seemingly paradoxical conclusion appears justified because *Civilisation* is so clearly a description of what the Webbs hoped and wanted the Soviet Union to be, and ought, therefore, to be seen *as the Webbs saw it*: as a reaffirmation of faith in what they had always believed, but in a version better suited to the new insights and circumstances of the Thirties.

The controversy arises from the incompatibility which some writers have seen between the Webbs' deep and lifelong commitment to 'a complex and varied democratic pluralistic society'[8] and their supposed eleventh hour approval, indeed espousal, of soviet 'totalitarianism' in *Civilisation*.[9] On this view, the *Constitution* is *the* definitive statement of the Webbs' political views and *Civilisation* must, therefore, be seen as an aberration, easily accounted for by advancing age and a gullibility fostered by the disillusionments of the preceding decade.[10]

[7] On this point see e.g. M. Cole, op. cit., pp. 103-5; L. Radice, op. cit., Chapter 14, pp. 291-309; and L. Woolf, op. cit., pp. 262-3.

[8] L. Radice, op. cit., p. 13. See also M. Cole, op. cit., *passim*.

[9] See e.g. L. Radice's comments (op. cit., p. 13) on D. Caute's account of the Webbs' reaction to the Soviet Union as portrayed in his *The Fellow Travellers* (London, 1973).

[10] See e.g. M. Cole, op. cit., p. 103. and L. Radice, op. cit., pp. 13-4 and 291-3. It is worth insisting on the fact that *Civilisation* ought *not* to be seen as a work about the Soviet Union, except in the most attenuated and indirect sense. If it were, it would be of no interest to us here, concerned as we are with what the Webbs thought and only very secondarily with their description of what was done elsewhere.

On the face of it, of course, there is a certain contradiction between at least the letter of some parts of the *Constitution* (and other earlier works) and the Webbs' approval of certain things they imagined to be going on in Soviet Russia. The question we must face then is, where these accounts differ, which should we accept as representative of what the Webbs themselves thought? There are, I think, three arguments for regarding *Civilisation* as superseding and in many ways clearing up the intended and unintended ambiguities present in the *Constitution*.

The first argument centres on the different contexts within which the two books were written. The *Constitution* was commissioned by the Fabian Society and written at a time when Sidney was not only prominent in the Labour Party, but about to launch a career in national politics. In spite of the obligatory disclaimer to represent any views other than their own, it seems implausible that the Webbs would be totally uninfluenced, either by the views of the Fabians or by those of the Labour Party in whose fortunes Sidney so clearly had an interest. It is surely of some significance, then, that their later book on Soviet civilisation was written at a time when the Webbs' public career was clearly at an end and when they were beyond caring what effect their views might have on the Labour Party or anyone else.

This suggests that the early Webbs may have 'tailored' their public pronouncements to suit their political objectives and this is, indeed, my second argument. The Webbs' public commitment to scientific objectivity and 'letting the facts speak for themselves'[11] was, according to Margaret Cole, somewhat overstated, for '... as some of their assistants afterwards discovered, if an awkward fact turned up, the Webbs were apt to regard it with grave suspicion and to tell its inconvenient discoverer to go away and find a more amenable one'.[12] This view is confirmed by Leonard Woolf, himself one of the Webbs' researchers. Woolf has written that the Webbs,

It is precisely in its almost total lack of any relation to the reality of Stalin's Russia and its perfectly consistent elaboration of the themes originally set out in the *Constitution* or, put another way, the fact that the Webbs 'only saw what they wanted to' which justifies the attention I am devoting to it here.

[11] T. Simey, 'The Contribution of Sidney and Beatrice Webb to Sociology', *British Journal of Sociology*, 12: 2 (June 1961), pp. 117–18.

[12] M. Cole. op. cit., p. 99.

... were so certain of the rightness of the ends which they were pursuing that they did not worry very much about the means which they used to attain them. The first time I worked closely with Sidney I was puzzled and troubled by this extraordinary mixture of scrupulousness with regard to ends and an almost ingenuous unscrupulousness with regard to means.[13]

It may thus be a confusion between the spirit and the letter of the *Constitution* which has led some students of the Webbs astray, a mistaking of the 'pluralist democracy' and 'checks and balances' for ends instead of the means which, I contend, the Webbs conceived them to be. One must bear constantly in mind, in this context, that the Webbs had a very 'personal theory of democracy',[14] and that this theory is itself a highly authoritarian and élitest one, impatient of those who would seek their private satisfactions rather than the Webbs' conception of the public good.

The third and final argument is that this interpretation is not only wholly consistent with the text, but perhaps more importantly, is the only one which does not require the patronising imputation to the Webbs of some weakening of the mental faculties or loss of acuity for which the evidence is slight at best. On this reading, not only does *Civilisation* appear as the natural development of the earlier *Constitution*, but the absence of the earlier obeisances to the 'ambiguities of social democracy'[15] and the niceties of constitutionalism becomes explicable as the mere discarding of means to other, more important and enduring, ends.

Perhaps most convincingly of all, Beatrice herself can be quoted in support of this argument:

What attracts us in Soviet Russia, and it is useless to deny that we are prejudiced in its favour, is that its constitution, on the one hand, bears out our *Constitution for a Socialist Commonwealth*, and, on the other, supplies a soul to that conception of government—which our paper-constitution lacked.[16]

---

[13] L. Woolf, op. cit., p. 258.

[14] As described in Chapter IV, above.

[15] N. Mackenzie, *Socialism and Society: A New View of the Webb Partnership*, a lecture delivered at the London School of Economics in 1978, p. 25.

[16] *Diaries*, Jan. 1932. Cited in M. Cole, op. cit., p. 104.

The one distinctively Webbian idea which did have to be
abandoned in *Civilisation* was, as might be expected, gradualism. Even before the Russian trip, as Beatrice pondered
the crisis of Western capitalism and the lessons that the USSR
had to offer in this regard, her conclusion was not that the
partnership had been wrong about their 'vision of an alternative order', but that they had failed 'to understand the
dynamics of the change which would bring it about'.[17] Far
from implying an abandonment of evolution as a theory of
social change, this implied a rather different *theory* of evolution
in which gradualism had no place. As early as 22 June 1930,
Beatrice was writing in her diary that,

...the Russian Communist Government may still fail to attain its
end in Russia as it will certainly fail to conquer the world with a
Russian brand of communism, but its exploit exemplifies the
Mendelian view of sudden jumps in biological evolution as against
the Spencerian vision of slow adjustment.[18]

Turning now to the detail of the Webbs' thoughts about the
organisation of political and social institutions, their theory
may best be described as one of *functional epistemocracy*. This
rather inelegant term is intended to capture the essence of a
view of government comprising two principal parts. *Epistemocracy* is rule by a 'comprehensive body of social facts',[19]
by an ever growing fund of scientific knowledge which the
Webbs believed would come to replace the arbitrary rule of
human will. The term, meaning the rule of knowledge and
not the rule of the knowledgeable or wise, is intended to
emphasise the *knowledge* itself, since it was held to be independent of and superior to the men who possessed it. Under
Webbian political institutions, men were not obeyed, nor did
they exercise authority. They were merely the instruments of
a body of knowledge to which rational men would naturally
want to defer.

Functional serves to accentuate those aspects of men which
were to be relevant to the organisation of social life and the

17 N. Mackenzie, op. cit., p. 24.
18 B. Webb, diary entry for 22 June, 1930. Quoted in L. Radice, op. cit., p. 292.
19 B. Webb, diary entry for 26 Sept. 1883; cited in S. Letwin, *Pursuit*, p. 359.

way in which the validity of claims to possess knowledge relevant to collective decision-making would be established. In this regard we can recall that the Webbs' view of man and his relationship to the 'social organism' comprised three distinct elements. There was, first, the end at which society aimed, superior to the ends of any individual; that end was to survive and flourish in the evolutionary struggle with all other social organisms. The second element was the idea that this survival could only be effectively pursued by maximising the production of utilities. The third element[20] saw the proper course of individual development lying in the efficient fitting of individuals to play their functional social role. Individual development was not seen as an end in itself, which society and individuals pursued for its own sake, but rather such development was pursued in an instrumental fashion, as a way of improving society's survival chances.

The Webbs saw all men as occupying three functional roles in the productive process and proposed a corresponding threefold organisation of socio-political institutions. Each leg of the 'tripod' and the relations between them were specifically designed to allow society to maximise production by making use of the expert knowledge that particular men have in each of their productive roles. The tripod was equally carefully designed to exclude from collective decision-making those human desires which can or do conflict with the maximisation of production. In a sort of countervailing force theory,[21] the Webbs sought to limit such socially dangerous forces by depriving them of a strong institutional base and assuming that they would be overwhelmed by the rational application of knowledge to social problems. As we will see shortly, it was the weakness of this countervailing mechanism in their *Constitution* which the Webbs thought was made good by the new Soviet model. This being the case, our attention is best

---

[20] In spite of the ambiguities present in their theory of human development discussed in Chapter IV, *passim.*, above.

[21] Without wishing to push the analogy too far, this theory is somewhat reminiscent both of certain theories of the separation of powers in a constitutional state (see the excellent discussion of this in M. J. C. Vile, *Constitutionalism and the Separation of Powers* (Oxford, 1967) and of A. Hirschman's account of seventeenth-century moral arguments about the merits of capitalism contained in his regrettably neglected *The Passions and the Interests* (Princeton, 1977).

devoted, in the first instance, to the theoretical framework of the *Constitution*. We can then see how *Civilisation* pursues and corrects the same themes.

Man, then, has three functional social roles: those of consumer, producer, and citizen. Examining each in turn, we shall see the socially functional contribution of each role and how the Webbs proposed to promote their desirable aspects while minimising their undesirable side-effects.

One of the Webbs' key criticisms of capitalism noticed earlier was its non-functional approach to both production and distribution. By making both depend on where the individual capitalist felt he could make the best profit, rather than on satisfying the *needs* which all individuals had to meet in order to be efficient producers, capitalism had eventually become an obstacle to production. Due to the market's inability to respond to anything but 'effective demand' (i.e. those lucky enough to have money), those productive social resources represented by the poor were inadequately provided for, impairing their productive capacities.

Profit-making in production had to be replaced, then, by what the Webbs referred to as 'production for use'. This required some mechanism which would give voice to each person's demands for consumption, regardless of their income, a mechanism which would see to it that everyone obtained the means to satisfy their needs. This role the Webbs believed could most appropriately be filled by an indefinite extension of the consumers' co-operative movement ('voluntary democracies of consumers') and the sphere of activities of local and national government ('obligatory democracies of consumers').

To the Webbs, the advantages of such a scheme over the market were obvious. Such associations of consumers respond to the demands of their members expressed, not through market forces, but via a mechanism like that which Hirschman has called 'voice',[22] or the ability to articulate one's needs to

---

[22] Hirschman argues that economists are usually so preoccupied with the 'exit' mechanism, that process whereby anonymous consumers abandon producers who are no longer offering what the consumer wishes to buy at a price he is willing to pay, that these same economists fail to notice an equally important mechanism he calls 'voice'. Voice is used by consumers who, concerned at the decline in the quality of a product, seek to influence their traditional supplier to return to his former standards. Whereas economists usually evoke the exit process as evidence that the market works

the person or group whose responsibility it is to meet them. Consumers themselves are thus given the job of saying directly what they want, rather than leaving it to the undemocratic and irrational vagaries of the impersonal market mechanism, for the consumer knows best what he wants. The consumer is hence elevated to the status of an 'expert' in this field; the Webbs are clear that the people themselves know what they want and 'democracy' therefore requires giving these experts free reign in their field of expertise.

This sort of expertise was explicitly limited, however, to the analogous 'expert' knowledge that a sick man has of his own symptoms. Hence, while no one knows better than the consumer what he wants, the simple fact of stating the desire is far from being a guarantee of its satisfaction by the responsible consumer 'representative'. Hence, the strict compartmentalisation of competences so necessary to the Webbs' constitution begins to introduce itself. The people, *qua* consumers, know what they want, but are not qualified to know: *a)* how best to turn this inarticulate desire into the most effective commands to industry for production; *b)* whether satisfying this want would have a positive or a negative effect on production and efficiency or; *c)* how, in a world of scarcity, to rank the relative importance of the satisfaction of this desire with other competing claims on production. The 'democracy' of production for use rather than for exchange is thus quickly hedged about with some quite radical restrictions.

The Webbs thought it perfectly acceptable, for instance, to let consumers set the broadest outlines of policy: they know that they want, e.g. more schools, better quality boots, more efficient and comfortable means of transport to work, and so on; but such knowledge does not fit them to decide how best to achieve these objectives. This is a matter of administration and as such is to be left to the administrators. This is a cardinal feature of all the Webbs' constitutional thought: a hard and fast separation of the spheres of policy and administration.

Democracy required, though, that those responsible for satisfying the expressed demands of consumers be elected by

to force out producers who do not produce what consumers want, Hirschman seeks to draw our attention to the process of recovery amongst firms who lose ground in the competitive struggle, but who *do* recover, sometimes because of the voice mechanism. See A. O. Hirschman, *Exit, Voice and Loyalty* (Cambridge, Mass., 1970).

and responsible to them, subject to recall and periodic election. But such a mechanism is obviously not neutral in carrying out consumers' wishes, and the representatives are not there to satisfy all demands equally.

By this I mean that, in replacing the market (or 'production for exchange') with production for use, the Webbs sought to eradicate the evils occasioned by the lack of 'effective demand' on the part of the poor. What they did not notice (or were indifferent to), was that their replacement put a premium on the satisfaction of those demands which were most widespread.[23] By letting the consumers' representatives decide which requests for goods would be successful, pressure would be strong to produce the lowest common denominator. More concretely, if *everyone* wants shoes, but a relatively small number would prefer a hat to an extra pair of shoes, to accede to this latter request might be seen as privilege if the total demand for shoes remains unsatisfied. The Webbs seem not to have grasped how the market functions to let individuals (with the means to create effective demand) in effect strike their own 'bargains' with producers for commodities they (the consumers) desire. Far from producing the explosion of diversity in production that the Webbs anticipated, it seems likely that their system would have reduced the range considerably.[24]

Furthermore, it would apparently be incumbent on the consumers' representatives to set prices which would reflect, not the cost of production of each particular good, but some other criterion, '... according to the relative desirability of encouraging the consumption or use of one commodity or service over another'.[25] One can thus well imagine, even where the consumer was lucky enough to prevail on the democracy of consumers to produce a good for which demand was slight and whose utility in increasing efficiency was

---

[23] It is thus no accident that Hirschman (loc. cit.) saw 'voice' and 'loyalty' as a necessary *complement* to and not a *replacement* of the market mechanism, which he calls 'exit', or the right to find a better supplier in the anonymous market.

[24] It is, however, equally conceivable that such a system *might* result in a greater differentiation within the range of products necessary to raising an individual's productivity, such as e.g. more different kinds of boots, to use a characteristically Webbian example.

[25] *Constitution*, p. 20.

doubtful, that the object of his desire would carry a high price tag.[26]

Now it seems logical that the consumer will normally use the mechanism of a democracy of consumers to press for all the goods he desires at the lowest possible cost. If this were to result in e.g. sweated labour and imprudent overworking of capital stock it would be contrary to the interests of society as a whole, and this is one reason why democracies of consumers cannot be allowed to have the final say in policy. The elected representatives of such 'constituencies', the experts in the economical satisfaction of their members' desires, are thus potentially in a position of conflict of interest with the needs of society. Their autonomy must therefore be circumscribed by allocating another, countervailing, sphere of competence to men in their role as producers.[27]

This next major sphere of sovereignty of competence was an explicit recognition of the different expert functional knowledge people possess and the different interests they have in their productive social role. One part of the Webbs' scheme for maximising production without succumbing to the vices inherent in total consumer sovereignty was to accord an autonomous sphere of control to 'democracies of producers'.

While superficially taking inspiration from the trade union movement, these democracies of producers would in fact be radically different in both theory and function. The elimination, in a socialist commonwealth, of the pernicious profit motive from production would necessarily result in the elimination of the 'enemy party' in labour relations: the new dispensation would see all of society's elements united in the

---

[26] To be fair to the Webbs, they did say, for instance, that any individual or group would be able to set up co-operatives to produce any desired good or service, and that private property and the right to engage in artisanal production would be untrammelled (see e.g. *Constitution*, Part II, Chapters 2, 5 and 7). But they also say that the distribution of productive resources shall be decreed by a central authority (to be described in detail below). When such an authority is expressly attempting to allocate *all* social resources in such a way as to maximise efficiency, how may a claim be expected to fare which merely seeks to satisfy the non-production oriented desires of individuals? Beer (op. cit., p. xxiv) strikes at the heart of this difference between the letter and spirit of the *Constitution* when he observes that: 'At all levels ... the institutions of state socialism are too strong to permit us to take very seriously the Webbs' claim that they have based the regime on a tripartite partnership of consumers, producers, and citizens.'

[27] *Constitution*, p. 23.

pursuit of maximum production. The desire to get more (wages and benefits) for less (work) would disappear because any increase in production would be shared out justly and equitably, with no 'tribute' to those functionless few who had hitherto 'lived by owning'. Democracies of producers would be freed from the need to 'oppose' the iniquities of capitalism and could turn their attention to what they know best: obtaining working conditions allowing all their members to function at peak efficiency. This entailed account being taken, not merely of short-term production goals, but also of the long-term productivity of each worker, protecting him against what might almost be seen as precipitate depreciation through undue wear and tear.

Working conditions would be the subject of negotiation between the expert representatives of the various functional roles, and would be conducted on the basis of purely objective reports of the ascertained needs of consumers (demands for production), the available resources, and the workers' evaluation of how much they could produce, consistent with the scientific exercise of their vocation and the demands of the National Minimum requirements governing all conditions of employment.[28] The representatives of the democracies of producers thus play the role of expert guides to their constituents, analogous to that played by their counterparts in the democracies of consumers. These experts help the workers to produce more and set out for them the scientific standards of production which they should, as socially responsible people, strive to meet.

Interestingly, the Webbs saw the elimination of capitalism as simultaneously eliminating the social basis of a broad working class consciousness. Such consciousness arose as a product of the growing awareness of the common interest all non-owners had in resisting their exploitation by the capitalist. Once production for use had eliminated this pointless social antagonism, the need for vocational organisations regrouping workers whose work was not functionally related would come to an end. Workers *qua* workers would cease to have a common interest. The sole purpose of vocational organisations in a

---

[28] Ibid., pp. 296-7.

Socialist Commonwealth being to secure to each clearly
defined functional group the autonomy necessary to exercise
their function in accordance with scientific principles (which
they are functionally best suited to discover), no role existed
for 'large and inclusive' organisations of workers such as the
TUC.[29]

The necessary corollary of securing such a vocational
autonomy to the democracies of producers, however, was that
they recognise the equally legitimate spheres of competence
of other experts, just as the sovereignty of the consumer was
constrained by the limits of *his* knowledge.[30] Thus it was noted
in the last chapter that the Webbs believed that on political
questions like the existence of the House of Lords, trade unions
cannot properly be thought to have relevant opinions. Here,
though, the restriction goes much further, cutting to the very
root of traditional working peoples' organisations.

Small wonder, then, that industrial democracy under the
democracies of producers seems to have very little indeed to
do with anything that might be described as 'workers' control',
or that Guild Socialism was seen by the Webbs as a pernicious
doctrine or, more prosaically, as 'damned nonsense', and
they devote some considerable attention to justifying their
opposition to both ideas.

In the last chapter, I argued that the Webbs believed that
the abolition of the dictatorship of the capitalist would usher
in a new era in which 'relations of authority' as we know
them would be swept away by the application of scientific
knowledge, of 'Measurement and Publicity', which would
make it clear that no one was subject to the arbitrary whims
of another, but only to the objectively ascertainable dictates
of impersonal science. They equally recognised, however, that,
even where it is democracies of consumers and not rapacious
capitalists who are determining what shall be produced and
giving the necessary orders to see that these desires are
carried out, for the workers, '... management ... is always
"government from above" '.[31]

[29] Ibid., p. 280.
[30] Ibid., p. 160.
[31] Ibid., p. 22.

However much sympathy the Webbs may have evinced for the workers in this regard, however, they were clear that someone had to issue orders if anything was to get done and '... the relationship between director or manager and workers "becomes hopelessly untenable if this director or manager is elected or dismissible by the very persons to whom he gives orders". '[32] The crucial question was how to convince the workers to renounce their out-dated oppositional mentality and to realise that scientific selection of the person most suited to fill any post (including in management) was the inevitable product of democracy itself.[33]

Democracy in industry, or in any other sphere, was thus held to depend, as noticed earlier, on the 'consciousness of consent' which comes from seeing that all social decisions are taken by representatives, popularly elected for the purpose, and given the best expert advice.[34] Since such 'objective' decision-making is done by democratically elected representatives, the fact that, as a result, workers may be given orders for which they do not care is not seen as undemocratic, any more than it is undemocratic for representatives of consumers to refuse to produce harmful or undesirable products, no matter how much their constituents might desire them. It merely points up the weakness of the mechanism for ensuring an awareness of the consent which is assumed.

On the face of it, the Webbs' arguments seem not to exclude the possibility of a national, vocationally based set of institutions which would give workers an indirect (through their representatives) but substantial input into social decisions based on their interests *qua* workers, and yet this too is firmly opposed by the Webbs.[35] Interestingly, aside from minor technical objections to the practicability of constituting such an assembly, the Webbs' main objection takes its force from their already noticed belief that, in a Socialist Commonwealth, workers as such would have *no* common interests:

[32] J. Tomlinson, *The Unequal Struggle: British Socialism and the Capitalist Enterprise* (London, 1982), Chapter 3 'The Possibility of Industrial Democracy: Cole versus the Webbs', p. 49.

[33] *Constitution*, p. 162.

[34] Ibid., p. 216.

[35] Ibid., Part II, Chapter VI 'The Reorganisation of the Vocational World', pp. 309-17.

... there would be, as it seems to us, no interest that the representatives would, as members of their several vocations, have in common. *To have interests in common, even when there is disagreement about them, appears to be indispensable for any effective assembly.*[36]

The objection seems, at bottom, then, to be related to the counterweight theory I have been advancing. While individual *vocations* have readily identifiable interests, putting representatives of all those interests together would not give an assembly which reflected their constituents' common interests. It would be a sectional body representing merely the 'vocational will' and not the ultimate 'civic will' which, according to the Webbs, is what binds all members of a social organism together.[37]

This brings us to the limits of the competence of democracies of producers. Within those limits, the sectional interests of producers coincide with certain functional interests of society as a whole: i.e. the maximisation of production and the provision of a participatory mechanism which helps to secure to producers the consciousness of consent.

There is a third and final social role to be considered, for the strengths of each of the first two do not exactly compensate for the weaknesses of the other. Consumers have a bias in favour of cheapness and abundance over the interests of the well-being of workers, just as they have an interest in immediate consumption over longer term considerations. Producers likewise have only sectional, unintegrated interests, just as they prefer to run their own lives rather than submit to the dictates of the whole community which, nevertheless, is utterly dependent on them for the means to survive.

For these reasons, no community which has shaken off the dictatorship of the capitalist can, the Webbs argue, dispense with the necessity of representing men as *citizens*, as people

---

[36] Ibid., p. 312. Emphasis in original.

[37] It is an interesting sidelight, in view of the interpretation being advanced of the Webbs' general political philosophy, to note that in this discussion they speak not so much of the 'interests' of workers or citizens being represented in elected assemblies, but rather 'the feelings and emotions' (ibid., p. 314) of those thus represented. In other words, people have vague feelings which they wish to see translated into policy, but it is their representatives' job to see not only that this is done in the most efficient way, but also to determine whether such feelings and emotions are in the interests of their constituents.

with a share in the formulation of the ultimate and overarching 'civic will'. Of course, the interests which citizens share are multifarious and there is no need to list exhaustively all that the Webbs intended to bring under this head. It must be noted, however, that citizenship was divided, in the *Constitution* into a political and a social aspect. The first concerned itself with,

... what used to be regarded as the primary functions of a self-governing community, such as national defence and foreign relations, the development of law and the execution of justice, which have no necessary or direct connection with either the production or the consumption of commodities and services.[38]

The second, social, aspect of citizenship encompassed essentially all that is not covered by the other aspects of men. A shorthand way of summing up its sphere is to say that this is where the conscious and purposive administration of men and things comes to replace the undirected and unconscious market mechanism: this is where economics exits and sociology is enthroned as the master science. Amongst its functions are:

... the management of the common economic life on which all production and distribution depend; the equitable distribution of the national income; the conservation and wise administration of the resources of the nation, for the advantage not only of the present but also of future generations; the determination and the maintenance of the kind of civilisation that the community intends and desires ...[39]

The civic will, as enunciated by the representative institutions created for this purpose, was thus to be the ultimate authority in social decision-making, serving to correct and guide the more particular wills of men represented in other, subordinate, institutions. To achieve this, the Webbs proposed the creation of two parliaments: a political and a social. Each was to have its own separate elections and institutional life, but the social parliament was to control the purse-strings, through its control of the entire process of production and distribution of wealth. It alone was to have taxation powers.

[38] Ibid., p. 103.
[39] Ibid., pp. 103-4.

On the other hand, in addition to the more traditional law and order, external relations, and defence functions which were to be its province, the political parliament's most novel and (for our purposes) interesting feature was its role as protector of individual rights against the encroachments of an over-enthusiastic social parliament.[40]

The claim that this institutional artifice could, in the end, act as a brake on a social parliament determined to trespass on individual rights hardly seems convincing, however. Not only was this the area which attracted the most hostile critical comment at the time of the book's appearance,[41] but the Webbs themselves acknowledged that, if push came to shove, the power of the purse-strings would probably carry the day.[42] It seems more likely that this unwieldy contrivance was a token nod in the direction of civil rights, an attempt to give more weight to their profession of faith in 'pluralism'. On this reading, such a brake would never have been intended by the Webbs actually to *frustrate* the purposes of the social parliament, whose sole objective was to determine by scientific means where the common good lay and to pursue it. The Webbs' higher individualism in social service could never have allowed the selfish desires of individuals to pose an obstacle to the greater good of the whole.

If I can anticipate some of the argument to come, perhaps the most convincing proof of this is that, years later, the Webbs saw no reason to criticise the absence of such a division of powers in the Soviet constitution: here political and social were united, and the idea of two parliaments sank quietly beneath the waves of Soviet Communism. What really mattered was that objective knowledge come to rule; if, in Britain, that required some concessions to individualism, this

---

[40] The rights-based justification of the creation of two parliaments is to be found ibid., p. 130. At least part of its failure to convince comes from the Webbs' almost disingenuous attempt to define the coercion of persons as related exclusively to the *criminal* law, apparently not seeing anything coercive or even potentially coercive in the exceptionally broad *dirigiste* powers granted to the social parliament. As long as the consciousness of consent implied in the election of representatives is assumed, coercion cannot take place. They also make a rather facile distinction between the administration of 'persons' and 'things' which assumes that they are always unproblematically distinguishable.

[41] S. Beer, op. cit., pp. xii–xiv.

[42] *Constitution*, p. 126.

was a small price to pay for a major step on the gradualist road. If, however, it could be got, as in Soviet Russia, without such obstacles, then functional epistemocracy, their one constant goal, was only thereby served.

This impression is reinforced by a detailed examination of the most interesting aspect of this part of the Webbs' constitutional thought: the operation of the social parliament. For it is clear that the Webbs did not seriously believe that conflict between social institutions was possible in the Socialist Commonwealth because the abolition of the Dictatorship of the Capitalist would eradicate the roots of social conflict.

The political parliament was to be endowed with a traditional party structure and cabinet-style executive because the nature of its functions required the ability to act decisively, subject to retrospective parliamentary criticism. In opposition to this, the social parliament was to have no executive as such, and hardly any executive functions. Its purpose was to discover the most efficient means possible of maximising production and distribution, given the actual state of knowledge. Its task was to set policy, not by means of political debate, but by scientific investigation and widespread popular education as to the results, i.e. by Measurement and Publicity.

Since the authority of the social parliament would flow from the disinterested nature of its conclusions, backed by the 'silent persuasiveness' of a duly informed public opinion, no rational basis would exist for opposition. Any conflict of purpose between the two parliaments would be a mere misunderstanding which patience and goodwill would not be long in putting right.[43]

Even within the social parliament, the possibility of conflict was discounted to the extent that not only was there no executive to enforce its policies, but there was no need for the chairmen of the various policy committees to be politically compatible. With only one scientific policy possible, disagreements between representatives responsible for carrying out that policy were simply not envisaged.[44]

---

[43] The extent to which the Webbs disbelieved in the possibility of really fundamental disagreement between the two institutions is reflected in the sort of issues on which they foresaw there might be disagreement; see ibid., pp. 124-5 and 129.

[44] Ibid., pp. 119-20.

The principal function of the social parliament was thus to be the organised and systematic application of all available knowledge to the overcoming of the problems of production and distribution. And this structure for the implementation of expert knowledge through research and publicity, coupled with a 'vocational freedom' for each functional group to fill its appointed role in accordance with the latest scientific principles, is reproduced at every level and in every part of the Socialist Commonwealth. No longer under the compulsion of pursuing his own narrow material interest, every member of the social organism was to find fulfilment in the knowledge of his effective and efficient contribution to the social welfare. At the pinnacle of this social vision was the scientific expert, who jealously guards his independence from every group, who 'invents, discovers, inspects, audits, costs, tests or measures' and whose disinterested work was to be the sword and buckler of 'a public opinion which the practice of wide and gratuitous publication of the [expert] reports will make both well-informed and all-persuasive'.[45]

Political parties, as they are known today, naturally find no significant role in the Socialist Commonwealth; the elimination of the selfish pursuit of sectional interest and the introduction of government in accordance with scientific principles also eliminates any functional role for them. The only recognition of their existence comes in a footnote (true, it *is* a two-page footnote[46]) in which the Webbs explain that '[t]he recurrent disputes among different vocations, or those arising between different sections of a community in which there is no "living by owning" may quite possibly produce no lasting division into political parties'. Instead, they predict the transformation of the roles of both special interest groups and elected representatives. With the necessity to pursue organised sectional interests gone, what becomes most important is the education of the public regarding specific problems and their scientific solution, a whipping up of the civic will by concerned and informed expert propagandist groups, using the force of published knowledge to advance their case. The elected representative too was to be transformed

45 Ibid., pp. 198-9.
46 Ibid., pp. 144-5.

into an impartial arbiter, seeking only the path of the common good amongst the choice of many competing particular goods.[47]

In summary, one finds in the Socialist Commonwealth an infinite faith in the rationality of man and in the eradication of social conflict through institutional reform. Most public policy is decided by the social parliament, not as the product of debate or the reconciliation of conflicting opinions, but as the outcome of a process of scientific evaluation. The implementation of such policy, however, is not the province of this central institution, but is properly left to each vocation, guided by independent experts.

As to democracy in the functional epistemocracy, it is found in the consciousness of consent. This comes from according to men, in each of their functional aspects, the right to elect those who will be advised by experts in the scientific determination of the policy appropriate to the efficient performance of that particular social function. This consciousness of consent thus depends not only on the application of the scientific method to the resolution of the problems of production and distribution, but on the vigorous dissemination of this information so that public opinion may demand and support the correct policies. Coercion plays a very minor role indeed because the key political problem is seen not as obliging people to do that which they have no wish to do, but rather in making clear to them what they *would* wish to do if only they knew enough.[48]

For these reasons it is perhaps not surprising that in a book purporting to be about political institutions, there is relatively little concern with the traditional instruments for dealing with social conflict: this is above all a work on administration. The police are mentioned only once, in a footnote about their efficient administration. The courts are hardly spoken of, except in the context of defining the legal powers of the respective parliaments. Their concern is certainly not to be found in the protection of the rights of individuals. Even in

---

[47] Ibid., p. 145 n.

[48] There would thus be no prisons (which are by their nature coercive institutions) in the Socialist Commonwealth, but only mental hospitals and 'convalescent settlements' whose function would be to get offenders to realise the irrationality of their behaviour, thus enabling them to return to their proper functional role in society. See ibid., p. 124 n.

the sphere of determining constitutional competence, the intention is not to create a sphere beyond the competence of *any* legislative authority, but rather to tidy up any annoying administrative overlap in what are seen as wholly separable functions. Certainly, only the simplest amendment procedures are proposed so that, should the courts interpret their powers in an awkward way, no real obstacle would be posed to the two parliaments immediately returning them to a more 'rational' basis.[49]

Fifteen years after the appearance of the *Constitution*, the Webbs were clearly in a less gently idealistic frame of mind. Mackenzie rightly suggests that this was not due to any inadequacy they perceived in their 'vision of an alternative order', but was rather seen by them as a 'failure to understand the dynamics which would bring it about'.[50] Woolf echoes this analysis, citing the Webbs' abandonment of gradualism in the face of the rise of fascism in Europe and the economic crisis throughout the capitalist world.[51] The gradualist road, the Webbs felt, had failed them: not only had people not turned to Fabian socialism in the crisis, but progress towards an evolutionary socialisation of the means of production (municipalisation, growth of the co-operative movement, and the growing influence of the Labour Party) had proved chimerical. Too much faith had been put in the growing rationality of the average sensual man, in his ability to see his own true interest.

Not only did this new mood of 'realism' make the Webbs turn their thoughts to the USSR, it made them realise the faults of their own *Constitution*. The latter's primary drawback lay in the weakness of what I have called their counterweight mechanism; in its failure to shield the constitutional structure against the selfish desires of ordinary men who persisted in refusing to identify their own interests with those of the social organism. Beatrice sums up both what she thought was right in the *Constitution* and the new insight afforded by the USSR when she wrote:

---

[49] Ibid., pp. 121-31.
[50] Mackenzie, op. cit., pp. 23-4.
[51] Woolf, op. cit., p. 262.

The Soviet constitution—the secular side of it—almost exactly corresponds to our Constitution—there is the same tripod of political democracy, vocational organisation, and the consumers' co-operative movement. And the vocational or Trade Union side is placed in exactly the same position of subordination that we suggested. Also the position of the separately organised consumers' co-operative societies is similar to ours. There is no damned nonsense about Guild Socialism! But the spotlight of intriguing difference between the live creation of Soviet Russia and the dead body of the Webb constitution is the presence, as the dominant and decisive force, of a religious order: the Communist Party ... [52]

There is no need here to look again at the essentials of the Webbian vision, which survived unscathed in the period between the *Constitution* and *Civilisation*. Even a cursory glance at the table of contents of the latter work reassures us: there are chapters on Man as citizen, producer, and consumer respectively, just as large chapters are devoted to such familiar themes as 'Science, The Salvation of Mankind' and 'Planned Production For Community Consumption'. In the chapter entitled 'The Good Life', the Webbs' positivist utilitarian philosophy is outlined, and the higher individualism in social service and 'higher freedom of corporate life'[53] are laid out without ambiguity.

The new and vital addition distinguishing this work from its predecessors is its fascination with the 'Vocation of Leadership'.[54] While the ultimate objective of transforming human beings by removing the distorting influences of capitalism[55] remained unchanged, the Webbs had now come to realise that this would not be accomplished by the mere elimination of the Dictatorship of the Capitalist. Their approving citation of the Moscow Sports Club's slogan, 'We are not only rebuilding human society on an economic basis: we are mending the human race on scientific principles',[56] is significant, for it sums up the move from the 'passive' transformation of men through institutional reform that

---

[52] B. Webb, diary entry for Jan. 1932; cited in M. Cole, op. cit., p. 105.

[53] Quoted in S. Letwin, op. cit., p. 376.

[54] On p. 908 of *Civilisation* the Webbs aver that this 'exceptional Vocation of Leadership ... may well be the dominant political feature of Soviet Communism'.

[55] Ibid., Part II, Chapter X 'The Remaking of Man', pp. 653-760.

[56] Ibid., p. 653.

characterised the *Constitution*, to the much more aggressive pursuit of human perfection in the USSR. Men were not expected to become rational of their own accord, but had to be 'mended' through both the transformation of the environment, and the active guidance of the Communist Party.

The rule of science could not depend, then, on the automatic and willing acquiescence of men in the findings of scientific experts. The 'consciousness of consent' which functional epistemocracy required in order to be 'democratic' was simply not strong enough. To foster this consciousness the Webbs now believed that an independent expert class was insufficient: what they proposed instead was an 'Order', dedicated selflessly to the public good through the application of science to human problems. The function of this order would be the ceaseless propagandising of the masses, through both education and example, inculcating in them the qualities necessary in the new Soviet citizen.

To the Webbs' eyes, the soul of the Soviet constitution was a leadership which put the improvement of Man above the improvement of self, a holy order which, without thought for the individual desires of its members, pursued a common good discovered by measurement and ratified by a highly centralised and hierarchical structure within the Party itself.[57]

This vocation of leadership rested on the division of the Party into two distinct halves. The first half 'individually fill nearly all the directing and managerial positions, whether these are reached by election from below or by appointment from above'. The membership of the Party being scientifically chosen so as to be the intellectual and ethical leaders in the new society, their filling of these positions was seen merely to be the natural fruit of this leadership capacity, and was in no way due to undue pressure or dictatorship.

The Party's other half were 'individual wage-earners continuing to work at the bench or at the forge, on the farm or in the mine, whose personal character and public judgments insensibly direct the mass of fellow workers among whom they live'. United, these two halves of the party 'formulate

[57] Ibid., p. 643.

industrial, as all other policy, and decide both the General Plan and its execution in thousands of productive enterprises'.[58]

For this to carry much weight, however, the Webbs needed to offer some sensible account of why Party members had proved to be such devoted servants of the public good when other ordinary men had shown their durable attachment to the irrationality of private desire. The Webbs offer five primary motivations. The first is what they had earlier seen as the higher individualism in social service.[59] With the vocation of leadership now in the linchpin role occupied earlier by disinterested experts, Party membership was, in the Webbs' eyes, the highest position to which a citizen could aspire.

Closely related to this was the sense of achievement or power which comes from being in a position of influence. Intellectual stimulation is cited next, as being the invariable by-product of the constant application of scientific principles to social problems. Even the mystical or emotional is not wholly excluded: the Webbs thought they perceived something akin to a religious fervour in the Marxist faith, a fervour that Beatrice, at least, was far from finding distasteful.[60]

In a class by itself, however, was the rigorous discipline which the Party imposed on its members, the constant surveillance by colleagues, the scientific weeding out of backsliders. The entrance to the Party was narrow, and few were admitted; the exit, however, was wide and put to frequent use.[61]

In all fairness, it must be said that the leading role accorded to the Party need not be as sinister as it may first appear. In this respect it is important not to overstate the argument being made. Soviet society appeared to the Webbs as a 'multiform democracy', distinguished by a bewilderingly diverse web of institutions providing channels upward for the expression of the popular will, as well as downward for the policies which were ostensibly a response to that expression. The leading role of the Party was in no way dependent on force or coercion, for the Webbs did not abandon the conviction that, in a

[58] Ibid., p. 642.
[59] Ibid., p. 643.
[60] Letwin, op. cit., p. 376.
[61] *Civilisation*, p. 643.

rational society, 'authority' would flow from knowledge, not people. While policy-making belonged to the Party, the latter was seen as the guardian of the common good and as the ultimate guarantor of that consciousness of consent which the Webbs found so elusive.[62]

This is why the Webbs insist upon the absolute lack of formal legal authority for the activities of the Party: its work proceeds purely by rational persuasion, the force of its arguments, and its members' personal example.[63] One representative passage to this effect suggests that the power of the Party members in every establishment (and there were Party members *everywhere*) over their colleagues and co-workers,

... has to be entirely educational and persuasive in character, not authoritative. The Party members ... cannot, as such, give any orders, either to the management or their fellow-workers. They can impose no policy. They can change nothing but the minds of the men and women among whom they work.[64]

But while the Webbian faith in the persuasive power of rational science remained unaltered and hence they by and large eschewed the use of force or coercion to bring about the new socialist civilisation, it was clear that they had changed to some degree in this respect. They had hardened their hearts against two classes of people whom they had been prepared to treat with relative equanimity in the *Constitution*, and this change is indicative of a subtle but important change which *Civilisation* illustrates in their thought.

The first such class are those who 'live by owning'. In their earlier, gradualist, days, the Webbs were content to let the implacable forces of evolution and rationalism work to weed them out gradually, as a by-product of the extension of democracy to production and consumption. By 1935 this had been replaced by a hard reappraisal. These capitalists were now intolerable social parasites, undermining the very fabric of the new civilisation which depended on the definitive crushing of the old forms of individual motivation[65] and their

---

[62] Ibid., p. 263.
[63] On this see e.g. ibid., p. 271.
[64] Ibid., p. 272.
[65] For the new 'socialist motivation' of the individual through public honours, shame, etc. see ibid., Part II, Chapter IX 'In Place of Profit', pp. 569-652, and particularly pp. 617-23.

replacement by a consciousness of the 'higher freedom of corporate life'.

The other class were those who, for whatever reason and in whatever form, wilfully opposed the spread of the new rational social organisation. Even here, however, the Webbs were true to their conviction that such opposition could not possibly have a rational basis. To them, one of the most promising aspects of Soviet Communism was its placing of ethics and morality on a firm footing of facts and facts alone and its utter identification of individual and social morality:

... to the properly instructed soviet communist, scientific ethics is simultaneously both social morality and individual morality, because these are fundamentally and inevitably identical. Any breach of the moral code, whether by the community or the individual, is a failure on the part of one or the other accurately to realise the facts; a failure due either to mere ignorance or to a weak and partial intellectual conception which is overborne by an emotional storm out of the depths of the subconscious mind.[66]

Whereas earlier they had confidently believed that such irrationalism would wither and die under the onslaught of Measurement and Publicity, opposition was now seen to be based on deep-seated personality disorders. While somewhat muted in the first edition of *Civilisation*,[67] this aspect of their thought is unmistakable in the postscript to the second edition, in which the Webbs condemn those not prepared to subordinate their private desires to the dictates of rationality. The only good life at which the Soviet citizen aims, they tell us, 'is a life that is good for all his fellow-men, irrespective of age or sex, religion or race'. In this new life,

[t]he dominant motive ... must not be pecuniary gain to anyone but the welfare of the human race ... For it is clear that everyone starting adult life is in debt to the community in which he has been born and bred, cared for, fed and clothed, educated and entertained. Anyone who ... does less than his share of work, and takes a full share of the wealth produced in the community, is a thief, and should be dealt with as such. That is to say, he should be compulsorily

---

[66] Ibid., p. 843.
[67] Ibid., p. 911.

reformed in body and mind so that he may become a useful and happy citizen.[68]

Compulsory medical and psychiatric care for those whose delusions prevented them from seeing reality was thus to become an instrument of public policy. Presumably, the consciousness of consent on which this depended could be implied on the basis that one so reformed would gladly give his retrospective consent to being made to see the light.[69] Almost the very last thing the Webbs wrote for public consumption (the 1937 postscript), thus represents the logic of their life's work carried to its most unpalatable conclusion: the equating of their own thought with rationality itself, and therefore the identification of differing opinions with error and irrationality. It is a small step from this to the unshakeable certainty that one's opponents are the prisoners of forces which shield them from reality and to wishing to help them overcome this absence of freedom in their own interests.

To conclude, the Webbs found their early faith in the ability of facts to speak for themselves, and thereby to provide the motor force of a gradualist evolution to a Socialist Commonwealth, to have been too optimistic. They saw that the roots of human conflict would not be eliminated through the simple suppression of a vicious capitalism, a feat which Soviet Communism had achieved. This had to be supplemented by a long and hard struggle against the sources of irrationality present in the mind of the average sensual man who sometimes lacked the moral and intellectual insight, as well as the ethical discipline, to make the order of his thought conform to the order of things. Thus, the 'paper-constitution' of 1920 was improved upon by the new civilisation of 1935; a new civilisation which was similar in almost all structural respects to that of 1920, but which was now supported by a quasi-religious order whose selfless members devoted themselves heart and soul to the guidance of their less enlightened and disciplined comrades. The Webbs had made the body of the new society from the simple clay of utilitarian social planning, but it took the Russian revolution to breathe a soul into its lifeless form.

[68] Ibid., p. 973.
[69] This is, after all, only requiring the individual to compare his wayward order of thought with the 'ascertained order of things'. Ibid., p. 531.

VI

CHARACTER, DEPTH AND RATIONALITY: ON THE REALITY OF LIBERAL MAN

> The ideas of every philosopher concerned with human affairs in the end rest on his conception of what man is and can be. To understand such thinkers, it is more important to grasp this central notion or image, which may be implicit, but determines their picture of the world, than even the most forceful arguments with which they defend their views and refute actual and possible objections.
>
> Sir Isaiah Berlin[1]

This chapter examines the roles that rationality, reason, and responsibility play in defining the concept of the person or the self.[2] Through an examination of these three elements, I will show that the concepts of the self which inform utilitarianism and ethical liberalism, represented here by the Webbs and Hayek respectively, are confused and incoherent. They cannot, as a result, account for certain aspects of the self, such as character and depth, aspects essential to any intelligible kind of moral discourse. In other words, if beings such as these two variants of liberalism conceive human beings to be really existed, they could not be considered to have all the attributes of *persons*. I am thus aiming, as John Stuart Mill did, to 'identify features of human life which, though they might conceivably have been otherwise and so are in that respect contingent, at the same time are so much beyond our powers of alteration as to be presupposed by all sensible reflection on the conditions of our moral and political life'.[3]

Rationality, reason, and responsibility are not meant to be an exhaustive list of the qualities or characteristics which are

---

[1] Quoted in G. F. Gaus, *The Modern Liberal Theory of Man* (London, 1983), p. vi.

[2] For the purposes of this book, the terms 'self' and 'person' shall be used interchangeably.

[3] Quoted in J. Gray, *Mill on Liberty: A Defence* (London, 1983), p. 15.

part of our notion of the self. These terms simply describe characteristics which are all necessary to a person, without implying that, taken together, they are also sufficient. On the contrary, as the argument is developed, other elements which may also be necessary to a full concept of the self will be discussed.

Taking rationality as the starting-point, one might begin by asking, 'What is the essence of the economist's, the moralist's, and the political philosopher's concern with rationality?' They are trying to establish, *inter alia*, two propositions. Firstly, and most obviously, that man is a thinking animal; this is part of our very definition of *Homo sapiens*. Secondly, that only thought which conforms to certain standards makes someone a full adult person. This is the implication of the special treatment we reserve for those who are 'insane' or 'irrational' or those whose rational faculties are not yet fully developed (e.g. children). This second point furnishes us with a further clue to the importance of rationality: it is a faculty which permits a human being in full possession of his senses to act in a way which others in his society find intelligible.[4]

The importance of rationality goes even deeper in the field of moral and political philosophy, however, for there it becomes not merely a mode of explanation of human action, but also a faculty to which appeal is made in justifying our actions. Hence, the statement that agent A acted rationally in performing act Y, usually means two things. On the one hand, that A acted in a way that we can understand, or find intelligible. On the other hand, what is being said is that, in principle, A could offer an account of why Y was consistent with a larger framework of goals and values which he holds. This account need not be compelling. It merely means that the actions of rational man, in addition to being individually intelligible, are not discrete, unconnected entities: they are interconnected and interrelated in some sense; they make a more or less intelligible whole.

---

[4] No claim is being made here for the universal validity of certain modes of 'rational' thought. In this regard see, e.g. B. R. Wilson (ed.), *Rationality* (Oxford, 1970), *passim*, for an overview of the debate amongst anthropologists about whether or not there exists a universal criterion of rational belief and action.

I do not mean that men do not change with time, that what they may have wanted at one moment they may no longer want at another in such a way that one's wants *over time* may appear inconsistent. Two comments are called for here. The first is that rational man could, in principle, explain why his wants have changed, that he could say, 'Yes, I wanted *x*, but no longer want it for the following reasons...'. The second is that clearly even at a single moment, a rational subject may have goals and desires which, objectively, are inconsistent or incompatible. This must be explained by the fact that it is perfectly possible for someone to be unaware of the potential incompatibility of goals. The test of rationality here is the agent's reaction when the incompatibility is drawn to his attention. If he is convinced that the goals may not be pursued consistently, then this must cause him to reconsider and redefine them so as to remove the inconsistency. Consistency, then, is something for which the rational agent strives consciously over time, without it implying that all the goals he holds at any given time are objectively compatible.

Rationality carries a moral force, both because we feel that it is a part of what makes us distinctively human and because it is the bedrock of the shared social experience of human beings; society would be unthinkable if the actions of our fellows appeared irrational. Interest in the concept of rationality on the part of the political philosopher springs, in part, from this moral content. Any philosophy which aspires to guide action must offer a convincing argument that to follow its guide-lines is to act rationally. 'Rationality' has, as a result, been conscripted in the service of many philosophies, not all of them compatible. In the process the term itself has become confused and ambiguous.

For the present purpose, it is useful to distinguish two particular uses of the term rationality; one weak and the other strong. The importance of distinguishing the two is that some theorists have claimed their systems to be 'rational', wishing thereby to lay claim to the moral commendation which is implied in the strong sense of the term, whereas their rationality was in fact of the weaker variety which does not carry such a moral content. To avoid confusion, therefore, I will refer to rationality in the strong sense described above as *reason*,[5] and in its weak sense as rationality *tout court*. When discussing other writers' concept of rationality, I will indicate whether they use it in a weak or a strong sense.

This second, weak sense of rationality is the faculty of calculation by means of which individuals order their goals in a world characterised by scarcity of resources. Since all goals cannot be realised, are not desired with the same intensity, and do not have the same probability of realisation, man must organise his life so as to make more likely the achievement of the largest possible number of goals. The weak rationality assumption simply says that a rational man with a given set of wants will, within the constraints imposed by information costs, try to achieve the greatest number of most desired goals at the least cost to himself. And, like reasoning man, he will strive to make his goals consistent over time.[6] This is the superficial similarity which gives some plausibility to the conflation of reason and rationality: each one carries the implication of the agent *evaluating* different courses of action, and hence an ability, at least in principle, to offer an *account* of why he acted as he did. I want to show, however, that reasoning man's account of his actions is in fact different in kind from that of rational man's.[7]

It seems clear that this notion of a person being capable of offering an account of himself is very much bound up with a person being responsible for himself in an important way, although which way is a crucial matter of dispute to be discussed below. For the moment, it is helpful to explore further the idea that a person, on the one hand, is capable of evaluating competing courses of action and of explaining why he chooses one over the other and, on the other hand, is held to be responsible for the evaluations and judgments he makes. To be responsible for one's judgments, for one's ways of acting

---

[5] This idea of 'reason' is redolent, *inter alia*, not only of R. Beiner's concept of 'judgment' or 'judging' (*Judgment, passim*), but also of Margolis's discussion of 'normative rationality'. See his *Selfishness*, pp. 11-16.

[6] See Brian Barry, *Political Argument*, pp. 3-5.

[7] It is worth while to note that it would be mistaken to see here any suggestion of irreconcilability between reason and rationality, a notion which appears to be at least implicit in both Hayek and the Webbs. Quite the reverse: in opposition to this it shall be argued below that *both* these faculties are constitutive of human beings.

in the world, is to be responsible for who one is. It is, in popular terms, 'up to us' who we are, the implication being that we have some capacity to shape ourselves and hence our evaluations.[8]

Another way of saying this is that our concept of a full person includes a reflective capacity, an ability not only to have desires and to strive to realise them, but a capacity to formulate what Frankfurt[9] calls 'second order desires', or the ability to have desires about what we *ought* to desire.

This ability to 'step back' from ourselves, to look at and think about who we are and what we are doing is, therefore, also crucial to our notion of a person. To offer an account of what one does requires one to be able to reflect on oneself, to be at the same time both the subject and the object of one's own thoughts.

Something important is thus being said about the moral subject in his relationship to himself and his actions, and this something is a notion of responsibility. A robot, perfectly programmed to act as a human being in all social contexts, and physically indistinguishable from a person could not, on this view, be properly regarded as a person. Lacking the capacity to question whether he ought to act as he does relieves him of any responsibility for himself or his actions. His inability even to formulate the questions disqualifies him as a moral agent.

A man is expected to be able to offer an account of his actions, to offer reasons; and we expect this because we know that in principle he could have acted other than he did. This is not so with the robot, although the actions that they in fact perform may be identical in all externals.

This suggests that moral responsibility resides not in action as such, but in the sort of relationship which the moral subject maintains with his actions. To be responsible is to be able to account for one's behaviour. The analogy with knowledge is not inapt: to be truly said to know something, one must be able to offer an account of why one knows it. To *guess* the

    [8] See e.g. C. Taylor, 'Responsibility For Self' in G. Watson (ed.), *Free Will* (Oxford, 1982), pp. 111–26.

    [9] G. Frankfurt, 'Freedom of the Will and the Concept of a Person' in G. Watson (ed.), op. cit., pp. 81–95, at p. 83.

right answer to a question is not the same thing as *knowing* the answer; hence one can quite properly say, 'He doesn't know the answer, he is just guessing.' To be a person, then, is to be responsible for oneself, both by maintaining a certain kind of internal relationship with one's actions, a kind of interior stance of 'owning' those actions, and by being able, in principle at least, to account for them.

This is the very essence of the legal concept of responsibility. When someone is accused of, say, murder, establishing the fact that the person performed the physical action which caused death is not enough to prove the charge. A critical question will be whether or not the accused is held to be a normal person, i.e. fully responsible for his actions. Someone who has wilfully caused the death of another person may none the less not be guilty of a crime because he is considered incapable of maintaining a certain kind of responsible relationship with his actions. To be guilty, one must be deemed to have a certain internal relationship to the act itself, a relationship of responsibility.

I. UTILITARIANISM

It was suggested at the beginning of this chapter that a discussion of the relationships between rationality, reason, and responsibility would show that the notions of the self at the heart of both the branches of liberalism which have been associated here with Hayek and the Webbs were seriously confused and implausible. The first stage in the argument turns on an examination of the moral responsibility which the utilitarian model of rationality makes possible. The aim is to show how utilitarianism (whether direct or indirect) cannot offer a plausible framework for understanding the depth or character normally ascribed to individuals.

I am not attempting to offer a comprehensive survey and critique of utilitarianism: such an undertaking would too greatly exceed the scope of the present work. What follows will therefore be limited to a consideration of a few selected features of utilitarianism of particular relevance to the larger argument.

It will generally be admitted that utilitarian man is rational in the weak sense described above. He is the rational calculator *par excellence*. The utilitarian uses his rational faculties to wring the maximum possible satisfaction of his desires out of the world.

He equally has a reflective capacity, an ability (of a sort) to 'reason'. He can weigh up alternatives and put off the immediate satisfaction of one desire in order to maximise the satisfaction of more desires in the long run. To use Taylor's[10] example, he is able to reflect on his desires to eat and his desire to swim and to put off eating (even though it would be enjoyable to eat now), so that he can have the pleasure of swimming now and eating later. But this is not all we mean to imply when speaking about a person's ability to 'reason', to reflect on his wants.

The utilitarian reflection is a *non-qualitative* one, one which reduces all courses of action to a single (in principle quantifiable) 'medium of exchange': for Benthamites, the pleasure to be derived from various potential consummations; for the Webbs, the fullest possible individual and social development through the satisfaction of measurable needs; and for Hayek, the same maximisation of the aggregate of development but this time through the self-chosen consumption of socially compatible utilities.

This is not, however, our experience of being faced with alternative courses of action; it is not commonly supposed that ordinary moral dilemmas (do I take in my aged ailing parent, or put him in an institution; do I honour my earlier promise to sell my house at a price lower than what I now know I could get on the market?) can be reduced to the maximum satisfaction of some single value held by the moral subject. We have a sense that such questions are different in kind from those of the sort 'Do I holiday in France or the Caribbean this year?' or 'Blue socks or black today?'

The first kind of dilemma requires us to reflect in a *qualitative* way, to frame our search for an answer in terms of the sort of qualities we would like to have inform our life. Such a qualitative (or strong) evaluation requires an evaluative

---

[10] Ibid., p. 113.

vocabulary with which we can characterise and contrast possible courses of action, not merely in terms of the pleasure or utility we derive from them, but in terms of the sort of moral existence we wish to lead.

In principle, the utilitarian sees all possible courses of action as commensurables, and his behaviour must, in the final analysis, be governed by his calculation of how much utility is to be derived from any particular action. Reflection for him serves merely to establish which of several alternatives is the most attractive: realising that some X maximises his utility is sufficient; he need not be able to offer an account of why he desires it other than in terms of a calculation of the relative utilities of the courses open to him. Such a 'simple weigher' lacks an evaluative vocabulary, for when choosing between incompatible goals, his choice can only be justified on the inarticulate ground that he feels he desires one more than another. Desires are not, for him, a subject for reflection, except to determine which ones he has, and their relative strengths.

While such a minimal reflective facility might not wholly preclude the utilitarian offering an account of a sort of his behaviour, such an account would not be a morally adequate or weighty characterisation of his actions. The trade-off mentality of the utilitarian is premised on the existence of many possible combinations of 'goods', any one of which is, in principle, at least as good as any other in terms of the satisfaction or 'aggregate utility' to be derived from it. This is what allows economists to construct indifference curves, graphic representations of the different combinations of goods and services acceptable to a consumer with a given set of values.[11] These values are not themselves a matter of calculative indifference, however, and this becomes more true as one moves from the field of consumable commodities to the field of ideal-regarding judgments.

A person cannot describe all his motivations or desires solely in terms of the attractions of various consummations or in terms of indifference curves, for at least some of the desires themselves express something about the person who holds

---

[11] B. Barry, op. cit., pp. 3–15.

them; they express who one is in an important way.[12] A whole person would be able to give an account of his actions using a contrastive evaluative vocabulary which would express the kind of life he wished to lead. The 'compleat utilitarian' would thus not be a full person because his way of evaluating is too shallow; he 'would be an impossibly shallow character'.[13]

This is not meant to imply that a real self-avowed utilitarian would in fact lack an evaluative vocabulary of worth. Clearly Hayek and the Webbs, for instance, make considerable use of just such strongly contrastive words. If, however, the utilitarian is consistent, he may not hold that any action is desirable in itself, that it is worth doing *because* of the value he places on the sort of moral life it exemplifies. He may not, for instance, justify an act on the grounds that it was courageous, worthy, generous, etc. and leave it at that. While an ordinary person could quite well say that a courageous, worthy, or generous life is worth living in itself, the utilitarian must argue that it is incorrect to conceptualise choices in this way.[14] For him a courageous act is desirable, not *because* it is courageous, but because of the satisfaction the subject of the action derives from it, and the satisfaction he derives from it is, in principle, identical with that associated with any other consummation.

This admittedly crude account of utilitarian morality is clearly neither the Webbs' nor Hayek's. But while they represent particular forms of utilitarianism (of varying degrees of sophistication), *both* the forms that they endorse require the rational agent to calculate in precisely this manner. It is true that, for the Webbs, the rational agent is only the expert acting in his field of expertise, whereas for Hayek all men are equal in their rational capacities; this does not change the force of this criticism of their moral utilitarianism. In the foregoing account the simplest Benthamite model has been used, in which utility is conceived solely in terms of the satisfactions to be derived by the individual subject, whereas both Hayek and the Webbs offer us accounts in which utility is measured against other unquestioned standards. This leaves

---

[12] This recalls the arguments advanced in Chapter II, above, regarding the difference between ideal- and want-regarding wants.

[13] C. Taylor, op. cit., p. 117.

[14] See G. R. G. Mure, *Retreat From Truth* (Oxford, 1958), p. 28.

the principle unchanged. By removing the ends at which rational action aims from the sphere of reason, by simply taking them as given, the only course open to the rational agent is to act rationally (weak sense), because there is no object on which reason can fix itself.

It is also true that Hayek is only ambiguously utilitarian. He tries to marry utilitarianism with a concept of the individual who is to be valued in himself, finding moral value in the fact of freely willed choice itself. These moral values reside not in *what* the subject chooses, but in the *fact of choosing* in accordance with rational rules which are indifferent to this account of the dimension of depth. Value is attached to the act of choosing and not to the way in which choices are made. I shall show shortly why I think this move is unsuccessful.

To return, for the moment, to the utilitarian account, it is superficial, then, because utilitarians do not hold themselves responsible for the desires they have; the deeper self whence they spring is something which the utilitarian does not struggle to know. The importance of this distinction between types of evaluation of desires is perhaps best highlighted by referring to a matter of everyday human experience: what has come to be called the problem of weakness of the will.[15] The focus here is on statements of the type: 'I wish that I liked Prokofiev, but don't'; or, 'I wish someone would make me sit down and work today, because otherwise I shall waste my time'; or again, 'I know I should be faithful to my wife, but I just can't help myself'.

What is of interest in these statements is that each contains two statements, one of moral evaluation, the other of the relative strength of different desires, both made by the same subject. In other words, the dilemma of weakness of the will is precisely that we have within ourselves an idea of the sort of values that we wish to exemplify in our lives, of the sort of person we wish to be, an idea which is frequently in conflict with other sorts of desire. Such statements imply that, if only someone else could impose their own (stronger) will, we would be able to put into effect our ideal-regarding desires, which our own weak character prevents us from realising. This is

---

[15] See, in particular, J. Elster's book, *Ulysses and the Sirens*, revised edition (Cambridge, 1984).

somewhat reminiscent of J. S. Mill's contention that, given the opportunity to experience them, men will eventually come to prefer the 'higher' pleasures even though, at the outset, they may prefer the 'lower' ones.[16]

Weakness of the will must be unknown to the utilitarian. It is perhaps possible to convince him that he would derive more utility from some other set of desires than those he actually holds, but he could not intelligibly say that he desired *A* more than *B*, but wished that he didn't. Once he was convinced that more utility was to be derived from *B* he would, by definition, both desire it and act on this desire.[17] By assuming no ambiguity, confusion, or inconsistency about an individual's wants, utilitarians simply rule out weakness of the will.

Now while both Hayek and the Webbs offer some account of weakness of the will, it is not at all of the sort discussed here. In both cases, since the measure of the desirability of an action is the social utility it produces, conflict can arise between individual desires and long-term social survival. But these conflicting desires are seen to be based on imperfect rationality, a miscalculation regarding utility maximisation, and not a conflict between ideal- and want-regarding judgments. Human ignorance and the desire to maximise individual short-term satisfactions rather than social utility is precisely why Hayek and the Webbs are opponents of politics; their aim is to remove debate about ideal-regarding judgments from collective decision-making by arguing for the commensurability of all consummations and a unique 'rational' yardstick for choosing amongst these.

To sum up, this description of a utilitarian or simple weigher does not seem to encompass a number of elements which are

[16] See e.g. John Gray's account of 'Individuality, Happiness and the Higher Pleasures' in *Mill On Liberty*, pp. 70–3.

[17] This does suggest two types of internal conflict over values which a utilitarian might feel. The first is what to do in those cases where he faced a choice between maximising his personal utility and maximising the general utility. The second is where the utilitarian sees a conflict between his own long-term utility and his immediate and strongly held desires, a conflict, say, between a desire to study for one's accountancy exams and a (much stronger) desire to go to the pub. Here the problem arises of the current person's relation to the future person who will be the beneficiary of a decision *now* to study rather than to have a pint. I have never seen any evidence that either of these problems can be resolved satisfactorily within a utilitarian framework.

ordinarily held to be constitutive of man's moral nature. A thoroughly consistent utilitarian seems to be lacking something important. While clearly endowed with a rational faculty, he lacks the tools with which to reason about his desires; they are simply given. Without an evaluative contrastive vocabulary, and a sense of values, held to be worth while in themselves, on which that vocabulary is based, the utilitarian cannot hope to offer the deeper kind of account of his actions which we expect from a person. And without the tools to reflect on and evaluate his desires in terms of their intrinsic worth, he cannot be held, nor does he hold himself, responsible in the way that that term is widely understood. As was suggested in the discussion of Beiner's work on political judgment in the first chapter, he is capable of asking himself 'How do I get what I want/need?' but he is unable to formulate the logically prior questions 'Why do I want/need that?' and 'Who am I that I want/need that?'[18]

Of course rationality, properly understood, *is* an indispensable feature of a person. Some utility-maximising way must exist of resolving practical, everyday questions. What cannot be admitted, however, is that this is a satisfactory way to resolve most *moral* issues, which are questions of a wholly different order. It is not the existence or the usefulness of the means/ends category which is in question here—it is its universalisation.

On the other hand, utilitarianism does not fail *because* it prescribes a unique yardstick for rational behaviour; this criticism is only justified if the yardstick itself is inadequate to its task. Consequently, both Hayek and the Webbs could

---

[18] Attempts have been made to escape from the difficulty that this poses for utilitarians. Bernard Williams, for instance, in his critique of utilitarianism, suggests that utilitarians *can* have a concept of the intrinsic moral worth of actions. Here the agent's satisfaction or pleasure is found in performing the action which is intrinsically good. This seems unsatisfactory on two counts, however. First, it still does not resolve the dilemma of how to choose between incompatible but intrinsically desirable goods except with reference to utility. This is precisely the problem of moral shallowness being discussed. Secondly, this seems to require us to conceive utility as deriving or resulting from actions as such, rather than as a result of the significance or meaning the agent attaches to the action. This runs the risk of being a tautological explanation of the origins of moral behaviour: why do men act morally? because they derive utility from it; why do they derive utility from it? because it is moral. J. J. C. Smart and B. Williams, *Utilitarianism: For and Against* (Cambridge, 1973), pp. 83-4.

respond to my arguments by asking in what way *their* guide to rational action is incomplete or insufficient, since their position is precisely that the qualities here ascribed to men (such as 'depth' and 'character') are dangerous or misleading. By giving credence to these purely subjective and non-demonstrable beliefs, liberals may argue, men are prevented from achieving their fullest development according to the certain criteria of liberalism.

This resolves itself ultimately into an epistemological question. Liberals are preoccupied with the status of knowledge, with how we can know things, and this preoccupation itself is based on a passionate desire to be certain.[19] Rational (weak sense) men desire their actions to be efficacious, just as they wish to reduce the possibility of error (and hence of wasted resources) to the lowest level possible. What one thinks can, in principle, be *known* (as opposed to merely believed) will thus be an important determinant of what one will allow as a justification for and explanation of action. What liberals believe is that *knowledge* cannot be obtained from subjective individual interpretation of empirical experience, and that to think it can is a dangerous (and possibly 'irrational') illusion. Liberals do not deny the reality of empirical experience. What they question is whether this can constitute knowledge.[20]

Practical, 'common-sense', experiential knowledge has been mistrusted by philosophers since at least the time of the Greeks, and this for the very sound reason that things are not always as they appear to be, as optical and other illusions show only too clearly. Arendt argues that empirical knowledge received its most devastating blow, though, with the fall of the Ptolemaic universe.[21] If something as patently obvious to the human eye

---

[19] See, in this regard, M. Oakeshott, 'Rational Conduct' in his *Rationalism in Politics and Other Essays* (London, 1962), pp. 92–3; and S. Letwin, *The Pursuit of Certainty* (Cambridge, 1965), esp. the introduction.

[20] The absurd consequences of this sort of non-cognitivist philosophy can perhaps best be seen by looking at a field in which most people think that certain knowledge *can* be achieved: natural science. In the philosophy of science a number of what David Stove has called 'irrationalist' theories have been advanced which purport to show that really we can know nothing at all for certain. The difficulty in which these theories find themselves is well described by Stove in his book *Popper and After: Four Modern Irrationalists* (Oxford, 1982), *passim*, and esp. pp. 18–20.

[21] H. Arendt, *The Human Condition* (Chicago, 1958), pp. 274–5.

as the revolution of the sun about the earth was wrong, then no faith whatsoever could any longer be placed in human perception. More: it appeared that the further removed knowledge was from the empirical world, the more real and trustworthy it became. Certain knowledge could only be had by removing oneself as far as possible from the world, as in the case of mathematics, or of analytic propositions which are true because they are tautological. In either case it will be noted that such absolutely certain knowledge is self-validating; one does not, indeed one cannot, explain or justify such knowledge outside its own frame of reference. It is '... knowledge which does not require to look beyond itself for its certainty; knowledge, that is, which not only ends with certainty but begins with certainty and is certain throughout'.[22]

Mathematics is the paradigm of this view of knowledge. It treats the universe as an abstraction, and reduces it to numbers. Mathematics allows us to remove from our observations all that is contingent and adventitious by rendering them in a language which is itself abstract and 'value-free'. Furthermore, mathematics is a purely human creation, a product of the mind; numbers do not exist in nature.[23] This fits in well with the preoccupation with certainty: one can never be sure of what one has not made oneself. This is the attitude, indeed, of Arendt's *homo faber*: only what he has made himself is real.[24] The crucial thing to bear in mind, though, is this: mathematics provides certain knowledge because it can be tested against itself; in other words, a mathematical proof does not depend in any way on subjective interpretation of the snare-ridden empirical world.

One of the great objectives of the European Enlightenment, from which liberalism sprang, was precisely to find a system which would afford men knowledge of themselves and of the principles of morality, but which would be analogous to mathematics in that it would provide utter certainty and not be dependent on experience. Descartes, for example, believed he had succeeded in this by basing his knowledge on the

[22] M. Oakeshott, *Rationalism in Politics*, p. 11.
[23] H. Arendt, op. cit., p. 290.
[24] Ibid., Part II on 'Homo Faber'.

unquestioned certainty of his own awareness of himself as a thinking being—a certainty itself not based on empirical experience, but on a single flash of metaphysical insight.[25] Everything followed logically from that one certainty; whatever could not be deduced from it was 'merely' belief or opinion, because it could not meet his radically restrictive criterion of what constituted knowledge. Many thinkers have imitated Descartes, in offering a single criterion or yardstick of knowledge from which all else could be deduced through a process of *raisonnement*. Certainty of knowledge seemed to depend on one's ability to rise above the empirical world, and think in the abstract, to rise above the contingent and the adventitious.[26]

One of the political philosophies which draws heavily on this mode of thought is liberalism. Liberals, as we have already seen, put complete faith in the moral and epistemological superiority of abstract knowledge and the principles one can logically derive therefrom. In so doing they believe they can avoid the errors inherent in individual experiential knowledge. On this view, 'true' knowledge, the rational man's only dependable guide to action, can only be judged against one yardstick: the degree to which it is utterly removed and independent from the empirical world and does not depend on individual experience for its validation.

This unique criterion of knowledge is narrow and restrictive; I would like now to look at a few arguments suggesting that it is too much so. It is certainly true that there is a 'hierarchy' of kinds of knowledge, in the sense that there are certain sorts of knowledge which are 'perfect' (e.g. analytical propositions, mathematical proofs) because they are necessarily true and not contingent, and that not all sorts of knowledge can aspire to this exalted height. These other sorts of knowledge, obtained by progressively more empirically-tinged methods, may, in a sense, 'decline' from this pinnacle as they become ever more error-prone. Men understandably seek to frame their knowledge more and more in terms of propositions which comfortingly resemble knowledge at the pinnacle. This is why the scientific method was seen as such a boon by Enlightenment thinkers: this procedure winnowed out the contingent in

---

[25] M. Oakeshott, *Rationalism*, pp. 16–20.
[26] See J. L. Evans, *Knowledge and Infallibility* (London, 1978) pp. 29–43.

empirical experience, leaving behind only certain knowledge, thus freeing men from the tyranny of superstition and myth. One advantage of this was its basis in method: it provided a foolproof procedure which anyone could apply to the discovery of knowledge, thus liberating men from dependence on an authority whose pronouncements could not be questioned.

While a useful corrective to the intellectual stupor that had descended on Europe, bringing a breath of fresh, critical air into a society which had too long depended on the 'revealed truths' of the Church and the authority of tradition, the Enlightenment's heavy emphasis on empirical method and the powers of individual critical reason contained the seeds of new dogmas, including the two forms of liberalism being considered here.

The Enlightenment's decline into utilitarianism and ethical liberalism was brilliantly characterised by Thomas Spragens when he argued that the two models of reason that have come down to us from the original individualistic critical rationalism could be called 'technocratic' and 'value non-cognitivist' respectively:

The technocratic conception retains the belief that scientific critical reason can ascertain principles for governing political and moral action, but it has departed from the earlier conception of liberal reason by regarding access to these truths as limited to a relatively small élite who have mastered the tools of critical reason; the political models generated by this tradition have, therefore, tended to be authoritarian and tyrannical in varying degrees. The value non-cognitivist conception ... has retained the idea that true knowledge is certain, precise and objective, but it too has departed from the earlier paradigm by denying that political and moral principles are accessible to reason so conceived.[27]

Spragens' critique of the two liberal conceptions of reason, while general in intent, clearly corresponds to my earlier characterisation of the work of the Webbs and Hayek respectively.

The Webbian social scientific expert, for instance, is an excellent and telling example of the technocratic model of reason. Here more traditional and philosophical ways of seeing

---

[27] T. Spragens, *Irony*, p. 15.

the world yielded to the onslaught of empirical method. The Webbs were striving to move our knowledge of men and of the world up the hierarchy so that it became ever more 'certain'. Along the way certain kinds of knowledge, because they could not be measured and therefore translated into the new language, ceased to be 'know-able', and declined into mere error-prone 'opinion'. If, though, certain aspects of the world can only be known through unquantifiable empirical experience (the kind of knowledge most prone to error), then in seeking to abstract our knowledge of that world from empirical experience, what we know about that world will become more certain, but we shall know less about it *in toto*.

Similarly, the 'value non-cognitivist' position outlined by Spragens echoes many of Hayek's preoccupations: such liberals subscribe to a radically restrictive criterion of what is knowledge, but draw from this conclusions very different to those of the technocratic liberal. The latter believes that a vast range of certain knowledge is available to those who master 'the tools of critical reason', including knowledge of the principles of moral and political behaviour which can be rationally justified.

The value non-cognitivist, by contrast, accepts that liberalism's demanding yardstick of knowledge means that there are important areas within which very little indeed can be known, particularly in the field of values or ideal-regarding judgments. To be precise, Hayek argues that the most certain knowledge we have is that distilled impersonally from human experience into social institutions and tools; but no one can ever know exactly what that knowledge is, its origins, or why it works. The most certain knowledge we have is of what has utility, and this excludes any possibility of knowledge about 'the good', which cannot be 'known' at all since it depends on a purely subjective evaluation.

The technocrat, believing that he alone possesses the means of discovering knowledge, feels empowered to rule others in accordance with it since, by so doing, he makes them free. This paradox is explained by the technocrat's belief that men are incapable of acting in their own interests since 'true' knowledge is inaccessible to them. As the only source of knowledge, he saves men from hurting themselves through their (unintentionally) irrational acts. That men resist this external rational direction is regrettable but, as the Webbs so clearly believed, such resistance must be fought and overcome in the interest of the survival of the race.

Hayek's value non-cognitivism has the reverse effect: the nature of the good is such as to preclude any claim to knowledge of it compelling the assent of rational men. Any attempt to govern society in accordance with a particular notion of the good, then, is not rationally justifiable. All men can do is to govern themselves in accordance with a method which permits them to determine which of all possible desires can most usefully be pursued and how this can be reconciled with a like freedom for all other men.

The paradox produced by the strict application of this Cartesian measure of knowledge was something of which Descartes' great critic and contemporary Pascal was only too aware. He argued that 'the Cartesian desire for certain knowledge was based upon a false criterion of certainty'.[28] Pascal understood that this rationalist over-intellectualisation of knowledge led invariably to the conclusion that the only true knowledge was that which could be deduced from first principles, themselves wholly outside experience. Pascal's alternative was his doctrine of probability, the essence of which was alluded to above: certain knowledge is certain precisely because it is partial. By stripping away all that is in principle possibly erroneous, one is left with knowledge which is absolutely certain. The paradoxical conclusion is that the quest for certainty leaves us a legacy of much more certain knowledge, but radically restricts what is to count as knowledge.

There is, in fact, a multiplicity of ways of achieving knowledge of the world and of ourselves, none of which is definitive or exclusive of all others. The rationalist error (to which even 'anti-rationalist' liberals like Hayek seem to subscribe), is to believe that there is only one kind of knowledge: certain knowledge. There are other sources of knowledge, however, which, while more error-prone, draw from a much broader field of human experience (i.e. neither

---

[28] M. Oakeshott, *Rationalism*, p. 19.; also J. L. Evans, op. cit., pp. 38-9.

the objects of knowledge nor what is to count as knowledge are so artificially restricted).[29] If, therefore, the possibility of error is not the same thing as error, and if not all knowledge of the world can be reduced to empirical statements, rules of procedure, and logical relations between these, then the rigidly hierarchical view of knowledge must give way. It must be replaced by one recognising the limitations of each way of knowing, but also their unique strengths.

This proposition that there are many paths to knowledge is borne out by our common social practices concerning claims to knowledge. When someone claims to 'know' something, we take account of several factors in determining the validity of his claim.[30] First of all we examine the proposition of which knowledge is claimed, and we may try to verify it against other sources which we may agree are more or less definitive. Secondly, we will certainly want to examine the reasons or evidence advanced by the claimant to support his claim. Such reasons may be of varying kinds, drawn from diverse sources, and what is to count as valid evidence or reasons will certainly vary with the kind of knowledge claimed. Knowledge of scientific, historical, and philosophical propositions, for instance, will each demand different kinds of proof. In one case, only evidence of a long and deep acquaintance with the field may be admissible, in others, quotations from poets or personal observation may be sufficient, and in yet others, empirical studies will be *de rigueur*. The point is that all knowledge which does not meet a unique criterion of validity is not in principle excluded, and any suggestion that it ought to be would be seen as distinctly odd. Finally, we look at the credentials of the person advancing the claim. As Evans[31] suggests, we would be more likely to admit a claim to historical knowledge advanced by the Regius Professor than by a schoolboy.

The importance of how we are to evaluate knowledge claims is, of course, capital. By departing from the common practice admitting a wide variety of yardsticks of knowledge, liberals and other rationalists deny the status of knowledge to whole

[29] J. L. Evans, op. cit., p. 43.
[30] Ibid., pp. 44–7.
[31] Ibid., p. 45.

classes of propositions, especially those based on subjective empirical experience. This enables them to qualify such mere 'beliefs' as rational, irrational, or non-rational, whereas such words are inapt to describe 'knowledge'. The obvious advantage of this is that, by defining what one knows as 'knowledge', and what anyone else claims to know as mere opinion or belief, one can easily lay claim to the moral force which still attaches to the term rationality. To refuse to act in accordance with what is *known* is irrational, whereas refusal to concur in another's opinion is simply a perfectly normal conflict of beliefs. Such monistic epistemologies, then, allow their adherents to monopolise claims to rationality, and to condemn other views as opposed to rationality itself.[32]

Of great interest too are the implications of the liberal view for the relationship between theory and practice. The liberal view holds that any concrete activity is well done to the extent that it conforms to an abstract conceptualisation of how that activity ought to be conducted, a conceptualisation which exists prior to the activity itself.

Oakeshott[33] and others have argued that knowledge of any activity can be broken down into two types. The first is a knowledge of how to engage in the activity itself; how to do it. The second is a knowledge of the principles or theory which are a representation of the activity itself. In other words, it is perfectly possible to know how to do something, but to be quite incapable of explaining how it is done, or of formulating principles or rules underlying the practice of the activity. Similarly, it is an experience common to us all to understand perfectly well the theory of an activity but to be utterly incapable of engaging in it because we lack knowledge of how to apply the principles: we may know the rules, but still not know how to play the game. Furthermore, knowledge of how to do something can only be had by doing it and it cannot, in principle, be entirely reduced to consciously formulated rules. There will always be a grey area in which theory cannot substitute for experience.

The conclusion of this line of thought is that the theory of any concrete activity (how to act morally, how to cook, how

---

[32] M. Oakeshott, *Rationalism*, p. 5.
[33] Ibid., pp. 19-20.

to be a lawyer) is necessarily only a partial representation of the activity itself and is necessarily extracted from a familiarity with that activity. In other words, it is the validity of rules that is to be judged against the practice, and not the reverse. Liberals, then, confuse the source and the product of inspiration and knowledge when they argue that man acts rightly to the extent that he acts solely in accordance with a set of abstract rules wholly independent of and prior to the activity of in fact acting morally.

Now it may appear that this argument unfairly puts Hayek in the same rationalist category as the Webbs, when it has already been shown that Hayek himself makes great use of this distinction between two types of knowledge, arguing consistently that we always know more than we can say about our traditions and practices.

It is surely right that Hayek denies the power of critical reason to derive knowledge from abstract speculation, and for this reason he has a much more plausible theory of knowledge than the Webbs, whose belief that all values can be derived from the application of the scientific method to empirical facts Hayek rejects as absurd. His error, though, is an equal but opposite one, for while he rightly emphasises that we always know more than we can say, he seems to offer a very unsatisfactory account of what is to *count* as knowledge, whether it can be articulated in any particular instance or not. For him, knowledge comes exclusively in the form of what has proven utility, whereas human practices indicate that other forms of meaning grow out of the shared experiences of men in communities.

In support of this it is worth examining for a moment Hayek's belief that justice is realised by the absolutely universal and dependable application of abstract rules of just conduct to every particular case, regardless of whether or not any particular outcome this produces appears unjust, and in spite of the fact that the utility of any particular rule of just conduct (which may produce some unjust outcomes) cannot be demonstrated.

Here we return to the liberal preoccupation with method noticed earlier. Since, the argument goes, men cannot agree on what is good (e.g. what would be a good outcome in a court case), the best they can do is to agree on rules of procedure which, as long as they are neutral as between all possible socially compatible ends, produce just outcomes because they treat all men identically and non-arbitrarily. Hayek advances the spontaneously grown common law as an example of this thesis in action: judges lay down rules of just behaviour 'blindly', according to abstract criteria which are validated by their conformity with established usage. It is improper for the judge to take account of any particular circumstances, human justice being reducible in its entirety to abstract and universal rules which act to prevent injustice.

Interestingly for someone who has such a deep admiration for the common law, Hayek pays no attention at all to one of its most important features: the jury system.[34] Surely one of the most important reasons why the jury system began and has persisted to this day is because people are extremely wary of trusting to 'experts', wholly preoccupied with the application of abstract rules, to administer justice to concrete individuals. The jury system offers precisely that human dimension to justice which the strict application of abstract rules cannot produce.

This means that even within the common law tradition which Hayek regards as paradigmatic for his 'antirationalist, evolutionary tradition',[35] discovering rules of just conduct by applying a procedural rather than a substantive notion of justice, the acceptability of rules is dependent not only on their conformity with abstract criteria, but also on their conformity with certain substantive notions of justice. In his attempt to make justice utterly independent of morally contingent considerations, Hayek extracts from the law a subjective element which is crucial to its legitimacy. He does not argue that the law can be laid down in advance of experience; but he does argue that only those who have a very particular *kind* of experience, applying the abstract rules of justice in a concrete society, should discover the law. What

[34] The only mention of the jury system occurs on p. 218 of the *Constitution*, where Hayek argues that 'procedural safeguards' such as habeas corpus and trial by jury 'presuppose for their effectiveness the acceptance of the rule of law as here defined and ... without it, all procedural safeguards would be valueless'.

[35] Ibid., p. 63.

the jury system suggests is that there is another type of experience which is also crucial: the experience of attempting to act justly as a particular individual in unique circumstances, and here judgment can only be rendered by people steeped, not in an appreciation of the abstract rules, but in the business of living particular lives filled with contingencies.

Hayek's notion of a justice which is strictly procedural and not substantive is explicitly tied to our inability to know enough. Omniscient men would, according to Hayek, have no need at all of a concept of justice, because they would be able to foresee all the consequences of their actions. In other words, the idea of justice is nothing more than a practical second best to the impossibility of complete and certain knowledge.

Why omniscience would do away with discussion about a substantive notion of justice is, however, unclear. A man who could predict with certainty what would be the outcome of all his actions would still be faced with the question, 'What outcome would be most just?' Hayek is not saying that omniscience extends to moral knowledge and therefore *simplifies* the search for just conduct, he is saying that justice 'would have no meaning in a society of omniscient men'.[36] Indeed, one would think that the ability to know in advance all the consequences of one's actions would greatly sharpen the debate on the nature of justice, because responsibility for those consequences would be so much less attenuated than the circumstances of the real world allow.

Clearly, though, no adequate account of the ethical or deontological aspect of Hayek's liberalism, and therefore of his full arguments regarding the criteria of rational action, has yet been offered. As noted earlier, this aspect of his thought attempts to offer a guide to action which will reunite rationality, reason, and responsibility with the full moral force they are expected to entail. Briefly, liberals such as Hayek hold that there are certain truths that are 'knowable' or 'discoverable' by men by virtue of their reasoning faculties, properly used. These truths concern the principles which ought

---

[36] See e.g. *Mirage*, p. 127, where it is argued that, 'Both freedom and justice are values that can prevail only among men with limited knowledge and would have no meaning in a society of omniscient men'. But compare ibid. p. 39.

to guide men in their relationships with one another, precisely the area where utilitarianism proved so inapt.

Moral action, on this view, becomes socially intelligible because it is based on principles discoverable by any being endowed with reason, that is, by any person. Here responsibility for self resides in the fact of choice: this self is held to be free of encumbrances such as desires and wants; they are not given. Responsibility for self lies in recognising that one is not a victim of a given set of desires, which one must bear. On the contrary, to be a person, on this view, is to have the capacity to choose one's wants. Since the principles of morality are in principle discoverable by every reasoning being, and since any reasoning being, having once grasped them, would adopt them as the embodiment of reason, each person acts morally to the extent that he chooses his wants and values in accordance with these overriding principles.

This is very different from the Webbs' account, even though they too want to separate desires from the individuals who hold them. The difference is that in the Webbs' 'mystical holism', the individual is not the *locus* of choice concerning what wants or needs he should have. This is the province of the rational agent and the rational agent is not merely any person, but only the professional expert whose knowledge authorises him to choose on behalf of subrational men. The Webbs thus make no attempt to see men as responsible for themselves or for who they are: the only responsible agents are the experts who implement objective knowledge wholly independent of their will. The Webbs are thus excluded from having anything interesting to say about political theory both because they fail to make any place for the moral personality of the individual and because experts (the few men and women who *are* endowed with such a personality) merely implement truths revealed to them by the application of the scientific method. *No one* is responsible in the deep sense discussed above precisely because the Webbs regard Beiner's second and third questions as unintelligible. It is worth delving more deeply into Hayek's works because his view attempts to answer the second as well as the first.

2. ETHICAL LIBERALISM

Hayek's Kantian-inspired liberalism starts from the premise

that all men are essentially, 'autonomous beings—authors of values, of ends in themselves, the ultimate authority of which consists ... in the fact that they are willed freely.'[37] This is, in part at least, an attempt to overcome the objections raised earlier to utilitarianism: an attempt to give a moral foundation to a political theory which prizes the individual and his freedom and yet which is not destructive of our notion that certain things are to be valued in themselves. Ethical liberalism sees human beings as self-motivating and self-determining, and concludes that the ultimate values, those to be valued in and for themselves, are in fact individual men—the creators of their own values—and the values that they freely choose. No man may be seen as a means to another man's satisfaction, nor can there be any basis for preferring one man's values to another's. It is not true, though, to suggest that liberals like Hayek want to hold that *any* value is good simply because it is held by someone. It is rather that the values men choose when they are able to will them freely are, as Berlin suggests, ultimate values.[38]

The concept of 'willing freely' is crucial here. The argument runs along these lines: human beings are divided within themselves into a higher reasoning self and a lower empirical self. The empirical self is the source of our passions and desires, but these are not constitutive of who we are. What makes us truly human is *only* the higher reasoning self, the unencumbered, radically individuated subject of choice at the core. This universal human essence may itself be further subdivided into an ability to reason about what our values ought to be and an ability to choose our values, to will that our rationally chosen values inform our life. The 'ultimate authority' of our values and our ends resides in the fact of our having chosen them by means of our reasoning faculty—choice in accordance with rational (strong sense) principles validates them. The implication, of course, is that those desires which we have not freely willed in accordance with rationally chosen principles must be resisted, for to surrender to them is to act unfreely and 'irrationally'. We are authors of our own values, and

---

[37] I. Berlin, 'Two Concepts of Liberty' in his *Four Essays on Liberty* (Oxford, 1969), p. 136.
[38] Ibid., p. 136.

therefore free, to the extent that we subjugate our lower empirical self to our higher reasoning one, and to the extent that we choose (or 'give ourselves') the values in accordance with which we shall act. This might be called rational self-direction.

The extent to which we are free, autonomous, moral agents, then, is directly related to our ability to distance ourselves from the contingent and adventitious in our lives, from everything which cannot be derived directly from our ability to reflect, calmly and reasonably, on what our values ought to be. The more we can abstract ourselves from the empirical world, the world of experience and attachments, the more the choices we make will be self-validating guides to action.

Such a view does incorporate notions of rationality, reason, and responsibility. Rationality remains the calculative faculty which permits us to match available means and desired ends, a purely instrumental faculty which only functions when ends are supplied to it—and ends are the province of reason. Reason is a higher, abstract, reflective capacity, a potential which resides, more or less realised, within each of us. This view of reason requires its subject to deploy an evaluative contrastive vocabulary to describe its chosen values. Indeed, its very function is to arrive at an understanding of terms such as just, fair, etc. through the exercise of sheer reflective capacity.

Liberal man is responsible, too, in the sense that he chooses what his values are to be, or at least has the potential to do so. Even if he accepts uncritically one set of values, he has the capacity to change them at will because he is not touched at the core by them. If he decides that his values are mistaken, he can discard them without loss to himself. He is responsible for himself because he can be other than he is if he so chooses, and because the values he does hold must rest on a choice of which he could, in principle, offer an account. Finally, the account would be socially intelligible because the fruits of reason are accessible to all rational beings.

A classic example of this liberal concern with knowledge of the principles of just social and political organisation derived from abstract reasoning, untainted by subjective individual experience or morally contingent considerations, such as the good, is to be found in John Rawls' *A Theory of Justice*. In his famous account of the 'original position', Rawls sets out to explain a procedure by which one might plausibly discover such principles such that any rational man would recognise them as just.

His device is, of course, the placing of 'thin' people, stripped of contingent aspects behind the 'veil of ignorance' which isolates them from any knowledge of what their concrete and particular position will be in the order whose principles they are to lay down. What validates the outcome of this procedure is precisely that none of the participants can know what he will gain or lose by the operation of the order proposed. The presumed result is a system in which every individual's chances of realising a rationally chosen life plan is maximised over any possible alternative. Again we return to a procedural conception of justice, neutral with respect to particular ends.

Now the affinities between Hayek and Rawls, while perhaps not immediately obvious, are none the less of some importance, as Hayek himself has suggested: in his introduction to *Law, Legislation and Liberty*, for instance, he suggests that the differences between himself and Rawls are 'more verbal than substantial'.[39] Later, in *The Mirage of Social Justice*, Hayek seeks to substantiate this claim by quoting what he sees as a crucial passage from *A Theory of Justice*. 'I have no basic quarrel', Hayek suggests,

with an author who ... acknowledges that the task of selecting specific systems or distributions of desired things as just must be 'abandoned as mistaken in principle, and it is, in any case, not capable of a definite answer. Rather the principles of justice define the crucial constraints which institutions and joint activities must satisfy if persons engaging in them are to have no complaints against them. If these constraints are satisfied, the resulting distribution, whatever it is, may be accepted as just (or at least not unjust)'.[40]

It is the Kantian ideal discussed briefly in Chapter I which provides the thread linking these two very different thinkers, but it is an ideal that each of them is trying to modify in a different way. As Sandel[41] makes particularly clear, Rawls

---

[39] *Law, Legislation and Liberty*, p. xvii.
[40] *Mirage*, p. 100.
[41] M. Sandel, *Liberalism and the Limits of Justice* (Cambridge, 1982), *passim* and esp. Chapter 1, section 2 'Liberalism Without Metaphysics: The Original Position', pp. 24–8.

seeks to escape what he sees as the unsatisfactory Kantian metaphysic, grounding the principles of justice in the more plausible discovery procedure of the original position. Hayek, on the other hand, is trying, under the influence of Hume,[42] to escape the heavy Kantian emphasis on individual ratiocination. Put another way, it is not the *objective* of rationalist liberals like Rawls which Hayek rejects, but rather their way of getting there. His disagreement with Rawls (where it is not merely 'verbal') is thus a methodological one dictated by their differing views of the degree of certainty introduced by different 'discovery procedures'.

To Hayek's mind, the market and other spontaneously grown institutions act like the original position in Rawls. Via a mechanism inaccessible to rational analysis, such freely evolved structures bring about an overall social order which is just in precisely the way described by Rawls: it will improve the chances of any individual chosen at random to realise his self-chosen ends;[43] and the order is itself neutral as between any socially compatible ends. No agreement on the good is necessary since the good is something that individuals discover for themselves within the framework for choice offered by just institutions. The advantage for Hayek in this procedure, as opposed to the 'original position', is that he believes that such spontaneously grown artefacts make use of more knowledge of the world than men behind the veil of ignorance could ever possess, and therefore deliberate about. And since this knowledge is embodied in institutions, traditions, and tools which individual men use for their private purposes, these instruments are neutral as between socially compatible utilities.

As we have already seen, the fact that certain ends are socially compatible and others not is not, for Hayek, a violation of the autonomy of the individual because what is important is not that individuals choose any values in particular, but that they be free to choose something. Hayek's concern with coercion is that it removes from the individual the responsibility

---

[42] See e.g. *Constitution*, p. 63 and *Rules and Order*, p. 6. John Gray also has a very good discussion of this influence on Hayek in his op. cit., Chapter 1, esp. p. 8.

[43] The affinities between the Rawlsian and the Hayekian conceptions of justice are made most explicit in Chapter 10 of *Mirage*, the concluding passage of which (p. 132) is so Rawlsian in flavour that it might almost have been written by Rawls himself.

for choice which is crucial to moral development: coercion prevents the development of character that the act of choosing brings about. As long as no one is coerced (i.e. by another agent's will) to choose a particular end, the constraints on choice represented by e.g. (just) social institutions are not obstacles to self-realisation because no one is constitutively bound up with any particular set of goals. The freedom which matters is the freedom to choose those goals which the superior rationality of spontaneously grown institutions indicates will result in the greatest aggregate of commensurate consummations.

Hayek is thus clearly in the liberal tradition of Kant and Rawls, but with this crucial difference: his scepticism regarding individual rationality. He prefers to let the superior rationality of the market, which is itself ignorant of the particular ends of those who avail themselves of it, indicate the direction of rational choice. Individual rationality is reduced to the faculty to which one appeals in an attempt to get men to subordinate their primitive, antisocial, desire-ridden self to the discipline of the market order. Somewhat paradoxically, perhaps, Hayek's life's work is dedicated to the use of rational argument to persuade men that rational argument and deliberation are a dead end.

Thinkers like Hayek and Rawls are saying something of great importance here about the nature of the self, about what they think the people who will live under their political order are like. The first area that bears further examination is the division of the person into 'higher' and 'lower' selves in opposition to each other. We have seen that the liberal considers that he is freer, more morally autonomous, and therefore realises more fully his moral nature as a person, the more he can subjugate the desires emanating from his lower empirical self to the dictates of his reasoning faculty.

The implications of this for the liberal conception of the self are extremely important. Watson,[44] for instance, draws attention to the fact that we would not consider that we become more human as we progressively eliminated all passions and desires because our intellect told us that this was 'right'

[44] G. Watson, 'Free Agency' in G. Watson (ed.), op. cit., pp. 96–101.

or 'good'. Quite the reverse is in fact the case, for we define ourselves as beings with appetites or desires which exist quite independently of our volition. We would consider it a great loss and source of sorrow to no longer feel, say, strong erotic impulses because we had willed them away or, indeed, if they were permanently absent for any reason whatsoever.

But this may appear a caricature of the liberal position, which simply sees the self as a chooser existing independently of all desires. Desires are still held to exist within men, but there is a pure choosing self at the core which is not itself bound up with these desires amongst which it must choose. At first, this may simply appear to be the liberal theory's way of formulating an essential element of any ethical system: an account of how the self may overcome those passions or desires which conflict with what we are rationally convinced is our good. Without this crucial element, men are simply slaves to their passions and are unfree because they have no influence over, or choice concerning, what they do.

While superficially attractive, this liberal view of the self as a totally unencumbered and radically free subject of choice seems plagued with difficulties. It was argued above that liberals hold that '... man acts morally only in so far as he is able to rise above the heteronomous influences and contingent determinations of his natural and social conditions and act according to a principle given by pure practical reason'.[45] In the case of Rawls, this principle is what is discovered behind the veil of ignorance, and for Hayek, that which is thrown up by the impersonal market. Values are seen as self-validating to the extent that men hold them as the result of a process of choice in which they strip themselves down, remove or ignore all desires and empirical circumstances, everything that is contingent and therefore morally arbitrary, and then choose those values through a process of pure reasoned reflection (Rawls) or allow the choice to be guided by impersonal and impartial institutions such as Hayek conceives the market to be. Even supposing that men can, in fact 'thin themselves down' in this way, however, the advantage that liberalism might draw from this is unclear. The intention is to give a

---

[45] M. J. Sandel, op. cit., p. 36.

particular moral weight to such free choices because the special conditions under which they are taken prevent their being influenced by morally irrelevant considerations. While ingenious, I think that this approach is ultimately unsuccessful for several reasons.

First, it depends on an ambiguity of language. 'Choice' has a weak and a strong sense in English. Weak or 'arbitrary' choice takes place when an individual 'chooses' to follow one course of action over another on a purely arbitrary or capricious basis. No attempt is made to offer an account of why he made the choice he did, and he may well be incapable of offering such an account. Such a random, unjustified choice, while not, in real life, absolving its subject from responsibility for its consequences, would not be considered to 'engage' him as a person. In other words, such an arbitrary choice could not offer us any kind of clue as to the character, depth, or moral worth of its subject. Here again we encounter the idea that a morally weighty choice demands not only an expression of a preference between alternatives, but a special kind of internal relationship with the choice.

Strong choice, choice in which the self is 'engaged' in choosing, might also be called 'considered' or 'reasoned' choice. In this case, alternatives are weighed and assessed against a background of preferred outcomes and existing values. Clearly only the second type of choice, requiring a responsible assessment of alternatives, and an attempt to integrate each particular choice within a larger framework of values, carries the moral weight on which liberals wish to base their defence of the sovereignty of individual wants.

It is precisely this second sense, however, which is precluded by their 'thin' notion of the self. The theory suggests not only that an original choice of values is possible, but that on the foundation of his original choice each individual can construct a complete value system. Only in this way can man 'freely will' his values, and claim a right to have them respected. But how can this disembodied thin self make this original choice? It has no background, no ties, no commitments, no values. The original choice such a thin self might make about its attributes, goals, and values can only be of the first, capricious, kind, and is therefore arbitrary. Such a choice may be freely willed, but it has no moral impact. In fact it is hardly recognisable as a 'choice' at all.

The second argument which can be raised against the moral claims for the liberal self questions the extent to which one can distinguish between the moral subject, that is the thin self which is prior to its desires, and its desires themselves, which it is held to possess. Desires, wants, and aspirations can only be conceived by the liberal as objects possessed by a subject whose, 'identity is never tied to [its] aims and attachments'.[46] If the thinly constituted self making the original choices whence flow freely-willed values and wants is implausible, the more thickly constituted self resulting from that original choice fares no better. It cannot be right to argue that our goals, aims, and affections are not, in part, at least, constitutive of who we are. In fact we experience them, both in ourselves and in others, as expressing something of prime importance to us, as indicative of our deepest self. The moral force that deontological liberalism gains by positing a self prior to and independent of its contingent and morally arbitrary wants appears to be won at the cost of what makes us human. 'To imagine a person incapable of constitutive attachments ... is not to conceive an ideally free and rational agent, but to imagine a person wholly without character, without moral depth.'[47]

The force of this argument can be illustrated by concrete examples. Take, for instance, the idea of nuns participating in a religious community, the purpose of which is to devote one's life to the service and contemplation of God.[48] On the liberal view, such a commitment is merely what Mill might have called an 'experiment in living'; it is an attempt to 'try out' the life of religious contemplation to see whether or not it confirmed the hypothesis that life in a religious community would be fulfilling. Yet the very character of this activity is such as to exclude a self-conscious attitude of experimentation: nuns do not ask each other, 'How do you find the experience

---

[46] Ibid., p. 179.
[47] Ibid., loc. cit.
[48] I owe this example to John Gray, who used it in the discussion following his presentation of a paper on Mill's liberalism at the fortnightly graduate political philosophy seminar at the LSE in 1984.

so far?' for this would indicate an absence of the fundamental belief which a religious vocation presupposes.

Furthermore, the liberal view suggests that no experiment has any intrinsic value to the agent carrying it out; men simply try out various ways of living and reject those that do not suit them, remaining untouched by the experience. But what would be the consequence for a nun, to pursue this example, of discovering that she no longer believed that single-minded devotion to God was the form that her life should take? Assuming her original commitment to have been genuine, such a realisation would quite properly be seen as a crushing blow to a self-definition which had been centrally bound up with a faith which has now proved itself inadequate. Thus, even if one could regard such a constitutive commitment as an 'experiment', failure does not leave the person untouched: it can be personally disastrous and may well cripple one for further experimentation. This highlights the anti-individualism of Hayek's evolutionist arguments: the species' progress which continual experimentation achieves is purchased, at great personal cost and misery, by large numbers of 'experimenters'. Others can learn from our mistakes, but we are not regarded as having paid anything for this knowledge.

Literature provides many striking examples. A common literary theme is that of the man or woman who is deeply marked by some personal experience. The power of such stories lies in the fact that we are all aware that we can only know people by knowing how they have responded to their experiences, just as men can only know themselves by actually seeing their own reactions to events. If, for instance, Lord Jim's experience of his reaction to the apparent sinking of the *Patna*, had merely produced the reflection that the nautical life was not for him and some other experiment seemed in order, Conrad's novel would have had no point. Men ought to be diminished by their unworthy deeds and exalted by their worthy ones in a much more deeply engaged sense than that of 'experimentation' implies. If this was all there was to men's lives, they could not be judged as individuals by what they have done and still less would they be expected to bear an enduring responsibility for certain kinds of 'failed experiments'.[49]

A note of caution: if carried too far, this argument may lead to the opposite error of seeing men as *solely* constituted by their commitments and ties. This cannot be right either. A nun who ceased to believe in God would undoubtedly be deeply changed and marked by the experience, but it would be going too far to say that she had ceased to be the person she was and had become someone else. There is a continuity to the self over time, a continuity which seems to persist even in the face of the most radical changes. Thus, while it could intelligibly be said of such a lapsed nun that 'She is no longer the same person', such a statement is ambiguous, because clearly she *is* the same person in some sense or she could not also be the subject of the equally intelligible statement 'She used to be a nun'.

Liberals are certainly right, then, to see a choosing element in the self, an element which assures the self's continuity over time, even where desires and attachments have radically changed. If we can change deeply held commitments, then we cannot be constituted exclusively by these, but must be able to choose amongst them. On the foregoing account, however, such a choice cannot be of the kind liberals describe.

In spite of its attractive exterior then, liberalism appears to fail to offer a picture of a person who either reasons or is responsible for himself in the sense in which I have employed those terms. While claiming that the liberal self is pure reason and ability to choose, liberalism denies to the self a morally significant context within which either reasoning or choosing can take place. Similarly, this view simultaneously affirms the absolute responsibility of each person for his values and desires, because he or she has chosen them, but sees that choice as capricious and arbitrary. The person I am is not engaged in the first crucial choice of values, because that person, conceived as an agglomeration of wants, desires, attachments, and goals, can only exist *after* the choice.

[49] For a critique of both this separation of moral personality from personal experience and the belief that men are not deeply marked by failed experiments, see Nick Bosanquet's critique of Hayek's economic philosophy in *After the New Right*, esp. p. 95.

The central thrust of these arguments against the liberal self and rationalist epistemology is that the abstract nature of the conception, far from being its greatest strength, is its fatal flaw. A self without attributes and constitutive attachments cannot possibly choose, in any morally significant sense of that term, what its attributes ought to be, any more than a mind bereft of knowledge can 'reason' about what the world or the person ought to be like.

Yet the ability to adopt an objective posture, to strive to free oneself from immediate circumstance and step back to think calmly and coolly about a problem is in fact a valued resource.[50] Abstract conceptions of justice and moral principles are far from being wrong or wholly irrelevant. On the contrary, their appeal derives from their perfect legitimacy and validity in the appropriate context. Problems arise when attempts are made to universalise such values, to seek to impose them as valid guides to action outside this context. When, for instance, we are exhorted always to adopt the attitude of a disinterested observer, whose relationships with real people are subordinate to abstract principles which have been logically deduced from simply given and unchallengeable premises (e.g. the value of liberty or the certainty of the scientific method or the long-term survival of society), it is virtually impossible to *apply* these values. And yet this is often the form which the liberal project has assumed. It is, for instance, explicit in Hayek: '[The Great Society] admittedly means that we make our rational insight dominate over our inherited instincts'.[51]

Of course such objective attitudes are necessary to the proper conduct of certain kinds of relationship. We want the judge hearing our case, the teacher educating our child, and the civil servant applying government policy each to set aside, in so far as is humanly possible, his personal feelings and to apply impersonal criteria of evaluation and judgment to his relationships with the people with whom he or she comes into professional contact. Each of us, to the extent that we undertake engagements with others through the market, for

---

[50] 'We *have* this resource and can sometimes use it: as a refuge, say, from the strains of involvement; or as an aid to policy; or simply out of intellectual curiosity.' P. Strawson, 'Freedom and Resentment' in G. Watson (ed.), op. cit., p. 67.

[51] *Mirage*, p. 91.

example, agrees to let certain aspects of our relationships be governed by the abstract and impersonal functioning of the price mechanism. Strawson[52] rightly argues, however, that such objective attitudes must be seen as being in opposition to what he calls 'participant reactive attitudes'.

Someone who conducted his relationships with people in accordance with abstract criteria alone (i.e. justice, fairness, etc.) would be regarded as cold and, in popular parlance, 'inhuman'. He would be incapable of sustaining the kind of close warm relationship the capacity for which is part of being human.[53] There are contexts where (say) justice is an inappropriate principle to guide one's conduct because the objective attitude or stance which it demands is destructive of the very essence of human relationships (e.g. love, warmth, caring). In Strawson's terms, such objective attitudes, 'cannot include the range of reactive feelings and attitudes which belong to involvement or participation with others in inter-personal human relationships'.[54]

Again it must be emphasised that the objective stance has its place. It is particularly appropriate, say, in a context where one needs or wants to treat another human being, not as a subject like oneself, but as an object. Such a position is often assumed, for instance, in dealings with people whose actions appear to us as inexplicable, bizarre, or irrational: we assume them not to be fully responsible people with whom one can sustain a normal relationship as between fully developed adults.

Mental patients and children are also examples, albeit rather different ones because they are subjects but are not yet seen as fully responsible for themselves, or at least their self-responsibility exists as an (as yet) unrealised potential within them. Thus, to the extent that we do not regard them as responsible for themselves, as capable of reasoning, one may be justified in seeing them as the objects of treatment or care or education, etc., but only to that extent. To regard another person in this way is precisely to put them outside the sphere in which participant reactive attitudes can be

[52] P. Strawson, op. cit., pp. 59–64.
[53] See ibid., C. Taylor, op. cit. and M. J. Sandel, op. cit.
[54] P. Strawson, op. cit., p. 66.

engaged. Even amongst human beings whom we regard as otherwise normal and fully responsible for themselves, we retain some control over the degree or extent to which we adopt one attitude or the other toward them, and this will vary over time and with our knowledge of the person in question. In all cases, however, this is a matter of degree and of judgment.

What cannot be admitted is that someone could adopt only objective attitudes towards all other human beings in the world. Whatever else we might be tempted to call someone who saw all other members of the human race as objects of policy, treatment, or control, we would have difficulty seeing him as a whole person. Our commitment to participating in intersubjective relationships—with all the range of emotions, ties, and commitments that implies—is simply too deep-seated and all-pervasive. And yet it seems that this is precisely what both the Webbs' and Hayek's liberalism, carried to its logical conclusion, implies: the (near) universalisation of the objective perspective.

It ought not to be supposed for one moment, of course, that thoroughgoing liberals are so far removed from these aspects of human experience that they do not at least have an inkling that people are not as they describe. That, however, can only lead to the conclusion that the liberal view of the self is not descriptive, but normative; it is not about what we are like, but what we ought to be like. It is an attempt to 're-create' people such that we can have certain knowledge about them, and it does this by two means. Firstly, it encourages us to see ourselves in a new way, i.e. as radically individuated and unencumbered. Secondly, it argues for the creation of a society in which only objective attitudes inform our public relations with others and participant, reactive, intersubjective relations are completely privatised, being relevant only to face-to-face (primarily familial) relations.

It then becomes simple to show that if we learn to strip away the adventitious, the contingent, the capricious in our lives, we can act in accordance with what is *truly* (as opposed to only apparently) us: our rational intelligence. This is undoubtedly a large part of the rationalist/liberal project: to convince us to give up those aspects of ourselves which do not accord with rational abstract principles or, more precisely, to change the way we conceive those aspects, so that they come to be seen as contingent rather than constitutive of who we are.

This project's success would bring us certain knowledge of human behaviour, not because the latter was better understood, but because we would have eliminated from it all we had not understood. People would be reduced to those dimensions our conscious minds can easily grasp. It has thus been said with some justice that the nightmare of the social sciences is not that men are as they describe, but that they could become so.[55]

My concern to this point has been to show how commonly held notions of rationality, reason, and responsibility appear to rule out certain sorts of conception of the self, notably the utilitarian and the liberal. But testing the adequacy of these theories, while in itself an essential critical exercise, must depend on an alternative theory, however indirectly stated, of what the self is like. The time has now come to give shape to this implicit image through a further development of my account of the necessary attributes of the person.

First, the person is rational, in the weak sense described earlier. He is thus endowed with a calculating capacity, or ability to match means to ends, and there is a certain consistency within his (given) system of wants.

Second, the self is, and can only be, thickly constituted. There is no 'thin' self at the core. We cannot talk intelligibly about people without attributes, or people who merely possess their attributes and are not constituted by them. Neither can a person easily discard many of his attributes without calling his identity fundamentally into question.

Third, the self is permeable, it can be and is shaped and changed by its experiences and its environment. This follows from two realisations: one, that experience of the empirical

---

[55] Liberalism is not the only rationalist, monistic philosophy which is guilty of trying to mould men into a brave new form. Marxism, the liberationist ideologies, fascism, and many others suffer from this one-dimensional view of what man is, or should be. My preoccupation with liberalism springs from its deep influence on our ways of thinking and acting, not because it is inherently more defective than other ideologies.

world is a necessary prerequisite to knowledge, thought, and language and therefore individual experience is not merely contingent and arbitrary, but is absolutely necessary to any sense of self whatsoever; two, that participant reactive attitudes are a necessary part of a person's repertoire of relationships. A person must be capable of having relationships which engage him on a deep level, relationships which involve mutual consideration, reciprocal openness, and shared emotion, transcending objective relations; relationships, in short, which are intersubjective.

The fourth attribute of the self is that it can reason, but both the subject and the object of reason are quite different from what the liberal and utilitarian views suppose. Neither of these views required the reasoning self to have *depth*, or a dimension prior to reason. The utilitarian thus cannot offer a qualitative evaluation of his desires, because they are simply given. Similarly, the way in which the ethical liberal says he qualitatively evaluates his desires cannot possibly be true.

If, then, reason implies an ability to reflect qualitatively on oneself and one's desires, but reason cannot be a faculty allowing a thin self to choose its attributes and values, the question arises, 'About what does the person reason?' The answer must be that the self is endowed with reason as a means to understanding and bringing to consciousness that dimension of depth—that deep, inarticulate sense of self which necessarily precedes our ability to reason. In other words, it is the thickly constituted self, the self with goals, attributes, and attachments, with history and experiences, that gives the context which makes reason possible. Buried in that inchoate side of ourself is a sense of self, of values, and of what is of 'decisive importance'[56] to us. Reason is also about choice, but not the kind of which liberals speak. Reason is about striving to construct a self-consistent set of values and goals from amongst the chaotic universe of possibilities such a thickly constituted self presents.

The object of reason is therefore threefold: in the first place, it is to allow us to sift through our experiences, our knowledge of the world and our reactions to it. In the second place, it is

[56] C. Taylor, op. cit., p. 123.

a faculty which allows us to integrate that self-knowledge, to make it our own and to construct from it an articulated understanding of ourselves, of our deepest values. It does not merely 'report' what it finds; it is an active faculty which struggles to reconcile our deep moral sense and our conscious understandings of ourself and, in the process, transforms them both.[57] In the third place, reason is what permits us to adopt an open stance *vis-à-vis* our deep moral sense. By allowing us to reflect on ourselves, on who we truly are in our deepest sense of what is important, reason allows us to distance ourselves from our professed values, from our traditional understandings of who we are. Such understandings are by their nature partial because they are attempts to articulate our awareness of that which is often least accessible to us, and also because such understandings are attempts to extract from our deep self principles and rules to guide us in action. And such rules are, as Oakeshott suggests, only representations of the richer and more complex whole from which they are drawn.

Reason, then, is not a faculty which enables us to choose who we are in some radical and absolute sense. Through it we both discover who we in fact already are, and work to live our life in conformity with our best understanding of who we wish to be. It enables us to reflect on what we believe our values to be and to maintain an openness to the idea that our understandings might be mistaken, or that our deep moral sense has changed or evolved, as the notion of the permeability of the self implies it can.

Both utilitarianism and even Hayek's anti-rational de-ontological liberalism 'over-intellectualise' the process governing the formation of individual selves; far from being solely the product of conscious and 'rational' choice in which the

---

[57] Taylor (op. cit., pp. 123-4) puts the point masterfully: 'Our attempts to formulate what we hold important must, like descriptions, strive to be faithful to something. But what they strive to be faithful to is not an independent object with a fixed degree and manner of evidence, but rather a largely inarticulated sense of what is of decisive importance. An articulation of this "object" tends to make it something different from what it was before. And by the same token a new articulation doesn't leave its "object" evident or obscure to us in the same manner or degree as before. In the act of shaping it, it makes it accessible and/or inaccessible in new ways.'

self begins as an unencumbered pure subject of choice who proceeds calmly to decide which desires and values it shall have, we are also the product of many factors over which we have little or no control. What, then, of responsibility?

Responsibility for self here entails the realisation that our principles, our conscious values are (or ought to be) attempts to articulate to ourselves and others our own deep sense of what is right, a sense which is itself born in, and shaped at least in part by, our experiences. Values come from striving to bring about a coherent structure or pattern from experience and from our sense of self; from trying to discipline the many cross-cutting ties and commitments we have, the many experiences and diverse ideas to which we are subjected, into a whole which we may be said to have chosen responsibly. We are intellectually free to adopt uncritically popular or other ideas in this regard, but true responsibility for self lies in maintaining a stance of openness toward our own evolving sense of who we are.[58]

Our sense of self and our values, then, do not come to us uniquely from experience, which is but one raw material. They come also from responsible openness, from reasoning about who we are. Man does not simply choose who he will be, nor is who he is simply given (determined). Rather he has the *potential* to be autonomous, self-conscious, and responsible for himself, all attributes which I regard as important facets of a mature adult.

Recalling once again the example of the nun, the significance of this kind of reasoned choice can be made clearer. For there to be a unity between the person both before and after the choice to cease being a nun, there must be something binding them together which transcends this kind of constitutive tie, and it seems plausible to see this as something like the choosing agency posited by liberalism. But for this choice to be morally weighty and significant, it would have to be explained and justified and not merely arbitrary. Such an account might be framed in terms of a decision to live a life that was more in conformity with a growing self-understanding arising from exposure to new ideas. Similarly, it might arise from a

---

[58] Ibid., p. 126.

realisation that the original choice to become a nun had not been a reasoned and responsible one: perhaps it resulted from undue parental influence and was adopted uncritically. There might well be an internal conflict between a continuing desire to remain part of a community to which she feels deeply attached and a desire to be more autonomous and self-determining. Here the faculty of choice comes into play, but the choice itself can only be made with reference to other values, with reference to ties, commitments, and beliefs which have now assumed a different configuration through the exercise of reason.

Hayek's liberalism holds that each man is automatically and necessarily autonomous and responsible, and this leads logically to a defence of a market order in society: if man is free, autonomous and self-determining, then society should maximise each individual's opportunity to realise the largest number of his wants. If, on the other hand, our values are based primarily on our experiences and our self-awareness, mediated by reason, then it follows that the kind of society we have will itself influence the extent to which we are autonomous and responsible beings. Our relationships and our society will influence the values we hold because the self is permeable and therefore these influences become bound up with the self and are partly constitutive of it, making it an intersubjective and not a bounded entity. Here we return to Beiner's point: neither strain of liberalism is capable of formulating questions about the nature of the self, which is held to be unproblematical.

All this will, of course, seem quite unsatisfactory to someone whose primary concern is with certainty, and therefore with rules, principles, and guide-lines. As I have tried to argue, though, knowledge of what we ought to do and how we ought to act is neither a matter of certainty, nor is it susceptible to simple formulation in terms of universal and abstract rules or scientific truths.[59] Above all, it involves a kind of inner

---

[59] Hayek argues that the process of evolutionary competition is like that of scientific experimentation: one judges the results not by what one thinks desirable, but by the method used to arrive at the results. And since the development of morals and principles is not in any way different, one must be free to reject principles in which one has always believed when the operation of the abstract social order proves them not to be conducive to long-term social survival. The problem is that scientific facts

exploration which is different for each human being, and the kind of self-knowledge which results is notoriously prone to error.

There are two possible responses to this epistemological difficulty. One is to reject the position advanced here, in favour of one which admits of a far greater degree of certainty. I do not see, however, how such a position could offer a plausible view of the self or a sensible account of responsibility.

The other response would be to rethink the quest for certainty. In physics, a field where certainty was once thought to reign supreme, particle physics now requires the incorporation of an 'uncertainty principle'. Newtonian physics was ultimately superseded precisely because the degree of certainty it demanded could not accommodate the uncertainty of the empirical world. If the criterion of certainty proved too unrealistic for physics, can it really be supposed that it ought to apply fully to men? Rather than rejecting any view which offers us less than certain knowledge, the extent to which the search for certainty is necessary, or even helpful, must be questioned. As has already been argued, to have less than absolute certainty is not to be wrong: it is to admit that one *may* be wrong, and therefore human. In view of this, priority should be given, not to systems that produce only certain, but radically restricted knowledge, but to ways of detecting error in a wider range of knowledge which we can derive from many (admittedly potentially error-prone) sources[60].

Self-knowledge is not subject to the same kinds of verification as other, less esoteric sorts of knowledge, but it is not without any check whatsoever. The check, though, is just as uncertain and error-prone as the knowledge to which it refers: it is the self-knowledge or articulated self-awareness of others. This returns us to the consideration of a person's ability to account for his actions, or, put another way, to the social context of self-knowledge. Certain strains of Greek political philosophy are instructive here, for the Greeks clearly had a notion of the

---

can be 'true' or 'false' according to well-defined and plausible criteria. We *can* test them. Hayek offers us no such plausible criteria for testing the products of spontaneous processes. See my earlier comments in this regard in Chapter II.

[60] Evans, op. cit., p. 49.

self and of human nature, of a content to those concepts which man could seek to know, but which he did not choose.[61]

In this tradition, the highest human activity was to seek to know that human essence and to strive to live in conformity with it. They considered themselves rational or reasoning men, not because they could choose who they would be, but because they had a mind which allowed them to enquire into their own nature and to realise that nature by living in conformity with it. The ends of this activity were not deduced in advance from abstract principles because it was a speculative voyage of discovery: one cannot draw a map of a new land before having explored it. And if the thing to be explored is internal, then other men's explorations cannot be more than general guides to one's own. They cannot dictate in advance what one will find, but they do provide a background of accumulated experience and knowledge against which one can test one's own discoveries. Self-knowledge, then, can only be achieved in a social context in which each struggles to render intelligible to others what one has discovered. A being incapable of offering an account of his actions or of articulating his sense of self, cuts himself off from the best available check on error: the experience of other beings like himself.[62] In his *Utilitarianism*, John Stuart Mill expresses brilliantly the crucial epistemological function played by deliberation within a social context:

> [Man] is capable of rectifying his mistakes, by discussion and experience. Not by experience alone. There must be discussion to show how experience is to be interpreted. Wrong opinions and practices gradually yield to fact and argument; but facts and arguments, to produce any effect on the mind, must be brought before it. Very few facts are able to tell their own story, without comments to bring out their meaning... [63]

The social context of self-knowledge goes even deeper, however, for if the earlier arguments about the permeability of the self are recalled, it will be seen that the social context is not merely a check on error, but is partly constitutive of who

---

[61] H. Arendt, op. cit., Chapter 2 and p. 208.
[62] Ibid., p. 57.
[63] Quoted in John Gray, *Mill on Liberty*, p. 108.

we are.[64] This is where the full significance of our capacity for participant reactive relationships and attitudes comes through. We saw that the liberal self could not be touched at the core by relationships of this type because they could not be constitutive of that self, but only possessed by the self which remained aloof from them. A permeable self implies precisely that the boundaries of the subject or self are not fixed, but can be opened to the extent that one regards other people as subjects, not objects, and can therefore form constitutive, *intersubjective* projects and attachments with them. In this regard Sandel argues

... in so far as our constitutive self-understandings comprehend a wider subject than the individual alone ... to this extent they define a community in the constitutive sense. And what marks such a community is not merely a spirit of benevolence, or the prevalence of communitarian values, or even certain 'shared final ends' alone, but a common vocabulary of discourse and a background of implicit practices and understandings within which the opacity of the participants is reduced, if never finally dissolved.[65]

To realise our full potential as people, we must be capable of, open to, and engage in such intersubjective attachments while they, in turn, help to define who we are. Such relationships are partly constitutive of who we are, and to that extent our reflection on, and reasoning about, that part of our deeper self will entail the 'coming to self-awareness of an intersubjective being',[66] whose boundaries transcend those of the individuals it comprises. This underlines the importance of a social context for self-knowledge for, as Sandel argues, it is the intersubjectivity of certain types of relationship which lets us better understand those people with whom we form constitutive relationships. Without a certain minimum of shared language, practices, and self-understandings, such participant reactive relationships would be impossible, and

---

[64] On the difference between the 'sentimental' and the 'constitutive' notions of community in which '... on the constitutive conception, the good of the community [is] seen to penetrate the person more profoundly so as to describe not just his *feeling*, but a mode of self-understanding partly constitutive of his identity ...' see Michael Sandel, op. cit., pp. 160–1.

[65] Ibid., pp. 172–3.

[66] Ibid., p. 132.

other people could only be regarded as objects, not as subjects with whom one could engage in the full range of human relationships. This recalls the importance of a 'communication community', or the idea that shared language and therefore a minimum of shared meaning is indispensable to the fullest exploration and development of the self.

Let me emphasise again that it is not my intention to suggest that the self is wholly defined by its constitutive attachments, by its *de facto* membership or participation in intersubjective relationships. This would merely be a substitution of a radically situated self for a radically free one, and each of these denies the responsibility of the person. We *can* experience conflicts between senses of our self. The measure of a man is always taken when he is in a position where two values he feels equally deeply come into conflict. No automatic presumption can be made in favour of intersubjective or any other kind of attachments. We all hope that no incompatibility will arise between 'ultimate' values like, say, love of country and deep family obligations, but it is a fact of human existence that such conflicts do arise.[67] The only responsible way out is to look afresh at one's self-understandings and strive to find some new articulation of them which will transform the perception of the dilemma and of the self and which can itself be explained to others.

More will be said in the next chapter on the subject of conflicts of values, and especially on the adequacy of a conception of moral action as rule following for the resolution of these. The conclusion to be drawn from the present chapter must be that if the self is neither the pure (thin) choosing self nor the empirical (thick) self, it must be the unity of the two, in which the self chooses the kind of life it will lead and the values it will have, but against a background of ties and commitments (themselves not necessarily chosen) which give meaning and moral substance to those choices.

To sum up, the principal thrust of this chapter has been to show that if people are to be responsible for themselves and

---

[67] Thus, in 'Two Concepts of Liberty', p. 169, Isaiah Berlin suggests that 'the possibility of conflict—and of tragedy—can never wholly be eliminated from human life, either personal or social.' See also Taylor's discussion of the Sartrian portrayal of the dilemma of existential or radical choice, C. Taylor, op. cit., pp. 117-22.

if we are to consider them reasoning as well as rational beings, then the liberal self, and the social and political arrangements which flow from it, cannot be acceptable. Requiring as it does the virtual universalisation of objective attitudes, it reduces the potential for participant reactive relationships beneath a critical threshold, and yet the latter sort of relationships are part of the very concept of a person. Berlin sensed this when he wrote that modern liberals, '. . . do not allow for the variety of basic human needs'.[68]

Both Hayek and the Webbs, then, require us to conceive of ourselves in ways which conflict with our understandings of reason and responsibility, and therefore conflict with our deepest moral sense. Each of these views has an appropriate field of application, however, and problems only arise when they are improperly extended beyond this. This, of course, still leaves open the question of how we are to know when and where the liberal view of moral action as rule following *is* appropriate and, more importantly, what form an alternative conception would take to which we could appeal in cases where liberalism is clearly *not* appropriate. These are questions to which the next two chapters address themselves.

[68] I. Berlin, 'Two Concepts of Liberty', p. 162.

VII

PRISONERS AND ENTREPRENEURS;
TRADITIONS AND PRACTICES;
ECONOMICS AND EXPERTISE

> ... the man of maxims is the popular representative of
> the minds that are guided in their moral judgment solely
> by general rules, thinking that these will lead them to
> justice by a ready-made patent method, without the
> trouble of exerting patience, discrimination, im-
> partiality—without any care to assure themselves whether
> they have the insight that comes from a hardly earned
> estimate of temptation, or from a life vivid and intense
> enough to have created a wide fellow-feeling with all
> that is human.
>
> George Eliot, *The Mill on the Floss*

In the last chapter men were shown not simply to choose their
values, desires, and identity in isolation, but rather to discover
these things (among others) about themselves in a concrete
social context. If this is true, then it seems clear that a notion
of the good, as was hinted in the first chapter, must have
something more than a purely private, self-chosen meaning or
a scientifically demonstrable one. We discover an important
part of who we are and what we hold to be good by exploring
what it means to be the person we are in the context in which
we live. This has important implications for the liberal view
that the justification of political institutions reposes solely on a
notion of the right which is prior to the good. There are several
reasons for this.

The first reason is that such views hold that the rules of
justice are universal because they apply to a hypothetical
universal self not bound up with its desires and values. This
is used to justify political arrangements which are concerned
exclusively to apply the rules of universal justice to which any
such self would be forced to assent by virtue of its rationality.
But if we cannot plausibly separate a man from his values

and desires, because the rational faculty that would be left is not a whole self, then a theory of political obligation based on the just treatment of this part of the self alone is partial and incomplete.

The second reason why this is important is that since the question of what is good for me is no longer separable from the question of who I am, then the very notion of justice itself cannot escape the notion of the good. Moreover, since the question of who I am is not separable from the question of what place and roles I occupy, then my good must be relevant to the good for all the people within the communities which help to constitute who I am. A theory of justice which can take no account of what is good for me and what is good for everyone in my society is not a theory of justice for men at all, for it treats men as if they are something they are not.

It is open here to liberalism to make the following reply: all this misses the point, which is not, as Bentham argued, that 'pushpin is as good as poetry', but rather that for the formulation of public policy we ought to act *as if it is*. Whatever the nature of the self, there exist in our society conflicting views about morality and what 'normal' people are like. Given this conflict of views, surely it is preferable to have public institutions which do not favour one person's values over another's; in other words, political arrangements in which no individual's views of the good would *count* for more than anyone else's in deciding public policy.

In spite of a certain superficial plausibility, however, this sort of relativist defence of liberalism again falls back on a theory of the pure subjectivism of value judgments and asks 'Who is to decide which purely subjective values shall prevail?' But, as Sandel rightly argues,

[t]oleration and freedom and fairness are values too, and they can hardly be defended by the claim that no values can be defended. So it is a mistake to affirm liberal values by arguing that all values are merely subjective. The relativist defence of liberalism is no defence at all.[1]

This relativism cannot avoid moral evaluation because it can only be morally defended on the grounds that it furthers some

[1] M. J. Sandel, 'Morality and the Liberal Ideal', *New Republic*, (7 May 1984), p. 15.

good. Yet it is precisely this that it cannot do because it disclaims the tools necessary to mount such a defence.

Put another way, the problem is that while rational self-interest might explain why men would act as Hayek and the Webbs think they would within their rules of social behaviour, they cannot satisfactorily explain (within *their* framework) why men should prefer this set of rules to another. This question requires a moral discussion: it isn't enough to say that the rules maximise want/need satisfaction because this doesn't explain why *that* criterion is morally acceptable. This is not unlike Bentham's dilemma: he says that social rules should be such as to channel men's rational selfishness into actions which are to the general benefit, but why should men such as those agree to such rules? The problem is even more acute if men are not pure rational utility-maximisers, but value some things for themselves and not merely as means to greater want satisfaction.

Men obviously need to satisfy certain material needs and this must be a preoccupation of any society. What Hayek and the Webbs have done is to say 'Let us suppose that for all intents and purposes this is *all* that men want, and let us further suppose that men are such that they are prepared to act in whatever way is necessary in order to maximise the means available for the satisfaction of those needs'. What they have given us is their expert opinion on how to make these assumptions work. But this exercise, defensible in itself, must now be integrated into a larger framework to see where and to what extent it can be made compatible with a more realistic view of the self and society.

The problem that needs exploring is that by restricting rules of social behaviour to those appropriate to rational self-interested man, Hayek and the Webbs appear to require us to apply a calculating 'rationality' in contexts where such behaviour seems inappropriate to men with depth. Hayek and the Webbs believe that in cases of such conflict men ought simply to divest themselves of the attitudes which conflict with rationality (weak sense). If that move is not open to us, because these attitudes are constitutive of who we are, then what Hayek and the Webbs are in fact arguing for is a society where those wants and desires which cannot be accommodated within *their* institutional framework are to be treated as if they had no public significance. While we may have any desires we wish in private, the obligatory rules of social behaviour (the law) shall be blind to them. So while the moral defence of the liberal social order rests on its maximisation of the aggregate of personal development (satisfaction of wants), it in fact maximises the satisfaction of *certain* wants while ignoring others.

The notion that certain things may be valued in themselves and therefore cannot be accommodated within an institutional framework dictated by market rationality or a pseudo-scientific inventory of 'objective' human needs obviously requires further elaboration here. If men can denominate all their desires in terms of a common medium of exchange without having to act in a way inappropriate to their moral nature, then no problem arises. We need to look much more closely at precisely how these rules of social behaviour may cause such situations to arise, and the implications of such situations for moral action. Further, if market relationships and scientific objectivity *are* appropriate in some contexts, then some criterion needs to be found to demarcate the areas where they are from those where they are not.

I will proceed on two fronts. The first line of argument has to do with the kind of wants the market addresses. The second looks at the different but related problem of how the market may require choices between alternatives which men with depth may find morally incommensurable and therefore inappropriate objects of *market* calculation.

What we are really talking about is a form of market failure, a failure to provide certain kinds of desired 'goods'. Hayek deals with certain traditional forms of such market failure, such as pollution and the free-rider problem,[2] but he seems to have very little to say about the rather different but central form of market failure implied by the frequent failure of market *choices* to reflect the state of *preferences* of market actors.

Hayek defends market arrangements, in part at least, on the ground that within the constraints imposed by the market (i.e. the resources of which I dispose, which are the product

---

[2] See, for example, F. A. Hayek, *Constitution*, pp. 229, 341, and 349.

of how much anonymous others value my contribution to the market; and the various consummations on offer amongst which I may choose), I am free to make whatever choices I wish. Since these choices are my own, he implies, under the market I get more nearly exactly what I want than under any alternative scheme.

This obscures a very important distinction made by many economists[3] between what I *choose* under conditions of constraint and what I would *prefer* in ideal conditions. This choice/preference distinction shows that if everyone were obliged to act in accordance with market rationality, the outcome could well be a situation that none of the market actors want, in the very real sense that they would actively prefer another outcome.

Two examples can be invoked here. The classic 'gunman situation' illustrates the principle of the choice/preference dichotomy. Beattie describes the problem as follows:

> . . . to hand over one's wallet to a gunman is to choose pecuniary loss as more desirable than loss of life. It is, however, obvious that one cannot legitimately infer from the fact that *in this situation* most people hand over their wallets that they 'desire' or 'want' to hand them over. Their choice is constrained by the situation (i.e. the gun) and they may well wish (prefer) that this constraint did not exist: they would *prefer* to keep their wallets if this choice was available.[4]

So our choices are structured by circumstances and by rules such that (in this case) none of the alternatives which we are free to choose in any way expresses what we would regard as a desirable outcome. The rules act to close off certain alternatives no matter how desirable we might find them in themselves.

This particular example is not directly applicable to a discussion of market rationality, since it involves coercion of one man by another, something explicitly excluded under Hayek's rules. But a market situation can produce the same result. Consider the problem of the sale of guns in America. Under the current rules (i.e. virtual absence of any effective

---

[3] A. Beattie, 'The Character of English Constitutional Theory', Unpublished paper, 1979, pp. 25-6.
[4] Ibid., p. 25.

control on the sale of guns), it is impossible to prevent people from obtaining them and threatening me. As long as other people have guns, it is perfectly rational for me to buy one as a means of protection against them, assuming that the police and the courts are unlikely to deter them.

The result must be that (virtually) everyone buys guns, not because they wish to have guns as such, but because the unlimited (free market dictated) traffic in firearms does not leave them any choice. Virtually everyone might *prefer* that *no one* had a gun, but this is impossible under market rules since the only *choice* open is whether or not to buy a gun. Such an outcome would need some other mechanism for the translation of collective preferences into public policy. One possible solution would be to legislate (i.e. a political solution), but under Hayek's constitutional rules such a 'coercive' possibility is regarded as unjust unless the proposed rule has the approval of a legislative assembly conceived precisely so that its members would be insulated from such coercive opinions.[5] The good, being purely private, cannot be used as a justification of coercion by the state.

Here again we are confronted with the liberal argument that when conflict arises between our desires and what is possible under the rules of justice, it is open to us to rid ourselves of our 'inappropriate' wants. Men, of course, do live under such rules and do make such choices, but that does not mean that this is not a problem for them. Rather it drives home the importance of the choice/preference distinction. Under rules of this type, which they know they cannot hope to influence, people will accept those constraints because all the incentives are for them to act in this way. Because it usually pays to act according to the rules (if for no other reason than because failure to do so normally attracts penalties), it may well appear that people prefer the (in this case) market rules. But what people choose to do under institutional constraints may well not give us any clue as to what they would prefer to be able to do.

This leads to the topic of things to be valued in themselves. One of the assumptions of the liberal view is that *any* good I hold I can choose to give up, without loss to myself, i.e. I am unchanged as a person if I exchange one value for another: what really matters is to increase the aggregate of satisfactions available to me. On this view, it is perfectly reasonable to expect men to assign a value to everything they possess and to be prepared to exchange against it something of greater value (on the same scale of measurement, since all consummations are commensurables). Not to be prepared to 'price' and exchange such goods for socially compatible utilities (Hayek) or 'objective' needs (the Webbs) in this way is to fail to seek one's own fullest development and therefore to act irrationally.

To talk about things to be valued in themselves, things which ought not to be subject to this sort of weakly rational choice requires us to show why such goods are different in principle from goods which are an appropriate subject of such exchange, and we thus return to the demarcation problem.

The problem cannot be resolved by saying that there are certain things which cannot be priced on the market, nor by saying that they in fact have no price because they are not on the market. Taking the example of a spouse, one can say that their 'services' are not priced because their individual services are not on the market. This does not mean that the market value of the services cannot be determined by finding out what it would cost to replace the services offered by a spouse on the market. Companionship, performance of household duties, sex, and so on are all available on the market on an 'impersonal' basis, although obviously not the particular service provided by an individual.

Similarly, while we may feel that a da Vinci or a Michelangelo is 'priceless', it can be assigned a simulated market value which allows us to determine relative preferences. Insurance companies are faced constantly with precisely this dilemma: how does one assign a value to something (e.g. a Rembrandt) when it is not on the market? The answer is to assign it a nominal value for comparison purposes: how much would I take as compensation for it if I could no longer have it, or what would I be prepared to swap it for? In this way, even things which are not on the market can be assigned relative preferences which *simulate* the decision one is faced with in a market situation.

It would seem then, that some sort of market value can be assigned to virtually anything, and we know this intuitively from the sort of difficult moral choices we face constantly, in which we are forced to assign relative preferences to things we hold very dear. If I were a spy, and was captured by the enemy, I might well be forced to choose between betraying other agents (thereby ensuring their deaths and betraying my country), and my own life. Whichever alternative I chose, I would be pricing *someone's* death as relatively preferable to someone else's, and this is a simulated market transaction.

So under conditions of constraint (e.g. market conditions or rule by experts) people may behave in ways which can be predicted by the logic of those constraints, but this does not mean that they would prefer this if an alternative were open. To say that there are things which men would prefer to be able to value in themselves is not to say that these are things which in principle cannot be submitted to the dictates of market rationality or scientific analysis. They are not absolutes in themselves. What are they?

The best way to characterise them is comparatively. We have just seen that anything may, in principle, be made the object of a market transaction. Let us, following MacIntyre,[6] give an example which shall establish how we can regard two different types of good as incommensurable and therefore inappropriate objects of market transactions.

Consider the example of an author whose name is sufficient to guarantee substantial sales of any book he cares to write. He is perfectly free to see his books as merely a means to obtain money and thus not to be concerned, except instrumentally, with what he writes. But such rewards (money, fame, prestige, etc.) are not intrinsic to the production of a literary work: they are, in a very real sense, external to it because they can be obtained by anyone in any number of ways.

There are, however, other 'goods' involved in the writing of a book which are themselves intimately bound up with, or are internal to, that activity itself. In any literary tradition there are bound to be established standards against which particular books are judged in an attempt to assess their worth *as books*

---

[6] A. MacIntyre, *After Virtue* (London, 1981), pp. 174-7.

and not as e.g. money-spinners. While it is entirely possible to write books purely to make money, with no regard for the standards of what a good book is, success at this endeavour makes the writer a good businessman, and not necessarily a good author. To be the latter requires one to value the meeting of a standard intrinsic to the practice of his art, not because it will procure him some good external to it. The two are not commensurable, although they need not be incompatible.

In MacIntyre's own example[7] of teaching a child to play chess, he offers the child fifty pence for every game the latter plays with him and, guaranteeing that the standard of play will be demanding but not impossible for the child, he offers an additional fifty pence for every game the child wins. At first the child plays in order to get the money, i.e. for goods external to the practice of actually playing chess. At this point in his apprenticeship, all incentives are for the child to cheat, as long as he believes that he can do so successfully. He has no reason to value a well-played game of chess in itself. And yet, in such a situation, one hopes that the child will come to value the game for the pleasures peculiar to it, its analytical and strategic demands, the challenge it offers, and the imagination that it demands; the things that come to constitute

a new set of reasons, reasons now not just for winning on a particular occasion, but for trying to excel in whatever way the game of chess demands. Now if the child cheats, he or she will be defeating not [his or her teacher], but himself or herself.[8]

So a distinction is being made here between two types of good: those 'internal' to practices and those 'external' to them, and it is important for us to observe the different qualities intrinsic to each type of good.

External goods, goods like money, power, prestige, honour, and influence, have no necessary connection to any particular type of activity, although some activities may be more likely to produce these goods than others. There are more wealthy businessmen than there are wealthy artists; politicians tend to wield more influence than dustmen, and so on. Because these

[7] Ibid., p. 175.
[8] Ibid., p. 176.

external goods are in limited supply (either necessarily or contingently[9]), they are the objects of competition in a zero sum game. There must be winners and losers in the pursuit of external goods.

Internal goods are those which relate to a particular practice (e.g. chess playing or novel writing) both because they are explicable only in terms of the practice itself and because they 'can only be identified and recognised by the experience of participating in the practice in question. Those who lack the relevant experience are incompetent thereby as judges of internal goods.'[10] Internal goods are thus those which allow someone to excel *at the practice* because it is considered worth while to do so in its own right, and not solely as a means to goods external to it. It is important to notice that such internal goods are subject (as in the case of the author used above) to the discipline and control of the established standards of how one engages in the activity and what the end of the activity is. It is therefore teleological: excellence involves an idea of what a good performance is and assumes that this is a standard to which practitioners aspire. Internal goods may also be the object of a competition to excel, but all those who engage in the activity benefit by the achievement of excellence since this raises the standard of what it *means* to excel.

External goods may thus be understood and desired by everyone, regardless of their field of endeavour. Internal goods, however, requiring a knowledge of what constitutes *excellence* in a particular field, as well as a desire to strive for that excellence, presuppose that one wishes to respect that standard for itself. Otherwise, there is no reason not to cheat.

Internal goods (what is judged to constitute 'excelling' at a practice) are thus obviously neither wholly defined by the individual, nor wholly consumed by him. For me, as an individual, to seek to excel at novel writing or chess playing is to choose to allow my work to be judged against a standard which it is not in my sole power to modify, although I can 'acknowledge' an established standard by rebelling against it. Departures from these standards, however, are criticised by other practitioners with reference to the standards, and not

---

9 Ibid., p. 178.
10 Ibid., p. 176.

with reference to external goods: if I propose to move my bishop in a way not allowed under the rules, other players will criticise me, not on the grounds that I will lose money, or not win great honours, but because to move in this way is not to play chess.

Furthermore, it is clearly not necessary to break the formal rules of the game in order to be deemed not to be playing chess when judged against the established standards of what it means to play chess. If my earlier argument is right that the rules governing any activity are necessarily a *post facto* and partial articulation of what it means actually to engage in the activity, then it is entirely conceivable to move the pieces on a chessboard in accordance with the rules and still to play very bad chess. To play the game is thus to acknowledge two standards of play: what is permitted (defined by the rules); and what is good (defined by the chess-playing 'community').

Anyone can (with a little effort) determine with precision what the rules are without ever having played the game and without knowing any chess players because the rules are abstract and universal. But this ignores the fact that no *chess game* is ever abstract or universal: knowing what is allowed cannot guide me in knowing what is good in the particular and very contingent circumstances of a real game.

One more interesting feature of this situation should be noted: the standard of what a 'good' move is is not something that can be established unilaterally. Since chess is a common object of knowledge for all chess players (i.e. is a case of *plural knowledge*), standards of good play, if they are to have any meaning at all, must be acknowledged by all who play the game in search of goods internal to it. These goods are thus collectively defined and consumed. I may sit at a chess-board making legal moves, but not 'playing the game' if I so choose, but I cannot claim to be playing 'good' chess, as recognisable by all who pursue its internal goods. Similarly, someone who does set a new standard of excellence, within the parameters laid down by the history and tradition of the practice itself, sets a standard for *all*, and not just for himself.

Goods internal to practices thus depend, for their very existence, on the meaning that practitioners attach to them. One can imagine a world where all chess players cheated because all that mattered to them was to win some external good. In this world, chess playing or novel writing or painting, etc. would only be pursued with the purely instrumental intention of obtaining something else, and not for the pleasure which measuring oneself against a standard brings; there could be no reason for wishing to play chess for its own sake.

As a question of meaning, a description of internal goods is only partly reducible to a factual description of the rules of the game, since recognition of excellence is also a question of discrimination, of taste, of connoisseurship, of the fruits of an experience which can never be wholly distilled in rules. In short, it is an acquired talent or faculty which is developed by those intimately involved with the practice itself, whether as actor or critic, and this talent or faculty is rooted in its possessor's desire for excellence, although a desire for external goods as well is by no means excluded. But without this *internalised* desire to excel, there are no incentives for anyone to respect the standards or even obey the rules; these are simply obstacles to be overcome by any means possible (including dishonesty, subterfuge, etc.). For this reason MacIntyre argues that goods internal to practices depend on a quality internal to the practitioner, a quality he calls virtue: 'A virtue is an acquired human quality the possession and exercise of which tends to enable us to achieve those goods which are internal to practices and the lack of which effectively prevents us from achieving any such goods'.[11]

This sort of valuing of standards (whether obligatory rules or optional conventions) as a good in themselves is something for which Hayek has difficulty accounting, since following the rules is, for him, *itself* only a means to some other, external, good or end. Indeed, he assumes that men will always break the rules, or at least seek to frustrate their intent, whenever there is a good chance that the privately consumable rewards to be gained will outweigh the potential penalties for breaking or bending the rules.[12] Rule-making is thus a battle of wits between men who see no reason to do other than maximise their immediate personal welfare (including engaging in market-destroying practices such as monopoly and price-fixing), and lawmakers who are constantly striving to plug the holes in the law that permit such antisocial behaviour.

[11] Ibid., p. 178.
[12] See F. A. Hayek, *Constitution*, Chapter 4.

This notion of things to be valued in themselves, not as absolutes, but as inappropriate subjects for the calculations of market rationality, has important implications for the adequacy of any theory which sees justice merely as rule-following which does not engage the whole person. Put another way, if justice is a practice engaged in by thickly constituted men pursuing many goods, both internal and external to their social practices, then no evaluation of the justice of a particular action could be wholly reduced to the question of whether or not the rules had been obeyed by its author. If acting justly is a practice in this sense, then any judgment of the worth of an action will depend in large part on our assessment of how that action measured up against a standard of just action. Such a standard would have to be established by others who sought to act justly for its own sake, and not exclusively as a means to some other end.

Since the standard of just action *as a practice* will only be observed by those who value the goods internal to that practice, justice may appear to become merely a question of the meaning that different people attach to different actions. Since an internal good is clearly an ideal-regarding judgment, no one can be compelled to hold it, compulsion by definition destroying its ideal-regarding status.[13] A man can be compelled to observe a standard, but this converts it to an external good: he observes the standard in order to avoid the application of whatever sanction is threatened for non-compliance.

There is a famous article by the economist R. A. Radford, based on his personal experience of the economics of German prisoner of war camps, which illustrates both the principle involved and the importance of the difference between these two conceptions of justice.[14]

The essence of Radford's story is that, in his camp, vegetarian Sikhs were refusing to eat the meat ration distributed equally to all members of the camp. Conversely, the British prisoners preferred a higher proportion of meat in their diet and were happy to part with some of their jam and margarine in order to obtain it. An Urdu-speaking British soldier quickly saw the

[13] See the earlier discussion of want- vs. ideal-regarding wants in Chapter II, above.
[14] R. A. Radford, 'The Economic Organisation of a POW Camp', *Economica* (Nov. 1945), pp. 189-201.

trade possibilities implicit in the situation, which permitted a classic Pareto-optimal solution: an exchange could be arranged in which British jam and margarine would be swapped for Sikh meat rations, leaving everyone better off. The interest in this situation for the economist lay in the fact that the person who arranged the swap was in fact an entrepreneur: he demanded a 'cut' of every such transaction he arranged.

Interestingly, the author concluded that objections to this demand (on grounds of immorality) were merely based on a lack of appreciation of the principles of the market mechanism. This, however, is surely not the only conclusion which might be drawn.

One alternative might be that while an exchange so facilitated undoubtedly did increase the overall welfare of the POWs, it was improper of the 'entrepreneur' to make a profit from it. One might legitimately ask what sort of man, *in these circumstances*, would make it a condition of improving the overall welfare that he gains thereby?

Assuming that this inmate was the only one prepared to facilitate this exchange (itself a market assumption), is it so strange that his fellow prisoners regarded him as immoral? An analogous case might be where a spouse asked for a similar 'cut' in return for executing such a gain from trade. Might this not (appropriately) provoke a hostile response from the other partner?

This example may show that market transactions are most appropriate when 'profit' is necessary if trade is to take place. One supplementary interpretation, however, may be that in intimate altruistic relationships (in the case of both spouses and the POWs), one might legitimately expect such increases in overall welfare to be arranged without personal gain. This suggests the very Hayekian view that the appropriateness of market rationality and market relationships might be determined not by any notion of things to be valued in themselves, but in terms of simple scale.

Hayek's argument here refers back to the moral code of 'face-to-face' tribal society in which men can know one another, form small-scale intimate attachments and, perhaps most importantly, agree on concrete common goals and objectives. This face-to-face contact and shared goals created a powerful incentive, on Hayek's view, for men to subordinate their individual development to that of the group *and* at the same time stunted everyone's development by inefficiently using the dispersed knowledge available. The Great Society is an advance because, as we saw, its scale makes shared *concrete* goals virtually impossible. Where such concrete goals are absent, men are freed to observe the abstract and impersonal rules of justice and incidentally to pursue most efficiently the fulfilment of their nature as consumers of utilities.

For Hayek, the POW camp example would illustrate well the drawbacks of face-to-face society: the individual entrepreneur whose actions increased the overall welfare was subjected to pressure to provide his service solely for the benefit of the 'tribe', foregoing his potential personal gain. It was precisely this which prevented tribal man from developing both himself and his fellows: because membership in the group presupposed an agreement to distribute wealth on the basis of some morally arbitrary criterion like merit, no incentive existed for men to produce as much as they possibly could, and this left everyone worse off. If, say, it were a condition of co-operation in the meat and margarine swap scheme that no one should personally gain thereby and this resulted in no swap taking place, then Hayek might argue (with considerable justification) that everyone was made worse off by the application of this rule.

The moral superiority of the Great Society lies in its anonymity, the distance it requires all men to establish between themselves and others, which in turn allows men, in the pursuit of their own, private and arbitrary good(s), to provide goods to anonymous purchasers, guided in what to produce only by the impersonal price mechanism and not by any form of coercion.

There are thus, for Hayek, three possible organising principles open to men in their relations with others. The first, the intimate, small-scale, love relationship, has an extremely limited scope, and with good reason. Hayek recognises that *this* sort of relationship cannot, by its nature, be conducted on an impersonal basis and that, again by its nature, it requires men to reduce, if not eliminate, the 'distance' between them. Because in this kind of relationship what is good for me can frequently only be understood in terms of what is good for the relationship, for its sake I may be led to forego strictly private increases in utility. By confusing my awareness of my own boundaries, such relationships make virtually impossible the objectivity that I must display if I am to treat others justly.

Hayek is prepared to recognise that immediate family relationships constitute a special case,[15] but in general he argues that to subordinate one's private good (as indicated by the market) to the desires of known others is immoral. The immorality, we can recall, arose from the fact that failure to follow the market rational course was to fail to produce the maximum of utilities which the market indicates are desired by *unknown* others. While one may, in this way, gratify those one knows, overall everyone is made worse off.

The second possible organising principle recognised by Hayek is the coercive one, in which the distance between men, between what I want and what you want, between what I regard as good and what those around me regard as good, is again collapsed, this time by the application of sanctions which interfere with my liberty to pursue my self-chosen goods. This is immoral because it prevents me from pursuing my good, not because I have chosen to do so in response to market indicators, but because I am actively prevented from pursuing it by others. Since their good is just as arbitrary as mine, there can be no *moral* justification for this, and this violates my autonomy as a choosing agent.

The third possible organising principle is, of course, the anonymous Great Society, in which the distance or space between men becomes vast and unbridgeable. With the single exception of intimate family relationships, where rational man still has trouble sorting out his own private good from that of the others in the relationship, the *moral* advantage of the Great Society is that it progressively encourages men to establish a distance between their good and that of others.

Just as the market form of society, and the market rationality which underlies it, encourages men to distance themselves from their desires and attachments, reducing them to commensurables, so it must encourage them to see other men as anonymous objects who serve them by being prepared to produce whatever the market indicates men desire. By leaving men

---

[15] There are many references to this subject throughout Hayek's works. See in particular, *Constitution*, Chapter 5, section 8 and *Mirage*, p. 37.

free to choose to produce and consume what they 'want' (under the constraints noted earlier), men co-operate to meet each other's wants without having to agree that those wants are good or bad in themselves. It is essential for the proper functioning of the market and for just social relations that men see each other literally 'objectively', as objects to be anonymously used and by whom we are, in turn, used.

On this view, the only interpretations of the POW camp entrepreneur's actions are those already suggested: either that he was a perfectly moral and rational market actor who took his just reward for making everyone better off; or that he failed to allow the intimacy of the camp to collapse the distance between him, his view of where his good lay, and the views of his fellow inmates on their good. Hayek's suggestion here is that by knowing men as individuals, we are led by our 'inherited instincts' to forsake our private good, and the objective good of all men (known and unknown alike) in society. The only choices open to us are the autonomy of anonymity or the heteronomy of community.

Might one not, with some plausibility, see this as suggesting some other possibility? For instance, the POW example seems to suggest the existence of something one might call a common good, that is, a situation where everyone could be made better off, an outcome which everyone desired. Now Hayek seems to be arguing that such a concrete common good, as opposed to an abstract one, depends on the existence of a face-to-face society. Where the social scale is too grand and diverse, agreement on where the common good lies has to be reduced to questions of strict rule-following. I am free to do what I think good within a framework of rules which prevent me acting unjustly.

By regarding the POW case as an example of how scale alters our judgments of what is just, the camp entrepreneur's problem can be expressed in the question, 'In these small-scale circumstances is it proper for men to seek to profit from the promotion of the obvious common good?' In other words, the pursuit of a specific common good, as opposed to the following of rules blind to particular goods, is only possible where the scale of the 'collectivity' in question is so small that men known to each other can actually agree on this good. The Great Society, on the other hand, makes such agreement impossible, given the diversity and incommensurability of individual goods that it encompasses.

We have already seen, however, that men's wants are not so private and that real concrete men are in fact bound up with certain collectively defined goods; the good for individuals cannot be understood in isolation from them. Furthermore, the example of the unrestricted trade in guns in America suggests that it is by no means impossible to discover in a large-scale society at least a potential concrete common good whose realisation is prevented by the abstract rules of justice.

The rather different conclusion that could be drawn here, then, is suggested by the idea of goods internal and external to practices. Here the crucial variable is not scale, but the internal perspective of social actors and the meaning they attach to their actions. To return to the example of the chess players, we noted that those people who defined themselves as chess players, who were members of the chess-playing fraternity or community, could not accept that someone could set for himself a private standard of what a 'good' chess player was, since the goods internal to chess are no one person's property or possession. The members of such a community of meaning do not have a series of private and incommensurable standards of what a good player is, but rather they have a common standard established by long tradition and common effort, a tradition which each of them strives to interpret and put into practice.

To the extent that I belong to such communities of meaning, such communications communities, in which many social roles and practices are held to have goods internal to them, then what is good for me is intimately bound up with collective standards of what is good not only for me but for all who occupy those particular roles.

This recalls the earlier discussion about human depth. There cannot be a self that has no 'inside' other than pure rationality, and consequently any plausible political theory must concede that men are thickly constituted, and that the roles they play in a particular concrete society help to define who they are. This means that what is good for them cannot be purely private, subjective, and separate from society. What is good for me depends on who I am, and that will depend on the boundaries of the self. If I define myself as not merely a universal and abstract rational essence, but as e.g. a parent, a scholar, a trade unionist, a professional, a citizen, and so on, then my good will be intimately bound up with the goods that attach to each of these roles. Such goods are not defined privately by me, but by all those who share the community of meaning and the traditions that constitute a practice.

To have a shared notion of something, in this case a social role, is to have, implicitly at least, the possibility of agreement on what the good is for those who inhabit that role, within a shared framework of meaning and established practices.[16] For example, the existence of the word 'son' in our language must imply a certain shared meaning of this word between those who communicate with one another by using it. If there is communication, such words cannot be mere noise or scratches on a piece of paper. As was suggested in the chess example, however, each person who uses it *interprets* this shared meaning for himself. This need not mean that different interpretations must be incommensurable, as Hayek implies they are, nor entirely attributable to factual error, as the Webbs believe. Some linguistic philosophers have suggested that a shared notion of what a 'good' son is is implicit in the existence of the common word and this implies that shared notions of the good exist, at least in embryonic form, in any communication community. And such a community of shared language and concepts, such a community of meaning is surely one of the most fundamental making up who we are, since it is what permits us to form the other ties and commitments on which our identity depends.

By viewing the good as potentially a matter of agreed meaning between thickly constituted men within an established society and set of traditions, one can see an important difference between justice as behaviour in accordance with abstract and

---

[16] This is argued, for instance, by Ludwig Wittgenstein: Beiner (*Political Judgment*, p. 141) writes that '[i]n Wittgenstein's phrase, communication in language presupposes "agreement in judgments", no matter how attenuated or oblique the community of judgment concerned'. Beiner himself adds much to this concept of a communications community; see his own comments, ibid., Chapter 1, *passim*. Finally, see also Michael Taylor's stimulating book on *Community, Anarchy and Liberty* (Cambridge, 1982) in which he considers communication as an essential element of community.

universal rules and justice as adherence to shared standards of social action.

For Hayek, goods are individual and incommensurable between men, but commensurable within a single man's life. As there is no rational ground for preferring one good over another, rules cannot be justified on the basis that they promote some good: this will not compel the assent of the purely rational and bounded self. Weakly rational man will obey abstract rules simply because they are neutral with respect to all socially compatible utilities, including those of his own choosing. Any rule which attempted to enforce a universal concrete good would be unjust since there is no such good which will compel the assent of rational men. What is not demonstrably, universally, and non-contingently true cannot form a morally justifiable basis for a compulsory rule of social behaviour. On the other hand, rules precluding certain types of action are not coercive because they leave the self free to choose amongst the alternatives not so precluded, all of which are commensurable.

On this view of the law, obedience is reducible to the fear of legal sanctions. The law obliges men to act in certain ways that, in the absence of penalties, they would not consider in their interest because such actions would not maximise their personal utility. Note that this view holds that there is no reason for valuing the rules as such; rules are simply a means to an end and one reluctantly obeys them to avoid punishment. Rules are seen as a more or less onerous external constraint that one bears.

This view of rules, and especially the compulsory rules of social behaviour we call law, clearly does not take adequate account of another aspect of the relationship between men in a community of shared values and and standards (including rules of behaviour). It neglects what Hart has called the internal aspect of rules,[17] or the relationship that thickly constituted men have with their community's established standards of behaviour. The essence of this internal point of view can be summed up in one word: obligation.

To speak of obligation is to speak the language of positive morality, and so it must be carefully distinguished from the

---

[17] H. L. A. Hart, *The Concept of Law* (Oxford, 1961), Chapter 5.

simple notion of being obliged to do something. As we saw earlier in Beattie's example of the gunman, men can, in conditions of constraint, be obliged to act against their will, even though it could be said that the victim 'chooses' to give up his wallet. Hayek's 'negative' view of law sees it exclusively in these terms: law exists to set constraints, to force (oblige) men to act 'rationally'.

This is a fundamentally different case from that of our chess players, for whom standards of good play (consisting only partly in formal 'rules') are not regarded as an obstacle to the pursuit of goods internal to chess. I do not respect the standards because I am obliged to, but rather because, as someone who plays chess for its own sake, I recognise them as an obligation I have in my role as a chess player. I do not refrain from breaking the rules because I wish to avoid the penalties attached; I obey them because I recognise that they set a standard which I have an obligation to uphold. Seen from the internal perspective of a chess player (and not of a utility-maximiser), a failure on my part to obey the standards of chess playing is a *reason* for criticism and penalisation, not only by others, but by myself (via regret, remorse, etc.). In the gunman example, one is obliged to hand over one's wallet, but one could not properly be said to have an obligation to do so; whereas in chess I may recognise that I have an obligation to respect a certain standard of play, even if I am not obliged to by the compulsory rules.

Put another way, if I am to benefit from the *collective goods* internal to chess then I have a duty to respect the standards which define what it means to be a good chess player. Observe that my feeling of obligation or duty here is not necessarily reducible to an obligation I feel towards known others. If I play chess with a stranger on a train, in an impersonal tournament, or even against a computer, I am bound by the same sense of obligation which is a part of being a member of the chess-playing fraternity. I would feel just as justly criticised by any of these opponents for a failure to observe the standard as I would by my regular chess partner who is also my best friend. Appealing as they do to a standard by which I judge myself, they can legitimately make claims on me for compliance regardless of the personal relationship I enjoy with them.

What, then, of our POWs? Might one not plausibly interpret this situation an analogous way? Here we might have a case where the interned men felt that, in view of their circumstances, they had a duty to one another to do whatever they could to further the general welfare without profiting 'privately'. The moral disapproval of our entrepreneur would then result from his failure to recognise this obligation, even though he claimed all the benefits of the society of men in which he lived. This legitimately exposed him to the criticism and other social sanctions which accompany such deviations from standards. This is a classic conflict between goods internal to practices and those external to them. Our entrepreneur was not interested in pursuing the good of the camp, for its own sake, as embodied in the moral standard of how a *good* prisoner would conduct himself with his fellow inmates. He was prepared to do his part only on the condition that he could profit from it, i.e. that he could realise some privately consumable gain as a result of doing what the others felt he had an obligation to do anyway.

Hart suggests that these social obligations have four distinguishing characteristics.[18] First, whether or not we consider we have an obligation to follow a standard of behaviour, in the present sense, is determined by the seriousness of the social sanctions which back it. Rules requiring one to stand for the national anthem, for instance, or to take one's hat off in certain circumstances, do not necessarily carry an obligation for us to do so, because the behaviour prescribed by the rule is not considered of great importance for the life of society; failure to observe the rule carries no particular sanction.

This leads us to the second aspect of obligations, where we begin to gain real insight into the significance of the internal point of view of those who have obligations. Hart says that the rules which *are* supported by serious social pressure and sanctions (and hence constitute 'obligations') receive this support because 'they are believed to be necessary to the maintenance of social life or some highly prized feature of it'.[19]

To put this another way, obligations constitute a recognition that certain standards of behaviour may legitimately be

[18] Ibid., pp. 84-6.
[19] Ibid., p. 85.

claimed of society's members, and that this collectively consumed good may be recognised as a good even by those on
whom claims for compliance are made (since this is an essential
element of the internal viewpoint). Hart puts this third point
as follows:

> ... the conduct required by these rules may, while benefiting others,
> conflict with what the person who owes the duty may wish to do.
> Hence obligations and duties are thought of as characteristically in-
> volving sacrifice or renunciation, and the standing possibility of con-
> flict between obligation or duty and interest is ... among the truisms
> of both the lawyer and the moralist.[20]

Yet it is of the utmost importance to recognise the fourth
and final aspect of the function of rules and standards: I can
perfectly well say of person *A* that he '*has* an obligation to do
x', without *A feeling* in the least obliged to perform *x* at all. This
must be due to *A* and I differing on the rule or standard
of behaviour which is applicable to him in those particular
circumstances. Even where no sanction is attached to a failure
to do *x*, one could still talk about whether or not *A* had an
obligation to do it, and from this Hart (rightly) concludes that
statements about the existence of obligations are not predictions
that punishment will follow non-compliance, 'but to say that a
person's case falls under such a rule'.[21]

This suggests something important about standards of social
behaviour. I argued earlier that only those who pursue goods
internal to practices are competent to judge the achievements
of other practitioners, and I noted in another chapter that
explicit and formal rules are only an incomplete description of
the (logically prior) activity of actually engaging in any practice. From this it follows that the determination of whether or
not *A* has an obligation to do *x* in particular circumstances is a
question of reflective and not determinant judgment, a distinction discussed in Chapter I. This is true not only for those
*x*s which do not fall under an explicitly formulated rule of
behaviour, but also for those which do, precisely because
(especially on the margins) the rule is itself potentially an

[20] Loc. cit.
[21] Ibid., p. 86.

inadequate articulation of what can be expected of actors pursuing goods internal to the practice concerned, whether it be acting morally or novel writing or even chess playing.

For our POWs this suggests not only that what was at stake was a difference of judgment on the part of the entrepreneur and the other men regarding which rules of social conduct applied to his case, but also something deeper. The entrepreneur, in Hayekian terms, recognised only one possible standard of just and moral behaviour: the kind of distant objectivism and lack of identification with the concrete men with which he shared the camp. By adopting this attitude, he transformed the question of his obligations into one of determinant judgment, because the universal under which his case fell was simply given.

This suggests (*pace* Radford) that the entrepreneur was criticised for a failure to discriminate and assign his particular situation to the universal which the other inmates felt embodied the standards of their community. By being seen to prize his individual welfare over that of the community of which he was a part, the others may well have felt used as objects by him and reacted against his failure to recognise that the correct standard of assessment of his actions could vary with his circumstances. By his inability or unwillingness to step back from his standard of judgment to see if it was appropriate, he showed himself to be morally 'shallow', untouched by the ties which bound him to the other inmates.

On this view, by assuming the self to be radically individuated, Hayek makes men alone the objects of a cool objective judgment, whereas holding men to be constituted at least in part by their ties and attachments means that it is also their standards of judgment which need to be held constantly at a distance. Only in this way can the meaning of such standards be interpreted in accordance with circumstances which, while contingent, may still be relevant to determinant judgments.

What about the question of scale? There is nothing about this stance of responsible assessment of the appropriateness of our standards of judgment, the universals under which we try to subsume particular cases that *necessarily* depends on a face-to-face relationship with others, although this may have played a role in the POW case. We saw, in the case of the chess players, that it is perfectly reasonable to see the standards internal to practices as relevant to relations with unknown others. Standards apply when one recognises that one has an obligation to observe them, when one judges that they are the universal applicable to a particular, and the fact that known others are involved is clearly a contingent consideration here. Although situations involving known others may frequently involve quite constraining or demanding standards of behaviour, this is not the only kind of situation in which such standards can be invoked.

The following of rules by people pursuing goods internal to practices is thus largely a question of the rules being seen as fallible guides in the pursuit of a good common to all engaging in such practices, but such rules must be supplemented by three things. First, a desire to pursue the internal good for its own sake, a good common to all engaged in the activity. Second, the acquisition of those virtues or moral qualities which make it possible for one to pursue internal goods for their own sake. Thirdly, the development of a faculty of judgment, based on each practitioner's experience of pursuing this particular good. But while the experience itself may be private, since experience can only be had by doing, it has a common object, and therefore certain shared structural constraints which give a common reference point for *all* practitioners. This common reference point, coupled with the desire to pursue internal goods (with the virtue that implies), is the basis of the conception of *politics* discussed in Chapter I. This conception is based on a tradition dating back to Aristotle, the central feature of which is

... the notion of a public good which is prior to and characterisable independently of the summing of individual desires and interests. Virtue in the individual is nothing more or less than allowing the public good to provide the standard for individual behaviour. The virtues are those dispositions which uphold that overriding allegiance.[22]

Unlike liberalism, however, this view of politics requires as a *sine qua non* of its existence that men who live together in a political society have the proper internal perspective on their

[22] A. MacIntyre, op. cit., p. 220.

relations with other members of the community, that they desire to judge their own good from the perspective of the common good, that they feel an obligation to respect the standards of just behaviour embodied in the optional and obligatory standards of social behaviour. Liberalism is not concerned to cultivate such an internal perspective because it seeks a justification of political obligation in the universal nature of rational man.

For liberalism, law is a way of forcing utility-maximisers to act in socially acceptable ways. While law prevents them from doing what they really want to do, men obey because they fear the penalties for non-compliance. They are *obliged* to respect the law because if they could be truly objective (purely rational thin selves), they would find the universal guiding their judgments of just action given, and they would be compelled by their rationality to accept this universal. Whether real, thickly constituted men would in fact feel an *obligation* to respect the law is held to centre on a mere matter of error-prone and subjective opinion, and is, therefore, irrelevant.

In political society, however, the law attempts to articulate and embody what any reasonable and intelligent man would prescribe to himself as a rule of just conduct *in that particular society* within the parameters of its common good. If this is the function of law and is recognised as such from the internal perspective of citizens pursuing the common good for its own sake, then citizens feel an obligation to obey the law as a guide to what good citizens would want to do. It is a standard against which men judge *themselves* in their role as citizen, and also against which their fellow citizens will judge and criticise them. He who shares and accepts the internal viewpoint, moreover, recognises non-compliance as a valid reason for others to judge and condemn him.

The making of law is thus the tentative attempt to enunciate those aspects of social behaviour that are judged so necessary to the maintenance of the common good that they are made compulsory, with the importance of different sorts of behaviour prescribed by the law being indicated by the relative severity of the penalties attached. For this reason, Hayek, for instance, seems incapable of offering an account of certain features of the law, not only with regard to juries, but in other ways as well. He does not see law as a system of politically arrived at rules: he assumes that rules with coercive sanctions are total prohibitions which exclude experimentation, but this is clearly simply false as a description of any actual legal system. This comes through very clearly in the *Constitution*, where he argues that voluntarily observed rules are superior because they make

... gradual evolution and spontaneous growth possible, which allows further experience to lead to modifications and improvements. Such an evolution is possible only with rules which are neither coercive nor deliberately imposed—rules which, though observing them is regarded as merit and though they will be observed by the majority, can be broken by individuals who feel that they have strong enough reasons to brave the censure of their fellows. Unlike any deliberately imposed coercive rules, which can be changed only discontinuously and for all at the same time, rules of this kind allow for gradual and experimental change.[23]

But there is a multitude of possibilities between total permissiveness and complete control. Laws may in fact be about changing the rational calculations of individuals in order to make them take more account of the indirect effects of their actions without actually prohibiting them. In practice, one is still left with the choice of whether or not to obey, but one knows in advance what the *costs* of non-observance will be.

Only in this way, I think, can we make sense of something as familiar as laws which prescribe no penalties for violators. Such laws may be understood as an attempt to indicate certain desirable sorts of behaviour, without them being judged so crucial to the maintenance of the common good that non-conformists need be penalised. Similarly, as opinion changes, so too does the effect of the law: two obvious examples being the laws relating to drug abuse and, as the recent Ponting trial suggested in this country, laws respecting government secrecy. As social mores evolve, the enforcement of certain laws becomes more difficult. Thus a legal system without Hayekian rigidity allows for adjustments within a framework of rules that carry coercive sanctions. In this sense, for those with the internal perspective of a citizen towards the law, laws become guidelines which themselves grow and change without the necessity of legislative reform; they are often not absolute prohibitions.

---

[23] *Constitution*, p. 63.

On this view it is not possible to separate the validity of law from the particular and contingent circumstances of the society whose values it is intended to embody. Its validity depends not on whether or not it would compel the assent of the thin liberal self. It depends instead on whether or not, in the considered judgment of people who have tried to live in accordance with the virtues that make possible the pursuit of the common good, the law is a reasonable summing up of the just rules of social relations.

But why should men agree to live in this way and how does this give rise to a sense of political obligation on the part of those who do not share the internal perspective on social rules? One difficulty with this notion is that it seems to be based on no clear and demonstrable criteria of justice or the right. How are rules formulated in this way to avoid declining into mere subjective definitional fiats which men who do not share them will none the less be required to respect? Liberals will rightly ask on what basis one distinguishes those standards of social behaviour which are to be made compulsory from those which remain optional, and how individuals are to be expected to *recognise* something as nebulous as the common good, let alone know how to judge when one standard of behaviour is appropriate in a particular circumstance and when another. Liberalism has the great virtue here of offering reasonably comprehensible principles for at least recognising unjust acts and makes a not unreasonable claim to a kind of objectivity which allows us to make law in accordance with criteria which require no agreement on the good. In the face of the deep divisions within our society about where the 'good' lies, these are claims not to be dismissed lightly.

I simply want to argue that, while liberalism does propose a workable set of criteria for judging the justice of particular social relations, these criteria are morally inferior to those made possible by political society. Just as political society requires men to attach a particular kind of meaning to their actions and relations with others, so does liberalism. But this latter kind of meaning cannot accommodate our sense of ourselves as beings with moral depth, and so requires us to renounce the stance of responsible openness which is necessary if any 'choice' of the values which guide our lives is to be morally weighty. Only political society makes possible this kind of openness.

This, in itself, does not meet the objection that nothing recognisable as a clear criterion of justice has yet been offered as an alternative to liberalism. Both the idea of a common good and that of standards of behaviour seem to depend on a retreat from the objectivity which any plausible theory of justice and political obligation must possess. In political society how can I *know* what standards are expected of me, how can I be certain that I am treated justly when compared to the treatment accorded other men? At least under liberalism, all men are treated alike, and no theory of justice can be adequate which does not treat similar men in a similar manner. There seem to be no clear criteria in political society for the determination of these matters.

One possible response to these objections takes us back to Chapter I, where it was observed that a common notion of justice was held by Aristotle to be one of two indispensable conditions of a political society. There it was noted that this was a desert-based notion of justice: it *requires* a notion of the good to operate because it requires some sort of agreement on what men deserve, and hence some criterion for separating deserving claims to just treatment from undeserving ones.

Hayek rejects this because he sees the right as prior to the good, and sees justice as merely a set of rules for authoritatively determining a whole set of just actions, without prescribing which particular just act *ought* to be performed. He assumes, largely without argument,[24] the impossibility of an agreed notion of the common good and from this concludes that the best society is the one where each person enjoys the maximum freedom to pursue his private and subjectively defined good.

The Webbs, on the other hand, believe that the common good is not a matter of argument, but of fact, of objective truth which compels the assent of rational men. Justice for them requires only that men get what they need and this can be

---

[24] Hayek seems to assume that the relative ignorance of men simply by itself precludes their agreement on anything like values: because we don't all know the same things or even have the same objects of knowledge, we simply have different values and that is the end of the matter. See e.g. *Mirage*, Chapter 7 'General Welfare and Particular Purposes', pp. 1–30.

determined without reference to the subjective opinions of ordinary people.

It is thus to a consideration of the nature of objectivity and justice in political society that I now turn, for until the objections regarding its apparent lack of objectivity, both in its judgment of the common good and the justice of social relations, is met, the arguments regarding its moral superiority will appear fatally weak.

VIII

HISTORY AND THE SOCIAL SCIENCES: EXPLAINING AND UNDERSTANDING HUMAN ACTIONS

> Knowing yourself means knowing, first, what it is to be a man; secondly knowing what it is to be the kind of man *you* are and nobody else is. Knowing yourself means knowing what you can do; and since nobody knows what he can do until he tries, the only clue to what man can do is what man has done. The value of history, then, is that it teaches us what man has done and thus what man is.
>
> R. G. Collingwood, *The Idea of History*

In the last few chapters I have attempted to undermine the radically individuated notion of the self which underlies both the utilitarian and deontological theories of justice and political obligation, arguing that the moral status of wants and needs can only be properly understood in a concrete social context, not in some abstract world of 'universal men'.

By assuming men to be impermeable bounded selves, with no insides other than a rational faculty permitting arbitrary choice, liberalism in the Hayekian tradition dismisses any sort of substantive notion of the common or public good as illusory. The common good is understood purely in terms of an abstract and impersonal set of rules, the following of which will maximise personal utility. Following these rules is rational because they represent an accretion of knowledge and experience and therefore surpass our mind's limited analytic and synthetic abilities. The 'common good' will thus be unconsciously achieved by applying the rules absolutely, without fear or favour, in every context, because whatever outcome these rules produce is *defined* as just. If we knew enough we would see why these rules promote our welfare; it is our ignorance of the world that makes the following of such rules rational.

Similarly, the Webbs' utilitarianism assumes men's insides to be limited to a rational faculty which, in principle, would compel them to acquiesce in the 'objective' determination of the common good by experts *if* men had sufficient knowledge to understand that good (it is the absence of this knowledge that makes rule by experts necessary and rational). They thus deny the relevance of subjective opinion to the determination of the common good, which is a question, not of moral evaluation, but of scientific fact.

Undermining the foundations of these denials, however, does not do away with the problem of what precisely the common good is or, put another way, of how competing notions of the good might be reconciled. The discussion in the last chapter suggested that this might be possible, but did not consider how it might be done.

The great strength of both strands of liberalism is that they attempt to find a universal and rational basis for a theory of justice which takes no account of any subjective notion of the good. This has the clear advantage of drawing our attention to the fact that if primary rules (in the Hartian sense of behaviour-constraining rules[1]) are to have validity in a particular society they must be in some sense objective, that is, they must seek to be seen as just by all called to abide by them.

The liberal approach says that such rules can be discovered or articulated by man's abstract rational faculty utterly removed from personal experience (or by speculating on what he would discover if he was capable of this). In the last few chapters this was several times likened to the search for scientific knowledge and the very specific kind of objectivity that that entails. It is instructive to consider for a moment this view of liberalism-as-science for the clues it offers to an understanding of this theory of political obligation and justice.

What many political theorists (and not just liberals) have sought, at least since the Enlightenment (and arguably since Plato[2]) is some rational ground for making *law-like*

---

[1] For a discussion of the concept of law as a combination of primary (behaviour constraining) and secondary (power conferring) rules, see H. L. A. Hart, *Concept*, Chapter 5 'Law As the Union of Primary and Secondary Rules'.

[2] A. MacIntyre, *After Virtue*, Chapter 8 'The Character of Generalisations in Social

generalisations about human beings which would produce a
science of man. This science, by recognising the essence of all
human beings, would disregard what distinguishes individuals
and permit the discovery of social and political arrangements
which would guarantee the just, i.e. equal and objective,
treatment of men, such equal treatment being morally justified
by the realisation of man's essential sameness. Further, such
a view, by concentrating on what men have in common, sees
them as units of unalterable and irreducible essence.

In the social and political fields the task of such theories is
to discover how to harness and control this essence in order
to achieve desirable ends. 'Desirable' here means in conformity
with what is necessary to permit the fullest possible development of that essence and this follows directly from a
proper understanding of its objective nature. The assumption
is that these human 'atoms' will react to stimuli in predictable
and constant ways. Once one settles on what they ought to
be doing, one has only to set up the institutional constraints
that will elicit that response. Failure to elicit the desired
response is seen either as a failure correctly to characterise the
essence or else as a failure to match the essence to the right
set of constraints.

On this view, an individual is seen not as John Smith, a
particular man in a particular society, but as an instance of
a universal man in his capacity either as rational chooser or
as uniform atom.[3]

There are several problems with this 'scientific' approach
(i.e. one that seeks to reduce all phenomena to their irreducible
basic units, removing all contingent considerations and aiming
at universal, non-contingent knowledge issuing in law-like
generalisations about the properties and behaviour of the
phenomenon under study). The first involves the subject-matter
(man) and the second involves the framework of analysis
(scientific method).

Unlike most other subjects of scientific investigation (animals
are a possible exception), men are not inanimate objects

Science and Their Lack of Predictive Power', pp. 84-102. See also the discussion
regarding generalisation in history, below.

   [3] See e.g. T. D. Weldon, *States and Morals* (London, 1946), p. 248, and Hayek,
Constitution, p. 161.

reacting unconsciously but predictably to the implacable forces of nature. Men are self-aware and have a perspective on what is happening to them—they attach meaning to their world and to events, a meaning which is not reducible to an empirical description of the world or events themselves.[4]

One of the key claims by both Hayek and the Webbs has been that it is possible to understand men and, more importantly, to be objective about them, only by stripping away their 'interpretations and experiences of the world', by emptying men's 'insides' so that that they become the same in principle as any other object of science. The flaw in this universal and aggregative approach to human behaviour is precisely that it forgets that the behaviour of the physical world and the actions of human beings are two quite distinct things. This is so, as has already been suggested, because human beings are agents, capable of action and guided by private motivations. When one observes phenomena in the physical world, one observes inanimate objects reacting to impersonal forces. When one observes such a phenomenon from the 'outside', one sees all there is to see.

What has characterised the self described in the last few chapters, though, is not its similarity to all others, but its uniqueness, which is due to its individual perspective on the world and its particular bundle of ties, attachments, and values. Rules of justice which derive their force from treating different men in exactly the same way are thus unjust because they take no account of who men are. Treating one man in his particular circumstances in a particular way may be just, but treating other particular men in other situations according to the same rules may equally be unjust, as was suggested, for instance, by the case of the POW camp.

Liberalism claims its rules are just precisely because they take no account of who we are and treat us objectively as uniform universal selves. From this perspective, the problem of politics is how to imagine an institutional structure in which men can be treated as whole selves, recognising their different wants and goods. If society recognises such contingent factors

---

[4] For a very interesting discussion of this role of meaning in human experience, see B. Parekh, *Hannah Arendt and the Search for a New Political Philosophy* (London, 1981), p. 11.

as relevant to the search for justice, how do we avoid sinking into mere arbitrariness? Surely any notion of *justice* in social relations must repose on a notion of similar treatment being applied to similar men, and surely the only way to treat *all* men objectively and hence justly is to treat them all as if they were alike, even if in reality they are not.

This concern with objectivity is certainly correct, but misleading because it is based on an inappropriate criterion of objectivity. In this we need to recall again the difference noted in Chapter I between determinant and reflective judgment.

Determinant judgment, being supplied with its universal, requires only the objectivity of the mathematician or the logician who knows that the solution to any problem in his field lies in knowing how to apply the given rules. That cases are similar (thereby attracting the application of the same rule) is known simply by correctly describing their given factual nature. There can be only one right answer, which is determined by the nature of the case, and objectivity therefore resides in the nature of the object being investigated. A wrong understanding of the facts will produce a wrong answer and that answer will be demonstrably wrong for anyone who knows how to apply the rules.

Reflective judgment, however, is the sort where the rule of interpretation itself is not implicit in the problem under examination, but is rather a question of the meaning that the judging subject attaches to the problem; that meaning will determine the rule he judges appropriate to guide him in resolving it. If meaning is purely subjective and private, without any means of resolving differences of interpretation between men, then no objectivity is possible, since different answers are simply different and incommensurable.

Liberal justice is objective in the first sense and is therefore bound to see men as universal and undifferentiated, but this is exactly what men are not. Justice means giving men their due, but if each person is unique, then the universal which makes rule-bound (determinant) justice possible is not given and it follows that justice is a matter of reflective and not determinant judging.

For each case in which men seek to act justly, the appropriate universal guiding their action must be posited by them. This means that justice requires not so much the mechanical application of a given rule (as seemed to be the approach of our POW entrepreneur), but the development of the faculty that permits one to judge, not merely what rule or set of rules will necessarily always produce just results in any circumstances, but rather to find which, amongst a number of potentially universalisable rules, is the one appropriate to apply in this particular situation. Put the other way around, what is sought is not a single universal standard of the right, applicable everywhere by all rational men. Rather it is a talent, ability, or virtue which allows one to recognise the standard of behaviour applicable to each situation, a standard which all men who pursued their particular good within the larger context of the common good of their community would prescribe to themselves in that circumstance.

While this points up the difficulty of trying to reduce justice to the following of abstract and universal rules when men and the circumstances in which they act are individual and particular, it obviously creates a whole new set of very difficult problems. On what criteria can one judge what is a just standard of action for one man in one particular circumstance in the absence of a notion of what is a just standard for all men? If the meaning men attach to the good is purely private and subjective, then how can any notion of justice which bases itself on reflective judgment make a plausible claim to some other kind of objectivity?

The reply comes in two parts. The first deals with the nature of objectivity itself, and the second looks again at the irreconcilability of private wants. Let me begin the discussion of objectivity by looking at its use, not in the study of science, but of history.

As Collingwood rightly observes, in *The Idea of History*, where human action is being observed, one must distinguish carefully between the outside of the phenomenon, the prevailing conditions, the forces present, the action actually taken, on the one hand, and its inside, the process of decision and choice by the agent or agents on the other. This is what sets apart, for instance, history and science: science need only concern itself with what is universal, with what all phenomena of a certain type have in common; the historian must offer us a coherent, sensible vision of what makes each historical event unique.

It is, of course, impossible to resolve definitively the question of whether or not the way any individual acts in any given set of circumstances is determined by genetics, or objective social class, or some other factor or factors. Both Popper[5] and MacIntyre[6] argue convincingly, though, that the future is by its nature unpredictable, not least because the conditions in which any human action takes place are too complex, shifting, and beyond human influence to be exactly reproducible, even in very similar circumstances.

This comparison of science and history can help to make clear how scientific objectivity which focuses on the outsides of its object cannot be sufficient in itself to help us understand the actions of men, who have depth or insides which are crucial to such an understanding. In the course of this comparison we shall also see that both the scientist and the historian *must* exhibit certain kinds of bias (depart from 'pure' objectivity) if they are to perform their respective tasks, and that this 'bias' is not only necessary, but desirable.

The most important similarity between science and history is one of method. To begin an inquiry in either discipline one must have a specific question to answer. One cannot merely sift aimlessly through the infinite data of the past or of the physical world, or one becomes neither a scientist nor an historian, but a simple archivist of facts unrelated to each other.[7] A choice must be made as to what the inquirer thinks is important and what is not, and this presupposes a *theory* which cannot be simply reduced to the facts. To this, trivial, extent neither the scientist nor the historian is 'purely' objective in what he does, since he must think something important if he is to find it worth investigating.

Once the question to be answered is selected, both the scientist and the historian must establish a point of view,

[5] Popper, *The Open Society*, Vol. II, Chapter 25.

[6] MacIntyre, op. cit., Chapter 8.

[7] 'The attempt at a universal history is foredoomed to failure. All history must be the history of something particular...'. R. G. Collingwood, *The Philosophy of History* (London, 1930), p. 15.

which might also be called a working hypothesis, which they think explains the problem at hand and offers them a framework within which data can be chosen, organised, and assimilated. Popper calls it a '... provisional assumption whose function is to help us to select, and to order, the facts'.[8]

The establishment of a working hypothesis, however, marks the point where science and history part company in their search for knowledge, and each follows a different path. This is true for two reasons.

First, science and history seek two different objects, which might be termed general and specific knowledge respectively. Simply put, science is only interested in any specific event in the world in so far as it illustrates some general law of universal applicability under specified conditions. History, by contrast, is only interested in general laws in so far as they can help to illuminate specific past events. To use the jargon of the profession, science is nomothetic while history is idiographic.

This can be well illustrated by an example.[9] We know that scientists, through the study of atomic chemistry and the properties of the elements, were able to predict not only the existence of certain elements before their discovery, but were able accurately to predict the precise properties which those elements would exhibit. This they could do thanks to knowledge gained through the study of all known elements and deducing from their behaviour the behaviour of certain hypothetical ones. Just as the fact that a hydrogen atom differs from a helium atom is sometimes important to know, it remains true that the difference is only important in terms of the universal and non-contingent truths we know about the laws governing the behaviour of atoms in general, of which the behaviour of helium atoms is but a specific case. It differs from that of the hydrogen atom in predictable ways because they are different instantiations of a universal and necessary truth and their differences are reducible to and explicable in terms of that truth.

The task of the historian, on the other hand, is never to determine how a certain type of man, whose existence is

---

[8] Popper, op. cit., p. 260.
[9] With apologies to Professor Collingwood, whose own examples inspired that one offered here. See his *Philosophy*, p. 10.

problematic, would act in certain hypothetical circumstances. Rather it is to determine how one man or group of men in particular did act in real and concrete circumstances. To think (to choose an example from modern British political history) of Keir Hardie as any man who was instrumental in the founding of the Labour Representation Committee is, as Collingwood suggests, 'absurd'.[10]

This leads to a consideration of the second reason why history and science diverge. Here we are dealing with the question of the 'testability' or 'verifiability' of scientific as opposed to historical hypotheses. The scientist's raw material differs greatly from that of the historian: the scientist deals directly with his subject and observes the phenomena in which he is interested at first hand, often in strictly controlled conditions. The historian, on the contrary, can never deal at first hand with the object of his interest since that object is past events which by definition no longer exist. The historian must study the past at one remove, through the examination of empirical evidence which is representative of the past but which exists in the present.

A scientific hypothesis, then, can be verified through testing and its operation observed at first hand, while an historical hypothesis cannot be validated in principle because it cannot be falsified. It is important in this context to bear in mind that, as many philosophers of science have emphasised, the simple statement that a theory explains all the known facts does not of itself constitute a proof of its validity. 'Only if we can look out for counter-examples can we test a theory.'[11] The historian's data being limited, and the direct object of his interest (the past) in principle irreproducible, then an historical theory which explains all the known facts may be a useful interpretative tool, but it cannot be said to be verified or corroborated in the sense that a scientific theory may be.[12]

A scientific theory which has withstood many efforts to disprove its validity may thus rightly be elevated to the status

[10] Ibid., p. 10.

[11] Popper, op. cit., p. 267.

[12] 'Of nearly every theory it may be said that it agrees with many facts: this is one of the reasons why a theory can be said to be corroborated only if we are unable to find refuting facts, rather than if we are able to find supporting facts...' K. Popper, *The Poverty of Historicism* (London, 1957), p. 111 n.

of a natural law.[13] By definition it is applicable where the necessary initial conditions[14] obtain, but,

... the fact that all laws of nature are hypotheses must not distract our attention from the fact that not all hypotheses are laws and that more especially historical hypotheses are, as a rule, not universal but singular statements about one individual event, or a number of such events.[15]

This means that one particular kind of 'objectivity', which we associate with the scientist, is by its nature *anti-historical*, because it is based on the belief that science and history must travel the same route to knowledge. This failure to distinguish between the provinces of scientific and historical method is called scientism by some and historicism by others. Whatever its name, its fundamental error is to assign to historical theories the force of natural laws, holding them to be valid in all societies at all times. Collingwood pertinently observes that 'Any idea of this kind is open to the fatal objection that it encourages the historian to plug the holes in his knowledge with something that is not history because it has not been extracted from his sources.'[16]

To engage in historicism, then, is to be misled by the initial similarity between science and history in that practitioners of both must choose a viewpoint, formulate an hypothesis, and use that framework to collect and order facts. Mistaking their theory for a natural law, such historians see its validity constantly reaffirmed because it agrees with their data, which have themselves been selected in function of the theory. Such theories may well have powerful analytical and explanatory value in the study of history,[17] but history cannot be put to the Baconian test as nature can and so it must always remain an interpretation of events whose validity cannot be measured by exactly the same criteria as scientific knowledge. It is a case of reflective and not determinant judgment.

[13] This in no way changes its logically prior status as an hypothesis. This is so since it may, in principle, be disproved at any time. A law is also at all times a provisional hypothesis and not an absolute. See Popper, *Society*, p. 260.

[14] For a discussion of the concept of initial conditions, see Popper, *Historicism*, pp. 122–7.

[15] Ibid., p. 107.

[16] Collingwood, op. cit., p. 8.

[17] See Popper, *Historicism*, p. 151.

The other kind of 'bias', or departure from pure objectivity with which we are concerned may perhaps best be characterised as 'imagination': unlike historicism, it is applicable (in varying degrees) to both science and history, and is a necessary ingredient for success in either as an intellectual discipline.

Imagination's role in history and science can perhaps best be illustrated by considering a domain which is more obviously its proper province: literature. Consider the task of the novelist. He wishes, whether consciously or unconsciously, to communicate a message to his readers. This message may be that human beings' evil nature is unleashed when placed beyond the restraining hand of civilisation (Golding's *Lord of the Flies*), or that man ignores the needs of his non-rational side at his peril (Dickens' *Hard Times*), or that Europe is cultured but decadent while America combines social dynamism with cultural impoverishment (James' *The Europeans*). He creates a cast of characters whom he causes to act out a story which illustrates his 'thesis' and he

... aims at making his picture a coherent whole, where every character and every situation is so bound up with the rest that this character in this situation cannot but act in this way and we cannot imagine him as acting otherwise.[18]

What is more, his picture, if it is to be an effective bearer of his message, must make sense to his readers. The world that the novelist creates must be consonant with his readers' experience of the real world because many features of that world must be common objects of experience to both the characters of the novel and the reader. A novel must assume a fairly high degree of plural knowledge of the structure of human experience, and it must assume that that common knowledge is sufficient to allow a character's interpretation of that experience, as manifested in his words and actions, to be understood by the reader.

Notice that the motivations or 'insides' of the novelist's characters must logically precede the creation of the characters themselves, who are but vehicles or receptacles for the thoughts which the novelist wishes them to have. Their 'outsides', or

[18] R. G. Collingwood, *The Idea of History* (Oxford, 1946), p. 245.

their physical world and their actions in it, are created expressly for the purpose of exposing those inner qualities which interest the novelist.

Now consider the historian. His task is in many ways analogous to that of the novelist, except that his constraints are greater and the rein he can give to his imagination reduced in proportion. As Collingwood effectively argues, the past in every historian's mind is wholly imaginary,[19] a kind of mental reconstruction, that must make a coherent and believable whole in the historian's mind. Where his task differs most importantly from that of the novelist is that the historian's vision must '... stand in a peculiar relation to something called evidence'.[20] In other words, the historian cannot create a world peopled with characters who will perform acts of his choosing. To a very large extent the 'outsides' of the historian's characters are settled for him by the empirical evidence. On this view, the historian's role is to present us with a credible picture of these characters' 'insides', one which will allow the student of history *now* to understand the actions of others in another time and other circumstances.

At the low end of the imagination continuum stands the scientist, not because scientists are by nature unimaginative, but because the nature of the subject-matter of the natural sciences severely circumscribes the imagination's field of operation. The object of the scientist's attentions—observable and measurable phenomena in the physical world—have only an 'outside'. Put another way, inasmuch as human beings are agents with an ability to act which is not wholly determined by their environment, the historian and the novelist must find the explanation, if not the origin, of their characters' actions within the characters themselves.

In the case of nature, this distinction between the outside and the inside of an event does not arise. The events of nature are mere events, not the acts of agents whose thoughts the scientist endeavours to trace ... the scientist goes beyond the event, observes its relation to others, and thus brings it under a general formula or law of nature.[21]

[19] Ibid., pp. 244-5.
[20] Ibid., p. 246.
[21] Ibid., p. 214.

This deceptively simple description of the scientist's work all but ignores the creative act which is his. Just as the historian must creatively apply his own world of experience to past events and people in order to explain them and interpret them, so the man of science must, through the observation of individual events, see the links between them and thus move from the specific to the general. Such relationships are not necessarily self-evident. A man plus an apple did not result in the theory of gravity. Newton plus imagination plus an apple did. The historian, then, makes intelligible the life of others separated from us by time and space through the telling of a story—a story that reveals something about the men concerned and which teaches us not only about them, but about the reality of human action.

To tell this story intelligibly, the historian must be able to see his characters' world *from the inside*, he must understand and communicate the meaning that they attached to their circumstances and their identity. This involvement with its object's insides makes historical inquiry different from the scientific because it presupposes a special interactive relationship between subject and object, a different relation of distance or objectivity.

Science can never, of course, keep wholly separate and independent observer and observed: for example, the very act of taking a measurement changes, however slightly, the character of the thing being measured.[22] This, however, leaves unchanged the very limited degree of the involvement or engagement of the subject in science. When the scientist correctly applies rules of scientific method, they necessarily produce certain knowledge (although that certain knowledge may be *misinterpreted*: this explains how agreed empirical data can give rise to conflicting scientific theories or interpretations). The application of strict rules of method to the treatment of objects with no insides by a subject wholly disinterested in the results *is* the paradigm of scientific inquiry and objectivity.

[22] For instance, David Bohm, Professor of Theoretical Physics at Birkbeck College, London, has written with regard to observation in particle physics that: '... one can no longer maintain the division between the observer and the observed (which is implicit in the atomistic view that regards each of these as separate aggregates of atoms)'. D. Bohm, *Wholeness and the Implicate Order* (London, 1980), p. 9.

The historian, however, cannot apply this standard of objectivity because he must, in the construction of his narrative, have a relationship of sympathy and understanding with his subject. Without this understanding of the insides of people in the past, an intelligible account of their actions cannot be had, for while a factual description is sufficient in science, it is wholly inadequate in history or indeed in any understanding of *human* activity. Every mere description of human action is susceptible to a large number of interpretations, and each action performed by a man may hold several meanings for him depending on the frame of reference used.[23] No account of human action is complete without some understanding of what the agent understood his identity to be, or what aspect of it he considered relevant.

But if a personal relationship must exist between the historian and his characters, is the historian in any sense objective and is there any distance between him and his object? Hayek, for instance, appears to be saying that the mere fact of personal involvement, of the sharing of a subjective conception of the good, of common projects, etc., must destroy the distance that must exist between men if they are to treat one another objectively. The Webbs echo this concern by emphasising that the expert must be prepared to apply the remedies which his professional knowledge dictate, no matter how much the patient protests.

The true historian, though, must be able to project himself into the position occupied by his subject, understanding and appreciating his insides, without allowing this understanding to collapse the distance between them. The historian claims to be able to render another's actions intelligible, to offer something like an account the character himself could have offered of his own actions, without himself becoming the character. When this distance is destroyed, the product becomes hagiography, vindictive attack, or defensiveness. Without distance, the historian's judgment becomes clouded, his assessment of his characters unsure; but without being able, through an effort of historical imagination, to occupy their actual contingent places and insides he cannot properly

[23] For a full discussion of the concept of 'frames of reference', see A. MacIntyre, op. cit., pp. 192–5.

account for their activities at all, nor reach valid judgments about them.

The suggestion, then, is that the historian's judgments about men in the past are neither possible nor comprehensible if individual actions can be evaluated against a single, abstract, and universal criterion of right action. Part of the fascination of history lies in its revelation of what real men judged was the appropriate universal to guide them in their actions, a choice which we can judge only when we are made aware of the tangle of circumstances as well as the values and goals of the actor. In forming such judgments we are concerned to decide, not whether a single abstract and universalisable rule of behaviour was always followed, but to decide whether or not the rule that was followed was the appropriate one for all men who might occupy similar circumstances. We search for the standards of excellence implicit in human actions and evaluate them on the basis of the kind of life they exemplify, on what they tell us about what it means to act by illuminating the past actions of individuals.

Historical accounts may therefore properly be evaluated with reference to other criteria than their strict empirical veracity. They may also be evaluated in terms of the meaning they convey. History, seen as a struggle to understand the past, will constantly be reinterpreted as men attempt to make a narrative on the past which will be intelligible to men now. This requires reinterpretation not least because we will be interested in different aspects of men's behaviour in the past depending on those aspects of our own lives on which we seek illumination, and this itself will change as the circumstances we face and the preoccupations we have change.

History as an activity presupposes that there are many possible stories to be told about the same events, each one reflecting what the particular storyteller found important to him in understanding the actions performed by men he did not know. Not knowing them personally, however, does not change the fact that they are men who shared with the historian and his audience a certain common structure of human experience and who are consequently linked to both through their sharing of certain ideas and practices.

Like any story, the historian's narrative will be shaped by his vantage point, and the hypotheses he uses to collect and collate the facts, but also by his perspicacity, his vision, his experience of similar events, his direct knowledge of those involved, and so on. And we may, by these and other criteria, judge any particular narrative/history adequate or inadequate for reasons only tangentially, or perhaps not at all, related to the objectively ascertainable facts. History and the past are thus not the same thing. The past leaves behind traces which become the objective data which history struggles to make sense of to men now.

Histories may treat of the same events and therefore share a common objective reality, but that reality may be seen from many viewpoints, each with its strengths and weaknesses. When we speak of an historian exhibiting judgment, we mean not just that he knows how to recognise an objective historical fact, but more importantly that he displays good judgment in choosing amongst the universe of facts about the past, forging from that potential disorder a cosmos of meaning which his contemporaries can find enlightening. To have good historical judgment is to have a well-developed sense of what men find relevant in the explanation of action. The historian is not free to write just what he pleases because of the discipline imposed by the facts; there is an objective world, but an objective world which may be observed from many vantage points.

As the epigraph at the head of this chapter intimated, narrative accounts of the past actions of men do not illuminate merely the circumstances and activities of men who are dead. Stories, and especially historical narratives based on empirical evidence, illustrate for us what actions men may perform in the pursuit of specified goods within the shifting contingencies of the world. As men who are bound up with communities which embody traditions and practices which others have striven to actualise in the past, such characters illustrate for us some of the possibilities and limitations inherent in our pursuit of those goods which we share with them. In fact, to the extent that such stories become part of the mythology of our culture, they may help to define for us what it means to perform well or badly the duties attaching to certain of the social roles we occupy.[24]

So, when we consider the actions of a man, we do not consider only his empirical circumstances and assume that anyone in those objective conditions should necessarily do as he did. On the contrary, we form judgments about historical figures (and about our contemporaries) on the basis of what their actions reveal to us about them as individuals, about their character and about the values they try to exemplify. Furthermore, such actions are not discrete entities, unconnected with the past and the future and related only to their immediate context. They are embedded in the life of a man and have meaning for him within the larger scheme of his life and his values—but here again, as a responsible man of depth, he is both the bearer and the interpreter of those values. He is not merely a prisoner of particular values, not least because our values and roles overlap and compete with each other such that we have to impose some degree of order on them, an order not necessarily implicit in them.

At least part of the (often) unspoken assumption underlying our interest in the actions of men in the past and the present is that we hold individuals responsible for their actions and expect them to be able to offer a proper account of them. Such an account would seem to depend not merely on a good set of reasons for a particular action, but on the integration of that action and those reasons within the larger framework of a life, a life which embodies and exemplifies the values and character of the person concerned. It is the existence of this framework of settled values that permits the judging subject to distance himself from any one value in particular, evaluating it responsibly against a larger background.

It is not even necessary that men have a choice in what they *do* for us to form such judgments: one of the great themes that tragedy explores is the reaction of men to the growing realisation that they are caught up in a chain of events which

---

[24] On the narrative mode of understanding oneself and others, see A. MacIntyre, op. cit., Chapter 15. See also R. Beiner, *Political Judgement*, Chapter 7, for a discussion of how the persuasive force of rhetoric, in the Aristotelian sense, depends to a very great extent on the shared values and experiences of a communal life, which help to lower for us the opacity of others, permitting a greater understanding of the unity and continuity of our lives.

must end in their destruction. What fascinates us in these circumstances is not the actions as such, since these are dictated by fate and contingent circumstance. It is rather to see how such men react to the certainty of the futility of their acts, the meaning they attach to them and to their life in the never-ending struggle against Machiavelli's implacable *fortuna*.

So we know that we must, in our evaluations and judgments of men, take account not only of what makes them men, but what makes them the particular men they are. The *study* of man cannot be a *science* of man in the way that the study of physics can be a *science* of physics. By reducing men to the universal anonymity of atoms, we rob them of what they must have if their actions are to be comprehensible and therefore morally responsible and we discount the concrete but almost wholly contingent circumstances which call forth action.[25]

Now clearly Hayek is not arguing that men are in some sense compelled to obey his rules of justice in the way that atoms are compelled to obey the laws of particle physics. His intention is a normative one, namely: to convince men in their social relations to surrender their responsibility for their actions by supplying a determinant universal by which to judge the justice of those actions. To the extent that men are successful in this, their actions would always by definition be just *because* they conformed to the rule and not because of any responsible attempt to choose the appropriate universal under which to subsume the particular. Similarly, for the Webbs, men ought to surrender their judgment concerning the good to experts who alone could master the tools of critical reason. But again, since the Webbs' theory gives no plausible account of human *choice* or values, it cannot attract our interest to the same extent as Hayek: the Webbs simply have nothing interesting to say about the critical issues.

On Hayek's deontological view, then, a separation is possible between the goodness (contingent) and the rightness (universalisable) of an action or a rule of behaviour: it makes

---

[25] 'Most of the things about which we make decisions, and into which we therefore inquire, present us with alternative possibilities. For it is about our actions that we deliberate and inquire, and all our actions have a contingent character; hardly any of them are determined by necessity.' Aristotle, *Rhetoric* 1357a 23–7, quoted in R. Beiner, op. cit., p. 87.

no sense to ask if an atom ought to obey the laws of physics, one is concerned only to identify those rules which correctly describe that behaviour. Likewise, men would not have to question whether or not it is good to follow the rules, they need only be aware that following the rules necessarily results in just outcomes.

An important difference between natural laws and such 'laws' of justice, however, is that the rules men follow partly constrain their behaviour; they are not purely descriptive. Even more than in the case of historicism, the elevation of a rule or set of rules of justice to the status of a natural law is crucially to misidentify the nature of men as moral and social beings. Just as the search for historical understanding requires us always to focus on the explanation of particular events and not on 'laws' of history, so the search for justice requires us to look at what justice demands in a particular context. In each case, the conclusions we reach may suggest some larger pattern permitting limited generalisation between cases, but to subordinate the interpretation of each case to the requirements of such an hypothesis is to mistake the tentative and provisional articulation of a non-scientific generalisation for the concrete reality it attempts to describe.

On this view, justice is not a natural law supplying a determinant universal, but is rather a provisional social hypothesis which cannot be empirically demonstrated, but which can be challenged and undermined. One of the most effective means of undermining such hypotheses is by producing examples of specific instances where the results of strict adherence to the rules produces an outcome which offends against other potential standards of justice. The evaluation of such 'counter-examples' obviously cannot take place against the background of the rules which it is designed to question. It requires the ability to distance oneself both from the rules and from the particular people involved, and yet to retain the internal perspective which gives meaning to the rules. In short, it requires us to bring to bear our sense of judgment, and to achieve this one must be able to occupy the acting person's place, to appreciate his circumstances, without letting that intimacy collapse the distance between actor and evaluator.

To occupy someone's place, to have the sympathy and understanding for another's predicament which can only come from the experience of having lived a life in which one strives to realise certain goods against a background of shifting contingencies, is thus not necessarily the same as collapsing the space between people. But to occupy that *particular place* is crucial to our understanding of it and our assessment of the actions taken by its inhabitant, judging what could properly be expected of that person in those circumstances. Following Beiner, then, one can identify some qualities which anyone who wishes to exhibit *this* type of objectivity, or judgment, must possess:

[t]he disinterested spectator ... evinces the formal requisite of judgment, namely distance. The active participant in worldly affairs, on the other hand, displays the substantive requisite of judgment, namely experience.[26]

This kind of objectivity, similar to that of the historian, is not necessarily only backward-looking, nor is it confined to an imaginary relationship between the living and the dead. For instance Beiner, following Gadamer, suggests that the phenomenon of friendly advice is analogous.[27]

When I ask someone for advice on what to do in a difficult situation, I normally do so for three reasons. First, because I believe that the person to whom I turn for advice wishes me well; that in formulating his advice he will think about what is good for me. Second, that he and I share a common conception of what the good is, at least with regard to the matter on which I am seeking advice. I thus must have confidence in his judgment of how to apply the universal we share. This tempers the first condition, without negating it, because I expect him, in tendering his advice, to be searching for my particular good within the larger context of a common good. Such shared meaning is essential, for without it there can be no rational ground for my asking advice.

Third, I must have some ground for feeling that our personal relationship of confidence (reason one) and our shared general conception of the larger good (reason two) will not serve to

[26] Beiner, op. cit., p. 105.
[27] Ibid., pp. 79–82.

cloud his objectivity, that in spite of our mutual ties he will strive to identify with me the appropriate standard of behaviour, no matter how difficult and painful that may be for me. It is normally precisely because we are so bound up with a moral or other dilemma that we turn to others for advice in an attempt to understand our obligations, what actions it is appropriate for others and ourselves to expect us to take.

That standard will not make reference uniquely to us, but to all men who share the larger notion of the good which, implicitly if not explicitly, contains the universal under which I must subsume my particular situation. In asking for advice in this way, I am asking someone to occupy my place, to appreciate my circumstances, but at the same time to maintain the degree of distance that will enable them to form a proper judgment. On this view, the judgment of men and their goods is an activity which demands the participant reactive attitudes which I argued earlier were crucial to an understanding of ourself and our goals, and this is in clear opposition to the Hayekian view that in order to be just in our relations with men we must *not* know them.

Returning now to the matter of standards of behaviour, it must now be recognised that within communities there are standards to which we are expected, and expect ourselves, to conform, even in advance of knowing what they are or how they will apply to us. By seeking advice I am recognising both that the standard to which I feel obliged to conform is something which I do not always find it easy to recognise or apply and also that this standard is not something purely personal, but is rather a common object of knowledge on which each person has their particular and unique viewpoint.

The question now is this: can this notion of 'historical' objectivity, of the ability to project oneself into the place of another without collapsing the distance that separates individuals as moral persons, have some bearing on a society's claim to treat its members justly and yet still treat them as whole and concrete human beings? In this regard Hayek offered us a stark choice. Either we could have a society where everyone attends only to his own interest, narrowly defined, and treats virtually all others as anonymous objects to be used for his own satisfaction, or we could have a society in which everyone's individual wants and interests are subordinated to those of the group.

The rather different notion of objectivity being advanced here suggests, however, that Hayek's choice is in fact a false one, and that there is a third possibility. This hinges on a rejection of the notion of the incommunicability and irreconcilability of individual systems of wants across the boundaries of the self. As we have just seen, for Hayek, either these wants are chosen autonomously and in isolation by a bounded self or they are heteronomously borne by a self whose boundaries have been collapsed and who has therefore been prevented from realising his good as a rational chooser.

This is far too passive a conception of human development. As I have already argued, people in fact seek their good through the actualisation of goods that are part of who they are. To this extent, what a man requires for his development cannot be defined in advance according to some abstract notion of a universal essence. This suggests that any society which aspires to justify itself on the grounds that it maximises its members' development cannot treat them objectively in the scientific sense. Human development, requiring as it does the co-operation and contribution of one's fellows, cannot proceed solely on the basis of a criterion of justice which abstracts from the good; this gives men no way in which to assess claims to different specific goods by particular people. It also offers no criterion or justification for choosing or discriminating amongst such claims when, as must happen eventually, they conflict.

Historical objectivity and the objectivity of a friend who offers advice are two elements of a possible response to this dilemma. This is a model of how, in certain conditions, men might be prepared to accept judgments about their good from other concrete men. But those conditions are specific and hard to fulfil.

To understand what is involved, we need to explore further the idea of advice and its relationship to rules in the determination of the good. We may recall that genuine chess players attempt to meet standards of play only partly embodied in the formal rules of the game. We did not, however, pursue the very interesting question of why the standard of what constitutes good chess is divided into formal rules, informal conventions, and contested marginal areas.

One answer is implicit in Hart's account of how one discriminates between those rules one has an obligation to obey, and those one doesn't. This depended on the gravity of the sanction applied to offenders, but we observed that rules as such existed because they were 'believed to be necessary to the maintenance of social life or some highly prized feature of it'.[28] Combining these two ideas, one could conclude that compulsory rules (those carrying the gravest sanctions) are compulsory because they are believed so necessary to the maintenance of the good pursued that it is held necessary and proper to make them universally binding. Such rules may thus be seen as the minimum virtue which must be required of all members of a community which pursues this end.

Optional conventions, by contrast, might be seen as somewhat more contestable requirements for the pursuit of the good in question. Here there is room for disagreements between 'schools', for differing interpretations of how best to realise the good or goods pursued. To the extent that such differing schools of thought agree to observe universal rules prescribing minimum standards, they are agreed on a provisional articulation of the standards to which one must conform in order to pursue the good *at all*. Players belonging to different schools or traditions within the broad practice may thus strive to realise the goods internal to this practice within a common framework of standards, while those who do not accept the compulsory minimum rules are thereby excluded from the community of practitioners. Membership of the community is largely defined precisely by an acceptance of such compulsory rules. In other words, the basic content of this good is not and cannot be self-chosen or defined, and a refusal to abide by this standard is seen by other members of the community as a refusal to pursue that good and not a choice to pursue it by other means.

Such a framework clearly leaves room for different approaches and interpretations which may give rise to supplementary 'rules' adhered to by members of competing

[28] Hart, op. cit., p. 85.

schools or traditions. Such refinements, while not incompatible with the community's good, do not represent a standard which the community can agree is so essential that they need be made compulsory. Finally, there will always exist idiosyncratic standards of play, and these too can be accommodated within the compulsory rules.

This does not mean that the essential minimum prescribed by the rules is definitive or immutable. As the activity to which the rules refer is more fully explored by practitioners in pursuit of internal goods, variations not envisaged by the rules are bound to be discovered, and standards once thought indispensable may come to be seen as optional, just as possibilities once thought discretionary may 'crystallise' into compulsory rules. There is thus a constant tension between the rules and the conventions, between what has been held to be a universalisable standard for all, and what remains only a potentially universalisable standard. And there may well be standards of behaviour not elevated to the status of rules which are none the less held by the community to be essential, and these conventions may well be backed with heavy social rather than formal sanctions.

As a chess player, I accept an obligation to respect certain provisional definitions of how chess is played. I also accept that other members of the chess-playing community will be able to advise me on how best to pursue my particular good because we share the basic provisional definition of the universalisable elements of that good. The practice is in part the challenge of applying the present understandings of the universal good to particular contingent circumstances. The seeking of advice is in part a recognition that, as a member of the community, my particular good is intimately bound up with that of the community; to this extent I will find my particular good in a co-operative exploration with others of my individual obligations under the good common to us all.

This must, however, be a case of advice and not of definitive determination. As a matter of meaning and interpretation, the questions on which one seeks advice frequently cannot be resolved in the way that one resolves mathematical equations: the answers will be tentative and open to dispute. Knowledge of the good, on this view, comes from sharing interpretations of experience, custom, connoisseurship, of knowledge which, while individual, is potentially universalisable because it focuses on an object of knowledge common to all members.

Chess playing, of course, is a matter of individual choice and as such poses no particular problem for Hayek's account. The original choice to seek the goods internal to chess is one we are free to make: no one is compelled to become a chess player. Hayek's concern is with individuals constrained to pursue goods they have not prescribed for themselves. Thus, choosing to adhere to the standards of chess playing is held to be different in kind from society using its coercive power (the law) to make compulsory observance of one arbitrary standard of the good.[29]

This, however, is crucially to misunderstand the function of rule-making in a society of men who are in part constituted by the communities of which they are a part. Many of the roles we occupy in life are not chosen by us, but are the result of purely contingent circumstance. We are sons and daughters, citizens of a particular country, members of a particular community of religious or other beliefs, and so on without this being a conscious choice on our part, and these ties influence and shape us throughout our life. We can distance ourselves from them, evaluate them, attempt to reconcile them with other values and beliefs we hold, but human depth suggests that our values are not something we choose arbitrarily, but are something we discover about ourselves and which we then shape and interpret as we understand ourselves and our roles better.

In this attempt to articulate and make coherent our deep sense of self, the communities of which we are a part play an important role. They set down, through compulsory rules and optional conventions, the behaviour currently seen as necessary to the pursuit of the community's collective goods. They tell us, in other words, how the community has hitherto judged its goods may best be attained, and those standards to which one must adhere if the resources of the community are to be called upon in the pursuit of these goods. And since society is the all-encompassing community within which all particular

---

[29] See e.g. Hayek, *Constitution*, p. 145.

goods are pursued, its rules of behaviour provide at least the minimum content of the concept of what men in society's past have found to be the good life.

But why should men consent to such rules, given that their validity cannot be demonstrated and they are necessarily contestable? Such ideal-regarding judgments may be acceptable where one chooses to belong to a community (like chess players), but it is difficult to see how they can be acceptable when consent is imputed on the basis of non-voluntary membership, as in the case of, say, citizenship.

The response to this is in large part a negative one: given the view of the self and the good I have put forward in earlier chapters, the project of finding a concept of the right that would abstract from the good and provide a rule of social obligation that would compel the assent of rational men seems simply mistaken. Political society, therefore, represents in some sense a 'second best' because it accepts that true political obligation can only ever be founded on necessarily contestable principles, never on empirically or rationally compelling ones.[30]

Political society derives its strength from its recognition of the uniqueness and distinctiveness of each man and of the impossible obstacle that this poses for theories of political obligation which appeal to man's hypothetical essential sameness. While such theories have a certain elegance and logical tidiness about them, this cannot compensate for the fact that their legitimacy is based on a vision of men which is false because incomplete. Defending the market or rule by experts on the basis that they would be in man's own best interest if only he could remove a good part of what makes him a full person is no defence at all.

Political society, by contrast, recognises that there will always be disagreements amongst people about how their common life may best be organised. Rather than counterfeiting the unanimous consent of ephemeral men, it accepts that *no* set of standards of social behaviour will be universally acceptable.[31] Instead, like the real men it mirrors, it sees its

[30] Beattie, *'Character'*, p. 25.
[31] Ibid., p. 25.

rules and standards of behaviour as a 'state of the art' articulation of society's understanding of what it means to seek the good life.

On this view, the first task of social institutions is to provide a framework within which men can co-operate in the ongoing search for a definition of what the common good is for them in their circumstances. That common good then becomes the framework within which all particular goods are pursued. In the discussion of political society in Chapter I, the name of Aristotle was invoked as one of the earliest thinkers to put forward this view of the nature of social and political relations. It is worth while here to quote at some length Pocock's analysis of the Aristotelian tradition, for it will help to draw together the diverse threads of the argument:

Aristotle taught that every human activity was value-oriented in the sense that it aimed at some theoretically identifiable good; that all value-oriented activity was social in the sense that it was pursued by men in association with one another; and that the *polis* or republic was the association within which all particular associations pursued their particular ends. Association with others, and participation in the value-oriented direction of that association, formed both a means to an end and an end—or good—in itself; and participation in the association whose end was the good of all particular associations, and the attainment of all particular goods, was in itself a good of a very high, because universal, character... [The citizen] took part in the determination of the general good, enjoying in his own person the values made attainable by society, while contributing by his political activity to the attainment of values by others.[32]

It is clear, then, that political society must be acutely aware of certain constraints. First, because it reposes on a living relationship of trust and confidence between all its members who share its internal point of view, it is, like any human relationship, fragile. Its maintenance can therefore never be

[32] 'Since this activity', Pocock continues in *The Machiavellian Moment* (Princeton, 1975), pp. 67-8, 'was concerned with the universal good, it was itself a good of a higher order than the particular goods which the citizen as social animal might enjoy, and in enjoying his own citizenship—his contribution to the good of others, his relationship with others engaged in so contributing—he enjoyed a universal good and became a being in relation with the universal. Citizenship was a universal activity, the *polis* a universal community.'

subordinated to the achievement of other goals except at the risk of undermining that which makes such a society possible.

Political society therefore requires its members to be able to put chains on their particular appetites, to accept that particular standards they might individually or as groups find desirable can never assume more importance than the relationship binding them all together. Political society cannot be merely a question of majority rule.

In addition to the desire to pursue the common good for its own sake, political society also reposes on the acquired ability of its members to be objective in both the formal and substantive aspects of the historical sense outlined above. In the search for the content of the compulsory standards of social behaviour citizens must distance themselves both from personal relationships and from their own conception of the good. They must not seek merely to impose their particular vision of the good which depends on the particular place *they* occupy, but to transcend that in the search for that which will promote the good of all. Because such judgment and objectivity can only be acquired through the activity of trying to exercise judgment and trying to be objective, and not through the application of rules of method, political society will again seek to involve the greatest number of people in deliberations about decisions affecting society as a whole, so that not only will they bring their particular knowledge to bear on the problem, but they will themselves be transformed through the process of seeking the common good.

Three further considerations shape this participatory search for the public good. First, it will be recognised that the tentative and uncertain nature of any particular conclusions requires that, whenever possible, decisions should be taken in a slow and deliberate manner, with ample opportunity for all sides to state their case and for arguments to be fully digested. Second, the fact that men are sometimes swayed by momentary passions and short-term considerations will be taken into account. Since the common good is based on a notion of the good for man as being something which is not transitory or subject to radical fluctuations, but draws on the experience of real men attempting to actualise it in the relatively stable conditions imposed by the structure of human existence, major change will require more than the momentary assent of the citizens. Finally, what is really the obverse of the second consideration, since the already established rules represent the accumulated efforts of generations of men to give substance to what the good life for man is like, some presumption in favour of them is justified, as against the immediate views of one generation at a particular moment.

These considerations suggest that a political society would be crucially concerned to do two things: first, to promote a level of participation which would both give legitimacy to the law and develop the faculties of judgment and objectivity on which proper law depends. Second, to create a set of secondary (power conferring[33]) or constitutional rules which would constrain political society in its elaboration of primary (behaviour constraining) rules. This suggests (*inter alia*) that it is the interaction of these two values of participation and constitutionalism[34] that make the deliberative pursuit of the common good, and therefore political society, possible.

[33] See note 1, above.

[34] Constitutionalism here refers to the concern with the structure of secondary or power conferring rules which provides the framework of constraints within which political actors attempt to realise the particular substantive good(s) they are pursuing. A very important distinction is thus being made between 'policy' questions (what ought to be done?) and constitutional questions (what means are regarded as acceptable in pursuit of our ends?). See Beattie, op. cit., p. 3.

IX

WHOLE MEN
AND POLITICAL SOCIETY

> ... there are two great enemies of politics: indifference
> to human suffering and the passionate quest for certainty
> in matters which are essentially political. Indifference to
> human suffering discredits free regimes which are unable,
> or which fear, to extend the habits and possibility of
> freedom from the few to the many. The quest for certainty
> scorns the political virtues—of prudence, of conciliation,
> of compromise, of variety, of adaptability, of liveliness—
> in favour of some pseudo-science of government, some
> absolute sounding ethic, or some ideology, some world-
> picture in terms of either race or economics.
>
> Bernard Crick, *In Defence of Politics*

A conclusion is, by definition, a bringing to an end, a summing
up, a leaving of a subject. Consequently, this conclusion is
perhaps harder to write than most, for it must 'conclude' a
work which has, in a sense, only just begun. For many reasons,
this book has been limited to a critique of two important
strands of the broad liberal tradition in Britain, leaving to
others the task of elucidating political theories which offer
more room than Hayek and the Webbs have done, both
for the fullest development of the reasoning, rational, and
responsible human self *and* for a theory of politics which is
neither too pessimistic nor too optimistic concerning the limits
of rationality and knowledge.

There is no shame, however, in limiting oneself to the
elimination of certain contenders from the field; political
theory has an important critical role to play in exploring the
adequacy of ideas proposed by others, as well as the somewhat
more glamorous one of putting forward one's own. Furthermore, I have tried to draw attention to the underlying
sympathies and affinities linking the works of Hayek and the
Webbs. These links are too often obscured by traditional

theoretical categories which, reflecting certain modern ideological preoccupations and intellectual interests, have conceived these authors uniquely as adversaries.

Obviously enough, however, even a 'critical piece' like this is not exclusively negative or descriptive, for it seeks to measure the strength and adequacy of certain ideas against other standards or ideas, themselves held to be sound. In this case, the purpose has been to lay the groundwork for a rehabilitation of the very concept of politics, to rescue it from the obscurity and desuetude to which both the utilitarian and deontological strands of liberalism have sought to consign it. The reason why politics is seen as so important is perhaps best understood by seeing in what the essential difference consists between these liberal approaches and the political one. The difference is this: both utilitarianism and ethical liberalism seek a *method* of arriving at social decisions whose validity compels hypothetical rational men to acquiesce in whatever conclusions or results it produces. Politics, by contrast, seeks the assent of real men to the results themselves as well as to the way they are arrived at, and does so through persuasive argument directed towards, and drawing upon, common experience and common objects of knowledge.

The liberal social order finds its justification in a realm of abstraction quite separate from the concrete and the contingent. It thus gives itself the appearance of objectivity, but this is the objectivity of the social scientist and not the historian, of the anonymous and faceless mass and not that of the man of character and judgment who has lived a 'life vivid and intense enough to have created a wide fellow-feeling with all that is human'.[1]

The burden of this argument is simple to state. Whether values are simply reducible to facts and are therefore not the product of any human will on the one hand, *or* they are merely exogenous and inexplicable whims to be excluded from the social order on the other hand, the sort of knowledge on which both of these claims is based is such as to preclude their carrying any significant moral weight. Indeed I would argue, although it is beyond the scope of this book to do so fully,

---

[1] This quotation is from the epigraph to Chapter VII.

that the whole project of searching for a notion of justice (e.g. expert scientific distribution of the means to satisfy measurable 'needs' or chance operating through an unpatterned market order) which can have some validity outside the hermeneutic questions of what is to be regarded as good, is simply mistaken.[2]

On the much more limited scale of the present work, it can be said that the Webbs and Hayek, in their search for some value-free justification of political and social arrangements, are obliged to define away as non-essential or merely contingent some parts of the self without which no sensible account of choice, responsibility, or moral agency seems possible. The notion of politics introduced in the first chapter was precisely about making possible a reclaiming of the definition of the desirable, the worthwhile, and the good from the abstract world of fact and method which must, of necessity, make no reference to the concrete experience of individuals. It is also an affirmation of the notion that men living in a community of shared experiences and language is the only context in which the individual and society can discover and test their values through the essentially political activities of discussion, criticism, example, and emulation. It is through the existence of organised public spaces, in which men offer and test ideas against one another, not for their truth value (which is better assessed in other ways) but for the common meaning which they embody and bring to consciousness, that men come to understand a part of who they are.

Politics offers a twofold opportunity. It makes possible a self-discovery and understanding which transcends the narrow limits of ascribed needs or inexplicable wants. And it provides for the arriving (by persuasive means which respect the autonomy of the reasoning responsible individual) at shared understandings of the obligations and rights which the pursuit of the common good requires in a particular society. As the examples of the POWs and the religious communities alluded to in earlier chapters indicated, these constituent elements of community are not universal and invariable; still less are they strictly a matter of personal choice and preference. They

---

[2] Many authors have given this question a much fuller treatment. A. MacIntyre's *After Virtue*, and M. J. Sandel's *Liberalism*, are two very good recent examples.

depend, like the lives of real men, on contingent factors and on ties and commitments, some of which are beyond choice.[3]

The constant adjustment of the lives and projects of men to each other, the making possible of the co-operative pursuit of self-realisation is thus both the objective and the justification of politics. In my criticism of Hayek and the Webbs I have, to some extent, echoed John Stuart Mill's criticism of Bentham, that 'man is never recognised by him as a being capable of pursuing spiritual perfection as an end; of desiring, for its own sake, the conformity of his own character to his standard of excellence'.[4] Going beyond this, I have suggested that at least some of the sources of such standards are to be found in the nature of human community and contingent relationships; sources which go deeper than either liberal theory of choice or human development allowed.

Before concluding, then, something more undoubtedly needs to be said about the intersubjective nature and justification of the knowledge of self, of obligation, of standards, and of the good which politics seeks. This can best be approached by recalling the central aspects of the case against politics put by Hayek and the Webbs and why this case was found wanting.

The Webbs offered us four reasons why their absolute standard of judging the worth and appropriateness of political and social institutions was valid. First, there was their theory of human development via utility maximisation. Second came their belief that the survival and flourishing of the social order, whose existence makes possible the satisfaction of all individual needs, takes logical precedence over the satisfaction of the needs of particular individuals. Third came a process of natural selection of social orders which favours those societies whose members are best able to satisfy their needs, needs being seen strictly in relation to one's ability to fulfil one's functional social role. Fourth and finally was the argument that both the definition and the measurement of needs *and* the direction in which evolution is pushing society is something which only scientific experts can know. Given the fact that men would

[3] On the binding nature of certain obligations which are not a matter of individual choice, see F. Canavan, 'Burke on Prescription of Government', *Review of Politics*, 35: 4 (1973), p. 462.
[4] Quoted in G. F. Gaus, *The Modern Liberal Theory of Man*, p. 270.

want to act in accordance with this knowledge if they had it, it is rational for them to acquiesce in rule by those people who alone have access to it by virtue of their special talents and training.

On the first three points there is broad agreement between Hayek and the Webbs, although Hayek sees a much greater distance between the social roles one occupies and the desires one has. Even so, while he attempts to offer both deontological *and* utilitarian (social survival) reasons why individual choices should be respected, he does not satisfactorily explain why the sort of choices made possible under a market social order are morally significant. With respect to the fourth point, Hayek and the Webbs part company, and radically, for while Hayek shares the Webbs' evolutionary perspective, he denies that the operation of the natural selection of cultural institutions is accessible to reason. Rather, for him, such a process spontaneously makes available rational guides to utility maximisation within social constraints (choice being limited to what I have called 'socially compatible utilities'). Such guides are superior to anything which could be arrived at by individual or collective reflection. Whereas for the Webbs, political values are validated by the objective scientific method of those who discover them, via an examination of 'facts', for Hayek they are validated by the fact that they are chosen by no one, but are thrown up by a sociological process utterly resistant to analysis.

Like so many forms of rationalist liberalism, these theories seek to exclude disagreements on morally contestable matters like the good by appealing to objective standards of the right, but this does not mean that such choices can be avoided. Such an exclusion is to evade responsibility for the choices to which the method points and to avoid those choices being scrutinised, debated, and changed by those who live under them.

Only by positing one unquestioned goal (in both cases with which we are concerned here, the survival of a social order which is rational for utility-maximisers), can the value-free method of liberalism make any plausible claim to universal validity. But this validity is purchased at a high price: the destruction of the moral community within which the criticism and evaluation of social institutions can take place and have some reasonable claim to evaluate the worth of those institutions at a deep level. Men in the ideal liberal worlds described had nothing which we could recognise as 'depth' or 'character' and did not struggle to know that dimension of themselves to which these terms refer. For this reason, among others, these examples of ethical and utilitarian liberalism provide an inadequate place for the public display of character and judgment and the exchange of experience and insight respecting the common social order which are crucial if men are to be said to hold their notions of the good responsibly.

Some other aspects of these two positions have also been rejected here on methodological and logical grounds, such as the pseudo-scientific claims made for natural selection: neither Hayek nor the Webbs were able to extricate themselves convincingly from the familiar trap of evolutionist arguments. This trap is that either the argument is circular (Why does this survive? Because it is sound. Why is it sound? Because it survives.) or it requires one to place an untestable faith in the process, untestable because its benefits are always 'long run': you may suffer now, but at some unspecified (and unspecifiable) future time this order will prove itself superior.

None of this emphasis on the many and important similarities between the philosophical foundations of the political thought of the Webbs and Hayek is intended to suggest, however, that their works are of equal *merit*. Hayek's arguments are both stimulating and challenging, whereas the Webbs merely refuse to take seriously the questions raised, *inter alia*, by these notions of politics, character, and community. This difference in merit can be ascribed at least in part to the different orientations to theory held by Hayek and the Webbs but also, and more importantly, to the critical perspective each has brought to bear on his own work and the proportion of human experience that each tries to encompass. At the very least, Hayek can address two of Beiner's central political questions (i.e. What do I want? How do I get it?), whereas the Webbs can make a place only for 'What does one who occupies this social role need to be most productive?'

If for no other reason, then, the Webbs can be rejected as serious theorists of politics because they not only have no credible place for choice, they have no serious conception of what choice is and no theory of human agency which is in any sense morally individualist. *No one* chooses because facts dictate to us the one and only possible answer to every question; no one is responsible because men are merely instruments of the social order, and experts are only the disinterested servants of the facts which they discover and publicise.

This is, of course, not an argument against the possibility of expert knowledge, but rather for restricting its field of application in political matters. It can no longer aspire to offer 'value-free' scientific guidance in understanding the good, for instance, but it does open up other possibilities.

One of the aspects of the development of the faculties of reason, judgment, and discrimination at which a political community of values, critically held, aims is learning to judge those people to whom decision-making power should be entrusted. It is not necessary, nor is there any suggestion, that political society be in constant 'general assembly', in which every decision is subjected to popular scrutiny at every moment, for this is clearly incompatible with the practical realities of the operation of a large-scale urban and in-dustrialised society. But a return to an idealised Greek city-state is not required for the freedom and growth which politics makes possible to flourish. There is no principle of liberty which is contravened by entrusting the care of certain of one's interests to others in those cases where judgment and experience indicate that they could look after them better than we could ourselves.

This is surely superior to (and a more communitarian sentiment than) the crude Benthamite assertion that no one knows my interests better than I: the kernel of truth contained in this resembles the identity condition discussed in earlier chapters. No one knows *who* I am better than I do, i.e. no one knows better than I do what interests I regard as important and constitutive of my identity, nor the relative weight I attach to each one. Yet I may still regard someone else as more competent than myself to promote what I regard as my vital interests.

The main limitation of expertise is that it is dependent on a necessarily prior choice of a good which is the object or end at which it aims. This affirmation of the good cannot itself be the province of the expert but is the necessary pre-condition of the very possibility of expertise. And in political matters, of course, while experts may be empowered to choose the means to achieve desired ends, it is not the experts who are the sole judges of the fruits of their labours, for *all* the members of the social order experience the results of political actions.

This is the value of the concept of plural as opposed to dispersed knowledge: every man is an expert in attempting to live the good life within the confines of a particular social order, but no one individual can hope to know it all. That is why public fora, common deliberation and discussion, and a desire to reach agreement on the issues of public life are necessary for the appearance, examination, and testing of that kind of knowledge which is concerned with contingency, experience, and meaning. Politics is, in part, at least, an active public life in which the insights of all can be heard and assessed by the 'experts in living'. To quote Aristotle: 'Each individual may indeed be a worse judge than the experts; but all, when they meet together, are either better than experts or at any rate no worse.'[5]

At many levels Hayek offers us a much richer theory than the Webbs were able to do, just as his work is more stimulating and exciting. While I have had much that is critical to say about Hayek, I have also tried not to understate his enduring contributions to modern political theory. The most important of these is undoubtedly in his clear and forceful restatement of the existence and value of spontaneous social processes such as the market and the consequent drawing to our attention of man's hubristic tendency to try to remake his world in accordance with his own limited awareness. As one of the most articulate modern bearers of an intellectual tradition stretching back through the Austrian School of economists to Edmund Burke, Adam Smith, and David Hume, he rightly reminds us of the importance of the independence of such processes from particular goals, and argues persuasively for the value of individual liberty and limited government. Much of my argument against Hayek's ethical liberalism can and does leave this intellectual legacy largely intact.

[5] R. Beiner, *Political Judgment*, p. 91.

In that deontological aspect of his work, Hayek wants to marry a theory of justice, which abstracts from, and does not depend on, a theory of the good, with a freedom for each individual to choose what he will regard as good. While this attempt is much more worth while and stimulating than the Webbs' efforts in a similar direction, it too fails. It fails in part because, by appealing to evolutionist arguments, Hayek creates a tension in his account between the values of individualism and social survival, a tension which he never successfully resolves. Clearly, however, this is not an essential element of a deontological account, for many deontological theorists of individual rights will assert the rights of the individual *whatever* the cost to society.

Hayek's theory fails in part too, then, because that aspect of the self which he empowers to make choices (the rational, utility-maximising self, unencumbered by ties and attachments) cannot make choices which justify an ethically based respect of individuals *qua* choosing agents. Worse, unlike Rawls, with whom he shares many aspects of the Kantian deontological ideal, he never lets even his equivalent of the hypothetical 'thin' people (the rational market actor) choose the principles of justice under which they will be expected to live. 'Choice' in this regard is to be left to impersonal sociological processes whose superior rationality is asserted but untestable.

While both Hayek and the Webbs would thus see in politics a retreat into arbitrary subjectivity and perhaps even superstition and 'tribal morality', it seems clear that neither of them can offer a convincing argument how their theories escape a certain unprovable 'act of faith'. Thus, my aim throughout has been to establish the limits (and limitations) of expertise and markets, not to prove their failure or invalidity.

So, while the Webbs' system is simply too limited to be credible as an alternative to politics, Hayek's is in a different, and more interesting, class. The limitations of his liberalism when compared with politics are, nevertheless, unmistakable. While both rely heavily on men learning from experience, politics extends the possibilities of learning: it not only allows tools, traditions, and practices to be passed on by discussion and persuasion as well as by less conscious processes, it allows concrete men now to benefit from that experience, and not just hypothetical future men. Further, it permits the sharing of the burdens of the experimentation which Hayek so rightly argues is essential to the discovery of new knowledge about the world and ourselves.

Learning becomes not merely a capricious possibility in which some men learn (and survive) and others don't (and are left behind) but the reasons why some do and others do not are simply unknown. Hirschman's insights into the wasteful and pessimistic nature of this approach, even in the competitive market, are useful here. If a firm fails in the market, that tells us something, but there are more possible responses to this than simply to say 'that's the way it goes, now someone more efficient must be meeting demand'.

Beyond this, in the sphere of human relationships, it has been suggested that ties and attachments, the centrality of participant reactive attitudes to the concept of the self, means that men are capable of more than simply looking at other men's failures and learning from them. They are also capable of concerning themselves with alleviating the costs of failure (since *all* benefit from the knowledge of what does not work). Politics recognises that success and failure in the market are not indicative of moral worth and seeks not merely to discard men whose attempts to realise the good life were unsuccessful, the way the market discards firms that are no longer competitive. But if men are to recover from failed experiments, if they are to learn now from their mistakes, and not merely leave them as a mute legacy to unknown others, they require a context in which discussion, reflection, and shared experience can be exchanged. This possibility the atomistic and pseudo-responsible market does not provide.

Thus, the existence of public fora, where whole men can attempt to convince others of a particular conception of the common good, by appealing to common experiences and standards of judgment, makes possible two goods of inestimable value. On the social level, it focuses attention on the fact that each person, while in principle equal in some respects with all others, is at the same time different, has a different viewpoint, and is the possessor of a unique set of talents and attributes. Politics humanises the formulation of the rules of social co-operation precisely because it must take account of the effect of the rules on real men and not on abstract and identical atoms. This conception of rules goes beyond the mere setting of the absolute minimum of co-operation necessary for any social order to exist (the essence of Hayek's concern with law). It concerns itself with defining those aspects of social life in a particular society which men prize highly enough to recognise them as explicit obligations on those who enjoy the benefits the social order confers.

The second good which politics makes possible is an individual one: a context within which our own self-understandings may be articulated and compared with others. This is the insight which comes to us from the discussion of historical objectivity and the narrative mode of understanding ourself and others. Politics both makes us test dialogically the adequacy of our present self-awareness and makes us aware of other dimensions articulated by other people. It creates, in other words, a context in which men can learn to *reason* and *judge*, in which they can learn to exercise a critical autonomy as beings with both constitutive ties and commitments and a choosing faculty. 'Judgment', as Crick has argued, 'is inherently social.'[6]

Politics, on the other hand, is not about everything. All political theories are concerned with the decisions or choices which shall be binding upon all members of a society. Liberalism restricts those decisions to what rational man sees as demonstrable truth. A political society sees a much wider potential scope for political decisions but recognises that since its decisions are inherently contestable, the rules laid down for making such choices must marry the difficult opposites of protecting the fragile living relationship of community (mutual trust, friendship, etc.) which brings acquiescence even where disagreement persists, and yet preserving the ability to act when action is needed. One has only to think of societies where this relationship has most obviously and tragically ceased to exist, such as Lebanon and Ulster, to see how its absence impoverishes and brutalises life and makes civilised social relations impossible.

---

[6] From B. Crick's 'Introduction' to Beiner, op. cit., p. xi.

The very possibility of political action (as opposed to action imposed on one group by another by force) requires as its basis an interpretation of society, of history, of individuals, and of the actions that particular facts and conditions call forth. Certainly in this men will often be guided by general principles, validated by experience. It may even be advisable to incorporate these in the ground rules governing political decisions and to insulate them from the momentary passions and humours of the citizens and their representatives. But that does not make the choice or discovery of these principles themselves unproblematic, nor does it make all such possible values self-consistent. Least of all does it make their choice the self-evident result of a logical syllogism or of the application of scientific method. If such a choice is to be morally responsible, it must be dictated by experience and recognisable only by an act of reasoning or judgment which is self-aware, self-critical, and open to the possibility of its own error.

The political approach thus privileges procedures designed to preserve the search for universal assent to such necessarily contestable principles. These are the conditions of political society set out in Chapter I. Unlike Hayek and the Webbs, who rely on objective method to arrive at very circumscribed definitional truths, politics relies on procedures to make possible and to encourage critical analysis in the constant search for agreement on the meaning of the good life and how it is to be pursued. This is not to imply that there is a definitive end to this search and that what is eventually aimed at is universal agreement on one particular vision. As long as there is diversity in human experience and different viewpoints on man's shared reality, there will be different interpretations of the good life. Diversity is an essential element in keeping us aware of the limitations on our knowledge and the tentativeness of our current self-understandings. Aristotle himself warned against the danger of seeking too great a unity in the *polis*:

The object which Socrates assumes as his premiss is ... 'that the greatest possible unity of the whole *polis* is the supreme good'. Yet it is obvious that a *polis* which goes on and on, and becomes more and more of a unit, will eventually cease to be a *polis* at all. A *polis* by its nature is some sort of aggregation. If it becomes more of a unit, it will first become a household instead of a *polis*, and then an individual instead of a household ... It follows that, even if we could, we ought not to achieve this object: it would be the destruction of the *polis*.[7]

What politics asserts is the right and power of the citizen, possessor of a unique perspective on a reality he shares with all other members of his community, to explore, criticise, contest, and try to change, by means of persuasive argument and appeals to common experience and shared standards, not only particular decisions, but the methods used to arrive at them.

Having shown why the attempts of Hayek and the Webbs to arrive at absolute standards for making political decisions (making them determinant rather than reflective judgments) seem inadequate, though, may simply leave the impression that there are no standards at all. In this case, politics would simply be about the purely arbitrary choice and enforcement of values. My point is rather to emphasise that values arise from the mixture of individual character and experience and that such experiences share a common object to the extent that they revolve around a social and physical world with a given structure, including a certain minimum of common language, history, and experience. The articulation of values which we hold is not merely an arbitrary, individual 'choice'. It is in part a coming to consciousness of the ties and obligations which shared experience of this kind creates and makes possible. It is also in part the exercise of a judging or reasoning faculty which we learn to use as we assume greater responsibility for ourself and our decisions, as we become progressively self-directed. This articulation of self and the struggle to make a coherent whole of the values one has are mediated by critical discussion and examination and the resulting knowledge is validated intersubjectively.

It must be granted that these standards of judgment cannot be chosen according to some objective measure independent of experience and they are, therefore, hard to recognise with the certainty to which Hayek and the Webbs pretend. This is merely a restatement of the inescapable difficulty involved in any judgment which, by its nature, is reflective rather than

[7] Crick, *Politics*, p. 161.

determinant. Such judgments are constantly susceptible to undermining and change as the result of experience. The central problem that this creates for politics is how to cultivate in men the ability to discriminate and judge, for, as Edmund Burke so skilfully put it,

No lines can be laid down for civil or political wisdom. They are a matter incapable of exact definition. But, though no man can draw a stroke between the confines of day and night, yet light and darkness are ... tolerably distinguishable.[8]

The very vocabulary to which one has recourse in describing these political activities (reason, judgment, discrimination, taste, evaluation, experience) helps to recall the very different skills, talents, and abilities which politics calls forth, in contradistinction to those necessary for the correct application of a method which requires only discipline and single-mindedness. While, again, one would need to write a separate book to deal adequately with the question of how these political attributes are to be cultivated and inculcated in the citizens, some directions can be sketched on the basis of what has gone before.

In particular, some of the ideas advanced in Chapters VI and VII offer us clues. In Chapter VI it was suggested that any theory, including one purporting to tell us how to act justly in the absence of any shared concept of the good, cannot logically precede the activity to which it refers. Theory is an attempt to capture in words and concepts an activity the whole of which may be unknown to anyone. As such, any attempt to articulate it, to lay down canons of performance, can never be regarded as definitive. It is always subject to the verification of experience.

Similarly, in Chapter VII, the concept of practices and standards was explored. One of the most important aspects of that discussion for this conclusion lay in a couple of realisations. The first is that the goods pursued by a community constituted by a shared core of practices were something not chosen by the individual practitioners, but were something which they

[8] Quoted in F. Canavan, 'Edmund Burke's Conception of the Rôle of Reason in Politics', *Journal of Politics*, 21: 1 (1959), p. 68.

learned to appreciate as a result of an apprenticeship, something which they came to value in itself. Such goods become a standard against which practitioners judge others and themselves as they develop an ability to judge for themselves, to appreciate and understand the standard from the inside, even though they have not themselves 'chosen' that standard in the way, say, that Hayek seems to indicate that liberal man 'affirms' what he shall find good.

The second realisation is that, within the broad parameters of the central (compulsory) rules, a living practice is constituted of practitioners whose activities are an exploration of the current interpretations of the goods which all practitioners affirm. Just as Aristotle suggested that a *polis* without diversity ceased to be a *polis*, so a practice without vigorous exponents of new, unorthodox, or simply different ways of achieving those goods or reinterpreting them would be dead or dying. When men cease to argue about the importance of different interpretations of their practices, when they cease to feel that any standard can be defended as so central to the practice itself that its observance must be compulsory if the community is to have any meaning, then one can be fairly certain that the practice itself is losing sight of its purpose and intention.

So the rational evaluation and persuasion of politics takes place against an articulable background of traditions and practices (arising from accumulated experience) directed towards the realisation of the good life for man. It is against this background only that we can come to an understanding of our values and that we can be said to exercise our choosing faculty in a morally significant way. But experience and dialogue do not reveal one principle (be it liberty or social survival) which overrides all others; it reveals instead the tensions existing between many elements which must be reconciled constantly if men are to live together in a free social order. By making the rules of social co-operation something beyond rational criticism and persuasion, there is no place for character, diversity, and the creative tension of disagreements over values and meaning which are the very stuff of politics.

Men, then, learn to judge, to discriminate, to distinguish what is desirable and possible through actually engaging in these activities. By being called upon to judge particulars in many contexts and then having actually to live with the consequences of their judgments, men learn the significance of judging. In addition, they learn about themselves through the exchange of values and ideas which politics calls forth. This suggests that this narrow view of politics could have quite a broad field of application: its implications clearly point to a highly participatory society in which many public spaces exist at different levels. In local affairs, in the workplace, in the school, and the organisation as well as at the national level, men would be offered many opportunities to exercise judgment and therefore to learn about it while simultaneously exploring and coming to appreciate the diversity and distinctiveness of individual human experience.

Sometimes this results in mistakes, for that is how people learn. No system eliminates human error, but some are more conducive to it than others, and each has its own characteristic ones. The dogma of rigid principle which will not allow its contours to be softened by the experiences that mark men's lives, by the knowledge of the strengths and weaknesses of real, human, three-dimensional characters is more likely to be destructive of men and their lives than a politics which sets out to create opportunities for men to give voice to what they have discovered about themselves and the world and to persuade others of its worth.

The deontological/utilitarian search for certainty is thus fundamentally at odds with politics, which explicitly accepts that it cannot escape the possibility of error but which equally denies that error can be eliminated. The most that can be hoped for is that error be made more tolerable by opening up the sources of error to potential improvement and correction. This can best be done by creating the conditions in which men learn to take responsibility for themselves by doing it. In this, as Macaulay so rightly suggested in the nineteenth century, there is no substitute for experience:

Many politicians of our time are in the habit of laying it down as a self-evident proposition, that no people ought to be free till they are fit to use their freedom. The maxim is worthy of the fool in the old story, who resolved not to go into the water till he had learned to swim. If men are to wait for liberty till they become wise and good in slavery, they may indeed have to wait forever.[9]

This does not mean that political society cannot learn to hedge its freedom with restrictions as it learns to compensate for its own errors. For instance, constitutional procedural guarantees and bills of rights can be justified on the grounds that, if politics is to operate at all, the greatest number of independent points of view on the common social reality must be preserved and their right to a hearing guaranteed. This may also prevent, or at least make much more difficult, the counterfeiting of rational agreement by clandestine and possibly coercive means.

In the final analysis, however, no constitution is better than the character of the men who live under it. Yet the theories of Hayek and the Webbs find no place for the character of individuals to be employed or displayed and, much more importantly, give little thought to the essentially social ways in which character is forged and developed. Because the character of individuals is the province of the historian and the story-teller, and not the social scientist, neither Hayek nor the Webbs is concerned with the conditions in which individual men will learn the value of politics, the significance of a co-operative search for meaning through persuasive means.

[9] Quoted in Hayek, *Constitution*, pp. 444-5 n.

BIBLIOGRAPHY

Arendt, H. *The Human Condition*. Chicago, 1958.
Ayer, A. J. 'Man as a Subject for Science', in P. Laslett and W. G. Runciman, eds. *Philosophy, Politics, and Society*. Oxford, 1967.
Barker, E., ed. *The Politics of Aristotle*. Oxford, 1948.
Barker, R. *Political Ideas in Modern Britain*. London, 1978.
Barnes, J., M. Schofield, and R. Sorabji, eds. *Articles on Aristotle*. Vol. II: *Ethics and Politics*. London, 1977.
Barry, B. *The Liberal Theory of Justice*. Oxford, 1973.
—— *Political Argument*. London, 1965.
Barry, N. *Hayek's Social and Economic Philosophy*. London, 1979.
Bay, C. 'Hayek's Liberalism: The Constitution of Perpetual Privilege', *Political Science Reviewer*, 1 (Fall 1971), 93-124.
Beattie, A. 'The Character of English Constitutional Theory'. Unpublished paper, 1979.
Beer, M. *A History of British Socialism*. London, 1929.
Beer, S. H. 'Liberalism and the National Idea', *Public Interest* 5 (Fall 1966), 70-82.
—— *Modern British Politics*. London, 1965.
—— 'The Webbs Confront the Twentieth Century', *Politics*, 9: 2 (Nov. 1974), 129-38.
Behrens, R. *The Conservative Party From Heath to Thatcher*. London, 1979.
Beiner, R. *Political Judgment*. London, 1983.
Benn, S. I. 'Freedom, Autonomy and the Concept of a Person', *Proceedings of the Aristotelian Society*, NS 76 (1975-6), 109-30.
Berlin, I. *Concepts and Categories*. London, 1978.
—— 'Two Concepts of Liberty', in the author's *Four Essays on Liberty*. Oxford, 1969.
Bohm, D. *Wholeness and the Implicate Order*. London, 1980.
Bosanquet, N. *After the New Right*. London, 1983.
Brennan, E. J. T., ed. *Education for National Efficiency: The Contribution of Sidney and Beatrice Webb*. London, 1975.
Buchanan, J. M. *Freedom In Constitutional Contract*. College Station, Texas, 1977.
Butler, E. *Hayek: His Contribution to the Political and Economic Thought of Our Time*. London, 1983.
Canavan, F. 'Burke on Prescription of Government', *Review of Politics*, 35: 4 (1973), 454-74.
Canovan, M. *The Political Thought of Hannah Arendt*. London, 1974.
Caute, D. *The Fellow Travellers*. London, 1973.

Cavell, S. *Must We Mean What We Say?* New York, 1969.

Clarke, P. *Liberals and Social Democrats.* Cambridge, 1978.

Cole, M. 'The Webbs and Social Theory', *British Journal of Sociology*, 12: 2 (June 1961), 93-105.

—— *The Webbs and Their Work.* London, 1949.

Collingwood, R. G. *The Idea of History.* Oxford, 1946.

—— *The Philosophy of History.* London, 1930.

Cooper, J. *Reason and Human Good in Aristotle.* London, 1975.

Cosgrave, P. *Margaret Thatcher.* London, 1978.

Crespigny, A. de. 'F. A. Hayek: Freedom For Progress', in A. de Crespigny and K. Minogue, eds. *Contemporary Political Philosophers.* London, 1976.

Crick, B. *In Defence of Politics*, 2nd edition. Harmondsworth, 1982.

Dent, N. J. *The Moral Psychology of the Virtues.* Cambridge, 1984.

Downs, A. *An Economic Theory of Democracy.* New York, 1957.

Drucker, H., ed. *Developments in British Politics.* London, 1983.

Dworkin, R. *Taking Rights Seriously.* London, 1977.

Elster, J. *Ulysses and the Sirens*, Revised edition. Cambridge, 1984.

Evans, J. L. *Knowledge and Infallibility.* London, 1978.

Feaver, G. 'Introduction to *Our Partnership*', 1975 edition, part of the LSE reprint series of the Webbs' work.

Flathman, R. *Concepts in Social and Political Philosophy.* New York, 1973.

—— *The Public Interest.* New York, 1966.

Gass, W. H. *Fiction and the Figures of Life.* New York, 1970.

Gaus, G. F. *The Modern Liberal Theory of Man.* London, 1983.

Gewirth, A. 'The Justification of Egalitarian Justice', in R. Flathman, ed. *Concepts in Social and Political Philosophy.* New York, 1973.

——'Political Power and Democratic Psychiatry', *Ethics*, 59 (1948), 136-42.

Goodin, R. *The Politics of Rational Man.* London, 1976.

Gordon, S. 'The Political Economy of F. A. Hayek', *Canadian Journal of Economics*, 14: 3 (1981), 470-87.

Gottschalk, L., ed. *Generalisation In the Writing of History.* Chicago, 1963.

Graubard, S. *British Labour and the Russian Revolution.* London, 1956.

Gray, J. *Hayek On Liberty.* Oxford, 1984.

—— *Mill on Liberty: A Defence.* London, 1983.

Greenleaf, W. H. *Order, Empiricism and Politics.* Westport, Conn., 1980.

Hall, J. A. 'The Roles and Influence of Political Intellectuals: Tawney vs. Sidney Webb', *British Journal of Sociology*, 28: 3 (Sept. 1977), 351-62.

Hamilton, M. A. *Sidney and Beatrice Webb: A Study in Contemporary Biography*. London, 1932.

Hamowy, R. 'Hayek's Conception of Freedom: A Critique', *New Individualist Review 1: 1* , (Apr. 1961), 28-31.

Hampshire, S., ed. *Public and Private Morality*. Cambridge, 1978.

Hardy, B. 'Towards a Poetics of Fiction: An Approach Through Narrative', *Novel*, 2 (1968), 5-14.

Hart, H. L. A. *The Concept of Law*. Oxford, 1961.

Hayek, F. A. *Capitalism and the Historians*. London, 1954.

—— *The Constitution of Liberty*. London, 1960.

—— *The Counter-Revolution of Science*. Glencoe, Ill., 1952.

—— *The Denationalisation of Money*. London, 1976.

—— *Individualism and Economic Order*. London, 1949.

—— *Knowledge, Evolution and Society*. London, 1983.

—— *Law, Legislation and Liberty*. London, 1982.

—— *New Studies in Philosophy, Politics, Economics and the History of Ideas*. London, 1978.

—— *The Road to Serfdom*. London, 1944.

—— *Studies in Philosophy, Politics and Economics*. London, 1967.

Hirschman, A. O. *Exit, Voice and Loyalty: Responses to Declines in Firms, Organisations and States*. Cambridge, Mass., 1970.

—— *The Passions and the Interests*. Princeton, 1977.

Kant, I. *The Critique of Judgment*. Translated by J. C. Meredith. Oxford, 1952.

Kovesi, J. *Moral Notions*. London, 1967.

Kuhn, T. 'Objectivity, Value Judgment and Theory Choice', in Kuhn, *The Essential Tension*. Chicago, 1977.

—— *The Structure of Scientific Revolutions*. Chicago, 1962.

Letwin, S. R. *The Pursuit of Certainty*. Cambridge, 1965.

Lewis, G. K. 'Fabian Socialism: Some Aspects of Theory and Practice', *Journal of Politics*, 14 (Aug. 1952), 442-70.

Lukes, S. 'Some Problems About Rationality', in B. R. Wilson, ed. *Rationality*. Oxford, 1970.

McBriar, A. M. *Fabian Socialism and English Politics, 1884-1918*. Cambridge, 1962.

McCormick, N. *Legal Reasoning and Legal Theory*. Oxford, 1978.

Macdonagh, O. *A Pattern of Government Growth*. London, 1961.

McDowell, J. 'Virtue and Reason', *The Monist*, 62: 3 (1979), 331-50.

MacIntyre, A. *After Virtue: A Study in Moral Theory*. London, 1981.

Mackenzie, N. and J. *The First Fabians*. London, 1977.

Mackenzie, N., ed. *The Letters of Sidney and Beatrice Webb*. London, 1980.

Mackenzie, N. *Socialism and Society: A New View of the Webb Partnership.* Lecture published by the London School of Economics. London, 1978.

McKibbin, R. *The Evolution of the Labour Party, 1910-1924.* London, 1974.

Macpherson, C. B. 'The Maximisation of Democracy', in P. Laslett and W. G. Runciman, eds. *Philosophy, Politics, and Society.* Oxford, 1967.

Malkiel, B. *Random Walk Down Wall Street.* New York, 1984.

Margolis, H. *Selfishness, Altruism and Rationality: A Theory of Social Choice.* Cambridge, 1982.

Mill, J. S. *Utilitarianism.* Edited by H. B. Acton. London, 1972.

Miller, O. *Social Justice.* Oxford, 1976.

Mink, L. O. 'History and Fiction as Modes of Comprehension', *New Literary History,* 1 (1970), 541-58.

Muggeridge, K. and R. Adams. *Beatrice Webb.* London, 1967.

Murdoch, I. *The Sovereignty of Good.* London, 1970.

Nozick, R. *Anarchy, State, and Utopia.* Oxford, 1974.

Oakeshott, M. *Political Education.* An Inaugural Lecture delivered at the LSE on 6 Mar. 1951. Cambridge, 1951.

—— *Rationalism in Politics.* London, 1962.

O'Hear, A. *Karl Popper.* London, 1980.

Olson, M. *The Logic of Collective Action.* Cambridge, Mass., 1933.

Parekh, B. *Hannah Arendt and the Search for a New Political Philosophy.* London, 1981.

Pateman, C. *Participation and Democratic Theory.* Cambridge, 1970.

Pennock, R. 'Responsiveness, Responsibility and Majority Rule', *American Political Science Review,* 46 (Sept. 1952), 790-807.

Pierson, S. *British Socialists: The Journey From Fantasy to Politics.* Harvard, 1979.

Plant, R. 'The Resurgence of Ideology', in H. Drucker. ed. *Developments in British Politics.* London, 1983.

Pocock J. G. A. *The Machiavellian Moment.* Princeton, 1975.

Polanyi, M. *Personal Knowledge.* London, 1962.

—— *The Tacit Dimension.* Garden City, NJ, 1967.

Popper, K. *Conjectures and Refutations,* 3rd edition. London, 1969.

—— *The Logic of Scientific Discovery,* 2nd edition. London, 1968.

—— *The Open Society and Its Enemies.* London, 1945.

—— *The Poverty of Historicism.* London, 1957.

Pratt, V. *The Philosophy of the Social Sciences.* London, 1978.

Radford, R. A. 'The Economic Organisation of a POW Camp', *Economica,* 12: 18 (Nov. 1945), 189-201.

Radice, L. *Beatrice and Sidney Webb: Fabian Socialists.* London, 1984.

Rawls, J. *A Theory of Justice.* Oxford, 1972.

Robbins, L. 'Hayek on Liberty', *Economica*, 28 (Feb. 1961), 66–81.
Rothbard, M. *Individualism in the Philosophy of the Social Sciences*. San Francisco, 1979.
Ryan A. *The Philosophy of the Social Sciences*. London, 1970.
Ryle, G. *The Concept of Mind*. London, 1949.
Sandel, M. J. *Liberalism and the Limits of Justice*. Cambridge, 1982.
—— 'Morality and the Liberal Ideal', *New Republic*, 190: 18 (7 May 1984), 15–17.
Schubert, G. A. *The Public Interest*. New York, 1961.
Scruton, R. *A Dictionary of Political Thought*. London, 1982.
Searle, G. R. *The Quest For National Efficiency*. Oxford, 1971.
Sen, A. and B. Williams, eds. *Utilitarianism and Beyond*. Cambridge, 1982.
Shaw, G. B., ed. *Fabian Essays*. London, 1948.
Shenfield, A. 'The New Thought of F. A. Hayek', *Modern Age*, 20: 1 (Winter 1976), 54–61.
Simey, T. 'The Contribution of Sidney and Beatrice Webb to Sociology', *British Journal of Sociology*, 12: 2 (June 1961), 106–23.
Smart, J. J. C. and B. Williams. *Utilitarianism: For and Against*. Cambridge, 1973.
Spragens, T. A. *The Irony of Liberal Reason*. Chicago, 1981.
Stevenson, C. L. *Ethics and Language*. London, 1945.
Stove, D. *Popper and After: Four Modern Irrationalists*. Oxford, 1982.
Strawson, P. 'Freedom and Resentment', in G. Watson, ed. *Free Will*. Oxford, 1982.
Swanton, C. 'The Concept of Interests', *Political Theory*, 8: 1 (Feb. 1980), 83–101.
Tawney, R. H. 'Beatrice Webb', *Proceedings of the British Academy*, 29, (1943), 285–311.
Taylor C. 'Interpretation and the Sciences of Man', *Review of Metaphysics*, 25: 1 (Sept. 1971), 3–51.
—— 'Responsibility For Self' in G. Watson, ed. *Free Will*. Oxford, 1982.
Taylor, M. *Community, Anarchy and Liberty*. Cambridge, 1982.
Unger, R. M. *Knowledge and Politics*. New York, 1975.
Vernon, R. 'The "Great Society" and the "Open Society": Liberalism in Hayek and Popper', *Canadian Journal of Political Science*, 9: 2 (June 1976), 261–76.
Vile, M. J. C. *Constitutionalism and the Separation of Powers*. Oxford, 1967.
Wallas, G. *The Great Society*. London, 1919.
Watson, G., ed. *Free Will*. Oxford, 1982.
Webb, B. *Diaries*. Edited by N. and J. Mackenzie. London, 1982–4. 3 volumes.

——*Diaries, 1924-32.* Edited by M. Cole. London, 1956.
—— *My Apprenticeship.* London, 1926.
—— *Our Partnership.* London, 1948.
Webb, S. *The Basis and Policy of Socialism.* London, 1908.
—— *The Difficulties of Individualism.* Fabian Tract no. 69. London, 1896.
—— 'Historic',in G. B. Shaw, ed. *Fabian Essays.* London, 1948.
—— 'The Necessary Basis of Society', *Contemporary Review,* June 1908.
—— 'The Place of Co-operation in the State of Tomorrow'. Pamphlet published by The Co-operative Union Ltd., London, 1910.
—— *Socialism and Individualism.* London 1908.
—— *Socialism: True and False.* Fabian Tract no. 51. London, 1894.
—— *Twentieth Century Politics: A Policy of National Efficiency.* Fabian Tract no. 108. London, 1901.
Webb. S. & B. *A Constitution for the Socialist Commonwealth of Great Britain.* London, 1975.
—— *The Consumers' Co-operative Movement.* London, 1921.
—— *The Decay of Capitalist Civilisation.* London, 1923.
—— *English Local Government.* London, 1906-27. 11 volumes.
—— *Industrial Democracy.* London, 1926.
—— *Methods of Social Study.* London, 1932.
—— *Soviet Communism: Dictatorship or Democracy,* 3rd edition. London, 1944.
—— *Soviet Communism: A new Civilisation?* London, 1935.
—— *The Truth About Soviet Russia.* London, 1942.
Weldon, T. D. *States and Morals.* London, 1946.
Wiggins, D. 'Truth, Invention and the Meaning of Life', *Proceedings of the British Academy,* 62 (1976), 331-78.
Wilhelm, M. W. 'The Political Thought of Friederich A. Hayek', *Political Studies,* 20: 2 (1972), 169-84.
Williams, B. *Problems of the Self.* Cambridge, 1973.
Wilson, B. R., ed. *Rationality.* Oxford, 1970.
Winch, D. *Adam Smith's Politics.* Cambridge, 1978.
Woolf. L. 'Beatrice Webb, 1858-1943', *Economic Journal,* 53 (June/Sept. 1943), 284-90.
—— *Downhill All the Way.* London, 1967.
—— 'Political Thought and the Webbs', in M. Cole, ed. *The Webbs and Their Work.* London, 1949.

INDEX